ON THE
WESTERN
FRONT

By the same Author

Military
Middle East Journey
Return to Glory
One Man's War
The Walking Wounded
Digger (The Story of the Australian Soldier)
Scotland the Brave (The Story of the Scottish Soldier)
Jackboot (The Story of the German Soldier)
Tommy Atkins (The Story of the English Soldier)
Jack Tar (The Story of the English Seaman)
Swifter than Eagles (Biography of Marshal of the Air Force
Sir John Salmond)
The Face of War
British Campaign Medals
Codes and Ciphers
Boys in Battle
Women in Battle
Anzacs at War
Links of Leadership (Thirty Centuries of Command)
Surgeons in the Field
Americans in Battle
Letters from the Front 1914–1918
The French Foreign Legion
Damn the Dardanelles! (The Story of Gallipoli)
The Australian Army at War 1899–1975
The Arab Armies of the Middle East Wars 1948–1973
The Israeli Army in the Middle East Wars 1948–1973
Fight for the Falklands!
The Man the Nazis Couldn't Catch
The War of Desperation: Lebanon 1982–85
Brassey's Battles: 3,500 Years of Battles, Campaigns and Wars

General
The Hunger to Come (Food and Population Crises)
New Geography 1966–67
New Geography 1968–69
New Geography 1970–71
Anatomy of Captivity (Political Prisoners)
Devil's Goad
Fedayeen (The Arab-Israeli Dilemma)
The Arab Mind
The Israeli Mind
The Dagger of Islam
The Arabs as Master Slavers
The PLO Connections
Know the Middle East

and other titles

ON THE
WESTERN
FRONT

SOLDIERS' STORIES FROM
FRANCE AND FLANDERS

1914–1918

JOHN LAFFIN

ALAN SUTTON
1985

ALAN SUTTON PUBLISHING LIMITED
BRUNSWICK ROAD · GLOUCESTER

First published 1985

British Library Cataloguing in Publication Data

Laffin, John
On the Western Front : soldiers' stories from France
and Flanders 1914–18.
1. World War, 1914–1918—Campaigns—Western
2. World War, 1914–1918—Personal narratives, British
I. Title
940.4′144′0922   D530

ISBN 0-86299-242-7

*Jacket photograph: Members of the 1st Division A.I.F. in a billet
at Ypres, October 1917, just before the Passchendaele offensive.
Australian War Memorial.*

Typesetting and origination by
Alan Sutton Publishing Limited
Printed in Great Britain

To the memory of the 947,000 British and Empire soldiers who died during World War I

John Laffin's interest in the Western Front, and in the 'Great War' generally, began in boyhood. His father was a member of the A.I.F. (Australian Imperial Force), first as a medical orderly and then as an infantry officer, while his mother was a nursing sister with the A.A.N.S. (Australian Army Nursing Service). Both saw much service in three different theatres of war – Egypt, Gallipoli and the Western Front of France and Belgium. Their son, John, grew up hearing about the war – the action from his father, the agony from his mother. He himself became a soldier during World War II and immediately afterwards a war historian and analyst. More than forty of his books concern war.

Since 1956 he and his wife, Hazelle, have spent much time on the old Western Front and they have a sense of mission about it. It is 'to make sure that the sacrifice, suffering and slaughter of the Great War is not forgotten.'

The Laffins take individuals and small groups to the battlefields to see family war graves and to explain to them the course of a particular battle. They have a private battlefield museum in their home in Wales.

Dr John Laffin is also a journalist, novelist, poet and specialist writer and lecturer on the Middle East and Islam.

CONTENTS

MEN – THE RAW MATERIAL OF WAR

The official histories of World War I – the 'Great War' – are accounts of strategy and tactics and political and logistical considerations and after reading them a reader might well wonder why they rarely mention soldiers, except in terms of military units. Even regimental histories devote much more space to plans and concepts than to the men who were used to implement the plans.

The experiences of millions of individuals were the raw material which made up the war. And the central reality of the war – shorn of its policies and propaganda – was concentrated suffering and slaughter in the midst of appalling conditions. In scores of thousands men were quickly trained, shunted to the battle zones and marched to the shell-torn trenches, there to take part in a conflict of relentless attrition.

The generals of all armies fought the war on the principle that if they could inflict more casualties on the enemy than they themselves suffered they must win the war. Nothing more subtle or sophisticated was considered. In any major attack, some generals assumed, the defenders must sooner or later run

out of bullets – or the the will to face the attackers' bullets. When that happened the survivors among the attackers would 'get among' the defenders with the bayonet and rout them. The phrase 'casualties are inevitable' appears over and over again in battle plans of the time. And after the battle the generals' reports would include the statement, 'As expected, casualties were heavy but lighter than expected – and certainly lighter than those inflicted on the enemy'.

It was easy enough for the writers of these reports to throw in the odd phrase complimenting the troops collectively – 'Our men were magnificent' or 'the Blankshire regiment fought like lions'. The Commander-in-Chief sometimes praised a division on its 'splendid achievement'. The greater the cost in life, the greater the praise.

Nobody asked the soldiers what they thought. I have read hundreds of battalion diaries and rarely find a comment by a common soldier – and, in truth, it is not the function of a battalion diary to record such comments. Few people were interested then, or later, in soldiers'

I

anger and frustration, humour and irony, despair and grief, enterprise and innovation. If Field Marshal Haig ever heard a personal story from the trenches he left no record of it. Some generals talk about 'the troops' in their memoirs but rarely in any personal way; at best they are no more then patronising.

At its lower level, the history of the war is made up of millions of trivial incidents, for something happened each day to each man – something that made him laugh or cry or sigh. The British Empire soldier laughed readily in that era and humour was simple and unsubtle. It didn't take much to make him cry either but he choked back his tears with another joke or with an apparently callous comment, a kind of safety valve to keep him sane. As for sighs – well, he sighed much of the time over a variety of things, such as women, food, leave, generals, sergeant-majors, the enemy, the cold, rain and heat, over injustice, unfairness, stupidity and life in general.

The stories the soldiers told and the things that happened to them reveal, collectively, much about the *real* war – that which took place in the minds of men. Most stories were for consumption within the army, and therefore more real and revealing than letters and diaries.

Similarly, behind the parades and inspections, the presentations of gallantry awards, behind the official and the formal there was another level of life – that as lived by the men in trenches and billets, in the Y.M.C.A. hut and in Talbot House in Poperinge. History was taking place in all these places just by the inter-action of man with man and of man with his environment.

The anecdotes which make up this collection are the first serious attempt, I believe, to show the humanity of the soldier on the Western Front. I cannot vouch for the authenticity of all of them and some are probably apocryphal. Nevertheless, even where I have no precise source of a story I am ready to swear that it *could* have happened and that it truly reflects conditions and attitudes and practices of the war.

My collection comes from many sources, including both my parents who served with the Australian army. My father began the war as a private soldier in the Army Medical Corps and finished as a platoon commander in an infantry battalion; my mother was an army nursing sister in Egypt, Lemnos (just off Gallipoli), France and England. Between them they had many stories to tell. Other anecdotes come from old soldiers – and I have spoken to thousands of them during a lifetime spent as a military historian. Some are taken from diaries, letters and published books several decades out of print. Several of the stories are mere trifles, nothing more than a piece of throwaway Cockney wit. Others are profoundly deep and evocative and have an enduring message so many years after the event.

The shortest story I ever heard – but it is also deep and evocative – concerns an Australian soldier who was repatriated to England in November 1918, just after the war ended. He was greeted at Victoria

Station by a well-meaning woman, one of many who used to greet the returning heroes.

'What did you do over there, Corporal?' she asked.

The Australian looked her in the eye and said softly, 'I died'.

I wonder if she knew what he meant. If she could read this book she would understand.

I am grateful to Michael Chappell, the leading expert on the uniforms and equipment of World War I, for information about some of the photographs in the book. The photographs on pages 62, 70, 102, 107, 115, 135, 149, 159, 172 and 173 are from the collections of either the Imperial War Museum or the Australian War Memorial.

WOODBINE WILLIE'S SOLDIER POEMS

'Woodbine Willie' photographed by W.W. Dowty
(Copyright: Michael Dowty)

It is fitting that this book should begin and end with a poem by Padre Geoffrey Studdert Kennedy M.C., who was so well known on the Western Front. Each of the poems tells a story about life and about death in the trenches and Kennedy saw a lot of both. He gained the nickname 'Woodbine Willie' because he carried in his big pockets handfuls of Woodbine cigarettes – they then cost a penny for five – which he handed out liberally to the soldiers. Above all, the troops loved their fags; often they were all that stood between them and total misery.

Kennedy went into the front line to comfort and pray with soldiers, to bury others and to hand out his Woodbines. His dialect poems deserve to be better known; they were written not so much *about* the soldiers as *for* them. Written in the style evolved by Rudyard Kipling in his *Barrack-Room Ballads*, they were very popular with the men themselves.

THE SECRET

You were askin' 'ow we sticks it,
  Sticks this blarsted rain and mud,
'Ow it is we keeps on smilin'
  When the place runs red wi'
  blood.
Since you're askin', I can tell ye,
  And I thinks I tells ye true,
But it ain't official, mind ye,
  It's a tip twixt me and you.
For the General thinks it's tactics,
  And the trouble as he takes.
Sergeant-Major says it's drillin',
  And 'is straffin' on parade,
Doctor swears it's sanitation,
  And some patent stinks 'e's made,
Padre tells us it's religion,
  And the Spirit of the Lord;
But I ain't got much religion,
  And I sticks it still, by Gawd.
Quarters kids us it's the rations,

And the dinners as we gets.
But I know what keeps us smilin',
  It's the Woodbine Cigarettes.
For the daytime seems more dreary,
  And the night-time seems to drag
To eternity of darkness.
  When ye 'aven't got a fag.
Then the rain seems some'ow
  wetter,
  And the cold cuts twice as keen,
And ye keeps on seein' Boches,
  What the Sargint 'asn't seen.
If old Fritz 'as been and got ye,
  And ye 'ave to stick the pain,
If ye 'aven't got a fag on,
  Why it 'urts as bad again.
When there ain't no fags to pull at,
  Then there's terror in the ranks.
That's the secret – (yes, I'll 'ave one)
  Just a fag – and many Tanks.

By Padre G.A. Studdert Kennedy M.C., C.F.
(Woodbine Willie)

5

1914

Following the German invasion of Belgium, the British and French armies went confidently to war against the Germans. The Germans were also confident but their famous Schleiffen Plan went awry. Nevertheless, the British, French and Belgians retreated to a line which was to become the Western Front, that is, the German *Western Front. The officer corps of the British Expeditionary Force – the regular army – was practically wiped out between August and December. Still, the British believed that 'the war would be over by Christmas'. All the belligerents counted God among their allies. An English poet, J.C. Squire, wrote:*
God heard the embattled nations sing and shout:
'God strafe England' – 'God save the King' –
'God this' – 'God that' – and 'God the other thing.'
'My God,' said God, 'I've got my work cut out.'

THE FIRST SHOT

CHATEAU DU GHISLAIN, MONS–CHARLEROI ROAD

On the morning of 22 August 1914, C Squadron 4th Royal Irish Dragoon Guards under Major Tom Bridges D.S.O. was waiting under cover when a scout reported that enemy were coming down the road.

Major Bridges ordered, '4th Troop, dismounted ready for action! 1st Troop, behind, draw swords ready to go!'

A troop of Uhlans, the German lancers, rode down the road at a leisurely pace, the officer in front smoking a cigar. Then sensing trouble they turned quickly back. Captain Hornby was sent after them with the sabre troop. Another troop, including Trooper Fred Thomas, a drummer on ceremonial occasions, was sent in support and they galloped through the little village of Casteau. 1st troop used their sabres, scattering the Uhlans. When 4th Troop caught up with them Captain Hornby gave the order, 'dismounted action!'

Quickly the troopers sheltered their horses beside the chateau wall and Thomas, quick and athletic, was first into action. Four hundred yards away he saw a German cavalry officer standing in his stirrups giving orders to his men to take up firing positions. Thomas squeezed his trigger and the officer fell from his horse and lay on the road. . . . He had fired the British Army's first rifle shot of World War I. Neither he nor anybody else knew this at the time but later research showed this to be the case.

Thomas was promoted sergeant in the field at Messines on 5 November 1915 and was awarded the M.M. He transferred from the cavalry to machine-guns in 1916 and retired from the army in 1923. For many years he was a commissionaire at Brighton theatres, where he was well known by his tall, straight figure and his waxed moustache.

9

ENCOURAGING THE REINFORCEMENTS

RETREAT FROM MONS

Hurrying to support the hard-pressed, infantry near Mons in August 1914, the 3rd Hussars of the 2nd Cavalry Brigade were close to their objective, when they saw many wounded being carried back in horse-drawn ambulances. Behind this little convoy came an infantry transport driver, wearing a stocking hat and mounted on an old mule. Thrown over the mule, with the tail-end buttoned around the mule's neck, was a German's blood-spattered overcoat.

One of the 3rd Hussars reined in by the mule and said to the odd-looking solder, 'Many enemy up there, mate?'

'Millions', he said glumly. *'You* 'ave a go. We can't shift 'em. Taken root, I think'.

He dug his heels into the mule and as he rode on he turned to speak to the Hussars. 'Talk about Napoleon's blinkin' retreat from Moscow', he said gloomily, 'it ain't ruddy well in it with this'.

Thus encouraged, the 3rd Hussars rode on.

UNKNOWN HERO

THULIN, NEAR MONS

Lieutenant Colonel Arthur Osburn, medical officer of the 4th Dragoon Guards, tended a great many wounded men on 22 August 1914, when the British Army first confronted the Germans. In the subsequent retreat he became detached from his unit and that night entered the town of Thulin. The only building showing any light was the Mairie (Town Hall) and as he approached Belgian priests and nuns ran out and surrounded him. 'M'sieur is a doctor? Please come in

A wounded soldier of the Middlesex Regiment and another from the King's Own Yorkshire Light Infantry during the retreat from Mons. On the right is a sergeant of the Royal Army Medical Corps. The original caption with the photograph reads: 'Wounded British soldiers have only one thought – to get back to the front; different from the attitude of German prisoners who are pleased to stay where they are ... Compare this photograph with photographs of German soldiers and our superiority in intelligence and spirit is apparent at once.'   *(Author's collection)*

at once – in here. There are many English wounded! There are no doctors!'

Osburn found wounded lying down, crouching and standing; the stairs were crowded with sitting cases, the passages with stretcher cases – some men were faint and white from loss of blood. Sisters of Mercy and their peasant helpers were carrying in mattresses, straw, jugs of water and old sheets for bandages.

The surgeon induced the priests and older Sisters to keep the badly wounded cases on the ground floor in case of fire and, by bullying, cajoling and encouraging he brought about some order. One man was badly wounded in the head but conscious enough to point to the man lying next to him. 'Sir', he said, 'that man blew off his right hand recharging a fuse to blow up a bridge across the canal which the Germans had captured. He went back along to do it himself – the first charge wouldn't go off. If he hadn't stopped the Germans they would have enfiladed our whole line'.

Osburn thought that both men were Royal Engineers. He dressed the shattered stump of the hero and quickly scribbled his name and number in his notebook. 'You won't be forgotten', he promised. 'You deserve the V.C. – I'll see that the General hears about it'.

Minutes later a Sister ran in to warn Osburn that the Germans were in the town. He dashed outside to find that his mounted groom and orderly had actually rubbed shoulders with the Germans in the darkness. The three men galloped off, under fire. Finding his regiment he was once again busy with wounded men.

When he finally had time to reach for his notebook he found that he had lost it. In the subsequent confusion of the British retreat Osburn was never able to trace the wounded R.E. hero (who almost certainly had been taken prisoner) and never could recall his name to nominate him for a decoration. He may have been burnt to death as the Mairie was set alight by artillery fire.

This Engineer was only one of thousands who deserved an award for gallantry but did not get it. Sometimes not a single man survived a fierce action.

SELF DEFENCE

RETREAT FROM MONS

Strict orders against looting were issued during the retreat from Mons in August – September 1914, if only to maintain discipline and to prevent straggling. An officer, coming around the corner of a farmhouse one day, confronted a soldier in the act of wringing the neck of a chicken. The soldier also saw the officer – simultaneously, some witnesses said. 'Would you, you brute!' he snarled at the dead chicken. With the bird in his left hand he snapped a salute. 'Attacked me, sir', he said.

AGONIES OF THE RETREAT

RETREAT FROM MONS

At one point in the retreat Corporal Bernard Denore of the 1st Royal Berkshire Regiment was sent with three men to an outpost at a railway signal box and found that it was being used as a clearing station for wounded. Amidst the sounds of agony and suffering, one man kept shrieking for somebody to bring a razor and cut his throat. As Denore went to move a bundle of hay, someone called, 'Look out mate, there's a bloke in there!' Only a leg, severed from its body was visible, and he felt very sick. To Denore's horror an artillery man who was standing talking to him was killed right in front of his eyes. Wounded men still cursed and died, while one soldier spent all night kissing a string of rosary beads.

In the morning a corporal brought the order to retire from the outpost and, with his battalion, Denore deployed, fired at the Germans then retreated again. Marching all day they reached Mariolles on the 25th.

The Germans attacked at 9 p.m., sustained their assault, and killed or wounded about 25 of Denore's company. In the darkness somebody called out authoritatively, 'Has anybody got a map?' As the company commander stood up holding out his map, a German walked up and shot him dead at point-blank range with a revolver. In return, one of the Berkshire's bayoneted the German. And the retreat went on.

Corporal Denore was wounded in several places four weeks later at Zonnebeke, during the first battle of Ypres, and was invalided home. In the late 1930s he recollected his O.C's death as the most vivid incident of his war.

RIGHT MAN IN A CRISIS

ST QUENTIN

On the hot afternoon of 27 August 1914, the Grand Square of St Quentin was thronged with British soldiers retreating under the relentless German advance. Many of the men were exhausted and sprawled on the cobblestones, while others drifted around aimlessly. A few, wild drunk, were firing at imaginary German aeroplanes. The great majority were not only without their rifles but had either lost or thrown away their belts, empty water bottles and other equipment, as demoralised troops do. The only officer present was Lieutenant-Colonel Arthur Osburn, the same doctor who had tended the wounded at Thulin. He was appalled by the scene.

The men were demoralised all the more because some hours before a train had left St Quentin Station carrying most of the British General Staff and the soldiers felt abandoned.

Into the town rode Major Tom Bridges D.S.O. of the 4th Royal Irish Dragoon Guards, with some still-disciplined men – part of his own squadron, a few Lancers and other stragglers who had attached themselves to him. Riding into the Square he spoke loudly and clearly to the disorderly mob, encouraging and exhorting them. The men were sullen and one soldier shouted, 'Our old man (his colonel) has surrendered to the Germans and that goes for us – we'll stick with him. We don't want any bloody cavalry interfering!' At the same time he pointed his rifle at Bridges. The major stared him down.

A surrender document signed by two exhausted colonels had already been sent to the Germans but Bridges did not recognise it as valid. He sent his own men to commandeer all the carts and horses that they could find and after that they rounded up 440 men – Osburn counted them. The men with blistered feet or otherwise unable to walk were put in the carts.

At a toy shop in the square Bridges bought a drum for himself and a tin whistle for this trumpeter and together they marched round and round the fountain, where men were lying as if dead, playing 'The British Grenadiers' and 'Tipperary'. Slowly the men sat up and even began to cheer. 'I'm going to take you back to your regiments', Bridges said. 'On your feet!'

Bridges lined the infantrymen up in fours and induced one of the colonels, a limping middle-aged man sick with fatigue, to march in front. Bridges formed a 'band' of men who had whistles and Jew's harps and to the tune of 'The British Grenadiers' he led them out in the dark.

Shortly afterwards, Osburn discovered that he had left his map case in the Square and returned quickly to look for it, but couldn't find it. As he sat on his horse in the silence he heard the characteristic clatter of cavalry entering the town – from the other side. Bridges' column had left just in time and Osburn spurred after it.

At two in the morning, Bridges brought his 'army', tottering with exhaustion but now held up by discipline, into the villages of Savy and Roupy. These men would fight another day.

The two colonels who surrendered were court-martialled and cashiered. One of them, Elkington, joined the French Foreign Legion and worked his way up to a commission, was badly wounded and awarded the Legion of Honour. For his gallantry in the field King George V reinstated him in the British Army and awarded him the D.S.O. Major Bridges in due course became Lieutenant-General Sir Tom Bridges K.C.B., K.C.M.G., D.S.O. He retired in 1922.

'CHEER THE MEN UP'

RETREAT FROM MONS – NORTH OF ST QUENTIN

Frederic Coleman, a pioneer American motorist, was one of the members of the Royal Automobile Club who volunteered their services and their cars at the outbreak of war. Constantly on the move in the battle area throughout the first months of the war, Mr Coleman became even busier during the retreat from Mons. A staff officer told him to 'Cheer the men up and keep them on the move'. He tells two stories of the men he was supposed to cheer as he waited by the roadside.

I

As I was intent on my work of encouragement a voice commented, 'A close shave the little divil made that time, shure'. Turning at the soft brogue, what was my surprise to see a Jock, in a kilt that looked as if its wearer had been rolled in mud. Capless, his shock of red hair stood on end, and a pair of blue Irish eyes twinkled merrily. This was before I learned that an Irishman in a Scots regiment is not rare – nor a Cockney in a battalion dubbed Irish.

As if entering himself in a competition of close shaves, the Irishman held his right ear between finger and thumb. 'And what do ye think o' that?' he queried. Right through the lobe of his ear close to his cheek, a Mauser bullet – 'the little divil' – had drilled a clean hole. 'Close that, I'm thinkin', said the proud owner. 'And I niver knew how close me ear was to me head until that thing came along'.

II

A woebegone squad hove in sight, red-eyed from lack of sleep, barren of equipment, many a cap missing, and not a sound pair of feet in the lot. Every man looked done but every man had his rifle. 'It will take something to cheer this bunch', I thought.

I ascertained their regiment and gave them detailed instructions how to find it.

'We've been rearguardin'', said a cadaverous coporal who acted as spokesman. 'We're proper rearguards we are. Been doin' nothin' else but rearguardin''.

'Right', said I. 'Don't forget; take the third turning after the fountain. Plenty of food there.'

'Rearguards, we are', said the lugubrious one. 'Proper rearguards. Ain't done nothin' else for three days'.

'Cheerio!' I insisted. 'Three streets on after the fountain and then — '

'_Proper_ rearguards — ' he started again.

'But,' I interrupted, 'I'm telling you where there's _food_ my boy.'

'And _I'm_ telling you sir, if you'll not mind', he continued gravely, 'that we are _proper_ rearguards. And we _'ave_ learned one thing about _proper_ rearguards in this 'ere war right off, and that is that rearguards ain't expected to eat. So we 'ave give it up, we 'ave. It's a bad 'abit, any'ow. Ain't it boys?'

Off they trudged grinning. The funereal visage of the spokesman turned and indulged in a sombre wink whereat they laughed to a man and I with them. He had had his joke and played it out to his heart's content. I had not been long at that roadside when I realised that many of us had been labouring under a great delusion. It was not that someone was needed to cheer up the _Tommy_; it was that most of us needed the Tommy to cheer _us_ up.

16

COLD COURAGE

NORTHERN FRANCE

During the first months of the war a company of Yorkshire troops were ordered to occupy a village which, their scouts said, was clear of the enemy. Hardly had they entered the main street, with swinging strides and singing a soldiers' chorus, a lad in khaki jumped out from the front door of a house and ran into the middle of the road. Rifles cracked and the boy fell to the ground.

Skirmishing forward, the Yorkshire men found the young soldier dead with eleven wounds in his body. From villagers they heard that he had been taken prisoner the night before. The Germans had obviously thought it was safe for them to allow him to go free in the house, while they set up an ambush – he would be aware that if he attempted to give a warning he was dead. But he was determined to warn the approaching British troops, and he did.

The Yorkshire men could not identify the dead hero so they buried him in a nameless grave under a wooden cross. On it someone scrawled, 'He saved others. Himself he could not save'.

BATTLEFIELD MURDER

VENDRESSE, NORTHERN FRANCE

The 1st Battalion Scots Guards were in trenches near Vendresse on 14/15 September 1914 and fighting hard to block the heavy German advance onto Troyon Ridge. Second Lieutenant Compton-Thornhill was wounded and, together with wounded Guardsmen and Black Watch soldiers, he crawled into a pit to avoid further fire. The Germans came up and fired on this party of 30 to 40 British, whereupon a Black Watch officer put up a handkerchief as a signal of surrender. Seeing this, the Germans walked in and shot the British wounded, point-blank. Two men escaped by feigning death and crawling back to the British lines at nightfall. Nearby a wounded medical officer lay on the ground and when the Germans came up he handed them his revolver; a German took it and shot him through both hands and left him. Eventually he was rescued and ɡ back to England.

This story came from Lieutenant Sir E. Hulse, Scots Guards, and I have included it to show the attitude of some German troops in battle at this early stage of the war. A number of atrocities attributed to them were manufactured in London and others were greatly exaggerated, but some were guilty of cold-blooded killing during the first six months of the war.

RUNNING THE GAUNTLET

MISSY, NEAR SOISSONS

Major A.A. Martin M.C. was serving with the Field Ambulance of the 5th Division during the retreat from Mons and with two other doctors was in Missy when German artillery opened up on the British troops, mostly Norfolks and Cheshires. On the morning of 15 September 1914, Martin found 84 seriously wounded men in an alley, where bearers had collected them.

In a little stone fowlhouse fourteen were lying closely packed together, while other wounded lay on the floor of a stable and a kitchen. All had been hit the previous evening while attacking Germans concealed in a wood.

Under shrapnel fire the wounded were carrried to a large house where cooks soon had a big fire going and were boiling water. The first case for Major Martin was a young soldier of the Norfolks who had been hit by a shell in the abdomen; he died painlessly four hours later.

There were many with head wounds and serious compound fractures were numerous, with much shattering of bone.

By nightfall Martin and his fellow surgeons had 102 wounded who had to be evacuated before the persistent shellfire killed everybody in Missy. They rounded up farm carts but there were too few for everybody to ride in and many wounded men, weak with shock, pain and loss of blood, had to walk.

They ran the gauntlet that night, led by a big horse-drawn wagon with a red cross painted on the side. A German searchlight probed the dark-ness and fixed on the leading wagon, then moved down the column. 'Keep moving!' Martin ordered as the men hesitated. He held his breath, waiting for the stutter of German machine-guns which would cause yet more casualties.

The searchlight played up and down the column again and was then turned in another direction – there was no attack on the column of agony. But it was a long trip – to Bucy le Long, Venizel and finally Mont de Soissons where ambulance H.Q was based.

WHITE FLAG TREACHERY

AISNE FRONT, CHEMIN-DES-DAMES

On the morning of 17 September 1914, the 1st Battalion North-amptonshire Regiment was holding a line from which a company made a bayonet charge. They reached an old trench and from there had a furious fire fight against the Germans in trenches a short distance away, until somebody shouted. 'They're surrendering!' White cloths and handkerchiefs were being held up all along the German trench and British fire was stopped. A few minutes later about 300 Germans moved forward, some with handkerchiefs tied to their rifles, others with their hands up, a certain number still carrying their weapons.

In the confusion Captain J.A. Savage of D Company and Lieuten-ant J.H.S. Rimmer of C Company, both of whom spoke German, walked forward to the German trench to try to organise a surrender. They stayed there for about five min-utes and then started to walk back to their own lines. The white flags were still up.

They had covered about half the ground when the Germans opened fire on them from behind. Savage pitched forward, dead; Rimmer threw himself down and crawled back to safety. Lieutenant Gordon, who was standing watching the proceedings, was hit in the stomach and died from the wound.

This breach of white-flag trust was too much for the machine-gunners of the 1st Queens, watching the episode from the flank. They immediately opened up on the Germans, who had changed their minds about surrendering and were firing down into the British trenches, and the vicious British Vickers-fire 'harvested' the Germans, as one young officer expressed it.

A British medium machine-gun crew with the arms and uniforms of the 1914 campaign. Machine-guns were few in the British Army but trained riflemen could fire 15 well-aimed shots a minute and when facing this rate of fire the Germans were convinced that the British were using machine-guns.

(Author's collection)

FIRING SQUAD

MESSINES

In mid-October 1914 Sergeant Paul Maze, a Frenchman serving on General Gough's staff as an interpreter-translator, had to tell a German soldier found in civilian clothing that he was to be shot as a spy. Divisional H.Q. at the time was in Messines and the prisoner was being kept in the church crypt.

Ordering the guards to leave the room, Maze told the German his fate and the man repeated what he had claimed all along, 'I am not a spy, I am a deserter'.

A few months before, during the retreat from Mons, Maze had himself been in extreme danger of death when 'taken prisoner' by British troops and sentenced to death by a divisional general who would not believe that he was a Frenchman working for the British. Sensing that this man was telling the truth he rushed to General Gough, to whom he had instant access, and urged him to spare the man. Gough replied that he himself was under orders to execute him.

Maze was on his way back to the cell to tell the German he had failed when he met the firing party marching up the road and marking the spot chosen for the execution. The German gave him a letter to his mother and another to his girlfriend. The escort was ready to take him but Maze rushed back to Gough in a final effort at reprieve.

The general was in his car, which was already moving, but Maze put his head in the window and said, 'Look sir, let's not shoot this fellow. One German more or less is not going to affect the result of the war'.

'Do what you like with him', Gough growled.

Maze ran back and caught up with the party on the march to the death spot. He took everybody into a house and explained the position. The firing party seemed relieved. The military police sergeant reponsible for the German said, 'Well, we had better give him back the souvenirs he gave to us'. They handed over his watch and chain and other property and shook him by the hand. The German spent the rest of the war as a prisoner of war in England.

Maze was a remarkable soldier. He served not only under Gough but later General Rawlinson and he was known to General Robertson, the Chief of Staff. He became such an institution that he could walk straight into the quarters of the senior generals to tell them what he had seen and heard. He won the D.C.M., the M.M. twice and the Croix de Guerre.

STRETCHER-BEARER IN BATTLE

STEINSTRAATE, YPRES

On the morning of 25 October 1914 stretcher-bearers of No 2 Field Ambulance were in billets at Boesinghe, Ypres, when they were ordered to collect wounded from part of the line.

The Regimental Medical Officer on the spot, short of trained assistants, asked that one of the bearers be left with him and a Glaswegian, Private John Kendrick, was detailed for this duty. Under fire, Kendrick helped to get two badly wounded men of the K.R.R.C. and five equally badly wounded Germans to a small house a little way to the rear. Because of the shells and machine-gun fire it was impossible to remove them further.

The British line was about to be taken over by the French and the R.M.O. and his orderlies had to move with their unit. Kendrick volunteered to remain with the wounded in the house, who were desperately thirsty. Their cries were pitiful and, having distributed his own water and rations which did not go far among seven, he was determined to obtain fresh supplies for the men in his charge. The nearest water was in the French trenches, across flat ground raked by gunfire. Undeterred, Kendrick started at a run for the French lines and slithered in on the surprised *poilus* who loaded him with as much food and water as he could carry.

The next day, and the next, Kendrick made the same dangerous journey. On the second night a shell broke down one wall of the house and Kendrick had to move some of his patients. He was constantly busy tending their wounds and had no sleep.

Convinced by the morning of 27 October that he had been forgotten, Kendrick fashioned a Red Cross flag and hung it from the front of the house. It was seen by his own Commanding Officer, Colonel Mitchell, who had the wounded men and their saviour evacuated. For his 54 hours of unceasing devotion to duty Kendrick was awarded the D.C.M.

A Trench too Far

HERLIES, NEAR NEUVE CHAPELLE

In October 1914, a soldier of the Royal Fusiliers known as 'Ginger' was sent out one night near Herlies, to call in the men of a listening post. When they failed to arrrive another messenger was sent and in due course he came in with the men of the L.P. Ginger did not appear with the dawn and at the end of the day the company commander assumed him to be lost.

That night an exhausted and disgruntled Ginger appeared. He had not located the L.P. but instead got into the German lines and after a dust-up he had got away. During the day he hid in No Man's Land until nightfall gave him cover to get back.

The O.C. was relieved but said irritably, 'What made you go so far as the enemy position?'

Scratching his head, Ginger said slowly, 'Well sir, nobody said anyfink to me abaht it being aht o' bahnds'.

SETTING AN EXAMPLE

HOLLEBEKE, YPRES

On 30 October, 1914, the Germans massed 40,000 men on a narrow front to attack trenches held by cavalry at Hollebeke. Under drenching artillery fire the 5th Lancers suffered particularly heavily and when the German infantry swarmed into the attack the surviving Lancers were overwhelmed. A battalion of Indian infantry was rushed into the breech, lost almost all of their officers in minutes, panicked and broke.

Lance Corporal Colgrave of the 5th Lancers ran in among the retreating infantry, striving by word and action to calm them, restore confidence and give them directions. Finding themselves with a leader, the Indians rallied and held. Colgrave brought several groups under his command in this way and still found time to carry in a severely wounded Indian officer lying helpless on the ground. The German attack was beaten off, almost entirely through Colgrave's efforts. Many acts for which the V.C. was given were less heroic and showed less outstanding leadership than Colgrave's but the supreme decoration was withheld; he did, however, receive the D.C.M.

THE FIRST GROUND-STRAFING

BAILLEUL

In October, 1914, No 5 Squadron R.F.C. was based at Bailleul aerodrome. One of the squadron's most enterprising fliers was Lieutenant L.A. Strange who decided that his Avro, capable of a top speed of 80 m.p.h., could carry a Lewis gun provided the plane was not required to climb higher than 7,000 feet. Until this time fliers shot at the enemy with rifles or pistols or tried to lob a grenade into the enemy's cockpit.

Attached to the aeroplane with metal tubing and rope, the aerial Lewis gun was a crude job, but on 21 October Strange, with Lieutenant Abercrombie as observer, managed to get close to a German Albatross, determined to use their new invention. The gun jammed after a few rounds. Next day Strange went up with Captain Penn-Gaskell, the squadron's Lewis gun expert, who yelled himself hoarse in the air trying to make Strange understand that he was merely the driver of the Lewis gun's carriage while Penn-Gaskell was the battery commander. He intended to attack a German train and troops at Perenchies siding.

Strange took the plane down and together the two airmen carried out what was probably the first 'ground-strafing' in military aviation. He and his observer later strafed the German airfield at Thielt. It was an easy game at the time, as there was no danger of enemy aeroplanes attacking from above. Had such strafing been used extensively it would have helped the hard-pressed infantry fighting the first battle of Ypres.

Strange finished the war as a Colonel, with D.S.O., M.C. and D.F.C.

A 1914 dogfight between a German plane (top) and a French plane. The pilot flew the machine from the rear seat while his comrade took potshots with pistol or rifle. Sometimes grenades were thrown or darts were dropped on the enemy. Top speed of the aircraft was about 60 m.p.h.

(From a German magazine)

25

SERGEANT'S CHATEAU

CHATEAU HARENTAGE, YPRES

On Wednesday 11 November 1914, the Germans made a massive attempt to break through the British line and take Ypres. The 1st and 4th Brigades of the Prussian Guards – 13 battalions in all – were rushed north from the Arras front and launched against Gheluvelt. They broke through the British front in three places and took the first line of trenches.

About three and a half miles from Ypres, just off the Menin Road, was the Chateau Harentage, 150 yards

Sergeant Clarke's defence of Chateau Harentage, near Ypres. Allan Stewart painted the scene soon after the war in the heroic style popular at the time.
(*From* Deeds That Thrill the Empire)

26

behind the British front trenches. Sergeant Edward Clarke of the 15th Hussars was ordered to defend the chateau at all costs. His garrison consisted of only 12 troopers, supported at that time by 30 French colonial troops in nearby dugouts.

After heavy artillery preparation, the Germans advanced in column and halted on the edge of a wood 100 yards away. Clarke ordered his riflemen to pick their targets carefully and open fire. The German commander apparently believed that the chateau was strongly held and did not wish to delay his general assault by attacking it. He therefore ordered his troops to advance across the front of the house towards the Menin Road. Many fell to the enfilading fire of Clarke's sharp-shooting Hussars.

Close to the road the Germans were checked by British reinforcements and retreated – again in front of the deadly riflemen in the chateau. Clarke held the chateau for two and a half hours; it was then given a stronger garrison and held out for three days against artillery and machine-gun fire. Sergeant Clarke was awarded the D.C.M.

COLD COURAGE

ARMENTIERES

In December 1914 the British front was still without proper trenches and the troops had to build emplacements above ground from anything they could find and then try to camouflage their positions. On one occasion a machine-gun section, commanded by a young officer, was having great difficulty in establishing a suitable position. The officer stuttered badly at moments of high tension; indeed, his men said he sounded rather like one of his own machine-guns at such times.

Not satisfied with the placing of some sandbags, he jumped out of the weapon pit in full daylight – in full view of the enemy – to make adjustments. A machine-gun opened up on him but the lieutenant finished his work and stood up to view it.

His men shouted at him to come down but he glared towards the enemy and said angrily, 'I b-b-be-lieve the bli-bli-blighters are shoo-shoo-shoo-shoo-ting at me!'

A corporal grabbed his legs and pulled him down – and everybody looked at him with awed respect. They recognised a cool, deliberate act of bravery when they saw one.

WORDS OF COMFORT

YPRES

During the first battle of Ypres, Captain W.L. Brodie V.C., of the 2nd Battalion Highland Light Infantry, was holding part of the line with his company. They had repulsed several German attacks and his exhausted men had given up trying to restore the trench which was being continually destroyed by shelling.

Their casualties were lying all over the place and everyone expected to be blown up at any moment. Among some Germans lying dead in front, in the open, was a wounded man who kept imploring the 'good Englishmen' to put him in the 'grave' – that is what he called it – 'grave' being the literal translation for the German *graben* (trench).

All the British were fed up with this man who kept repeating the phrase and in the same melancholy tone. At last a Colour Sergeant leaned over the trench and said in a friendly voice, 'A'richt, ma wee mon; dinna fash; in a wee whiley we will a' be in the grave'.

Brodie, then a lieutenant, had won the V.C. at Beselare on 11 November 1914, when he led a bayonet charge and 'relieved a dangerous situation'.

AND THEN THE LAUGHTER ENDED

ARMENTIERES SECTOR

Trying to drain water from the trenches was a continuous misery during the first winter of the war. The pumps were primitive and inadequate and the labour exhausting. Private Frank Richards and his friend Stevens watched one morning while a man tried to repair a hand-pump. He had his boots, socks and puttees off, with his trousers rolled above his knees and he worked in the cold, muddy water. When he slipped on his back and submerged the two men burst out laughing.

Then Stevens too dropped down in a sitting position with his back against the rear of the trench. This time it was no laughing matter. A sniper shooting from the right flank had shot him right through the head. He was buried at Bois Grenier cemetery.

MÉDAILLE MILITAIRE

METZ

Felix Klein was a chaplain with the French Army and much of his service was in military hospitals. Among the stories he tells of heroism, suffering and sacrifice is that of Sergeant-Major Louis Schoeny, 5th Regiment of Field Artillery.

Louis received two serious wounds, one tearing away the side of his face, the other fracturing his skull. Yet he had the super-human strength of will to remain at his post, half blinded by blood, and to serve his gun till a splinter of shell struck him in the stomach and knocked him down by the gun carriage.

Another brave man, the lieutenant-colonel of the 53rd Battery – himself under treatment for wounds – was appointed to hand him the Military Medal (Médaille Militaire) – on 10 November 1914. As far as circumstances would allow he kept to the usual ceremonial, such as the military salute. Comrades looked on

from their beds and the officers came from neighbouring wards to make up a fine audience.

Everyone present, nurses and patients, felt tears come into their eyes. The colonel recited the prescribed words, 'In the name of the President of the Republic, and by virtue of the power conferred on us, we award you the Military Medal'. The dying man asked to be raised so that he might kiss the glorious badge, and receive it with more respect. As he pinned it among the bandages on the panting breast the colonel's own hand shook a little. Louis Schoeny fell back and died shortly afterwards.

29

HOLDING THE LINE

SANCTUARY WOOD, YPRES

On 11 November 1914, during the first battle of Ypres, men of London territorial battalions held the battle line in Sanctuary Wood as German artillery pounded their inadequate defences. The bombardment was intense and some men broke under the strain and ran out to certain death in the open.

A corporal fell with a shrapnel ball in the head. He lay unconscious all day, nodding his head as if suffering only some minor irritation. A worried young soldier said, 'Shouldn't we put him out of his misery?' A more experienced campaigner explained that the wounded man felt no pain, and towards evening he lay still.

Another soldier had his belly ripped open and sat against a tree, while he gazed with fascinated eyes at the coils of his own intestines, which he held in both hands.

Before the shelling ceased the men were ordered to man the broken parapets to repel enemy infantry 'Stand to' came the command.

'Mother of God!' a trembling soldier said. 'This is terrible.!'

A tall, veteran N.C.O. shouted grimly, 'Ha-ha me boys! Now we're for it – and so are they!'

Six German army corps of perhaps 200,000 men paraded in the open and now they swept down on the weak British Army. The line broke in places, was mended, broke again and was put together again. Next morning, opposite the London Territorials in Sanctuary Wood a German was seen alive at the British wire. He dropped his wire cutters and made a friendly motion with his hand, intending surrender. The Tommies covered him with their rifles and Corporal John Lucy called to them, 'No, Save him'.

A bitter voice replied, 'No bloody fear! No Sergeant Benson tricks here!' And the German was shot dead.

Sergeant Benson had been killed by the Germans when attempting to rescue a wounded German soldier. Corporal (later Captain) Lucy who told this story said that the man with the fearful stomach wound survived. His intestines had not been perforated and bearers got him to a field hospital where he was stitched together.

PRIVATE PROPERTY

KLEINZILLIBEKE, YPRES

On 8 November the Grenadier Guards with the London Scottish and a good many French troops were in the woods at Kleinzillibeke. A German infantry attack was expected to follow their artillery fire and, to escape the persistent sniping, much digging was going on. That day a Grenadier guardsman appeared at Major G.D. Jeffreys' company H.Q. with a Zouave in his bright red and blue uniform. 'Beg pardon, sir,' he said, 'but we've found about 60 like him digging in *our* wood. What shall we do with them'?

He was surprised when Jeffreys told him that the French Zouaves were British allies and had a right to be in the wood. 'Well, they'd better not touch *our* trenches', he said.

Many problems of inter-Allied co-operation occurred, at much higher level than this. General French was notoriously unco-operative with the French high command.

MAN'S BEST FRIEND

ROCLINCOURT, ARRAS

On 12 December 1914, a Zouave sergeant was in the trenches at Roclincourt when a shell burst near him, killing his neighbour and covering the sergeant with earth and debris. Badly hurt and three-parts buried the sergeant was helpless with nobody near except his dog, Fend-l'Air.

The dog's licking revived the Zouave and the animal then started to scratch him out of the rubble. His wounds were serious: the lower part of his right leg torn off, the left struck in the calf, a splinter of shell in the thigh, two fingers gone and his left arm burnt. He was taken to a dressing station at Roclincourt, where his foot was amputated. During the next six days he was moved from one medical post to another and his dog was allowed to stay with him as far as Aubervbilliers railway station. The surgeon in charge there told him that he could not send the dog on the hospital train to a base hospital.

The woman in charge of the soldiers canteen offered to look after him, though the parting of man and dog reduced many people to tears. Having forgotten to ask his name, the canteen woman called the dog Tue-Boches (kill Germans). Nobody could induce the animal to eat, so a group of women took him to the American base hospital and explained how he had saved the Zouave. He was sterilised, admitted to the hospital and given a basket bed next to his master. He then started to eat again. The sisters later recalled that he did as much to save the Zouave's life in hospital as he had in the trenches.

FOUR YEARS 'SOLITARY'

BERTRY

During the battle of Le Cateau in August 1914, Trooper Patrick Fowler of the 11th Hussars was cut off from his regiment and for four months, with two comrades, he wandered the Cambrai district. In January, half-starved and unkempt, and now alone, he came across Louis Basquin, a woodcutter, who took him to the house of his mother-in-law, Mme Belmont-Gobert.

It meant death for any French person concealing a British soldier so Mme Belmont-Gobert hid Fowler in a squat wardrobe, less than six feet high. Germans were billeted in the house and it was dangerous for Fowler to come out. Except for two periods in a barn when house-to-house searches were being carried out, he lived in the cupboard for four years.

In 1916 the Germans told Madame that they needed her entire house but she managed to take the cupboard with her to a new dwelling. Soldiers arrived to search it after some alarm and this time Madame signalled Fowler to leave the cupboard and hide under a bed while her daughter delayed opening the door. The soldiers inspected the cupboard and Fowler saw bayonet points coming through the mattress under which he lay, but he remained undiscovered.

32

He lived in the cupboard for two more years until Canadian cavalry and South African Scottish troops liberated Bertry in October 1918. Then he was briefly arrested as a deserter!

His cupboard is in the Imperial War Museum. Anybody in Bertry will direct an inquiring visitor to the house where 'the English soldier lived in the buffet'.

ENTENTE CORDIALE

LOCRE–DRANOUTRE ROAD, FLANDERS

Captain W.G. Padstow, a staff officer, was in a car travelling along the narrow Locre–Dranoutre road late in 1914. Rain was falling heavily, making even more foul the thick mud on either side of the road. He was following a convoy of five-ton supply lorries which after a while stopped.

Padstow sat in his car for some time waiting for movement and when none came he climbed out and trudged through the deep mud and pouring rain to the front of the column. He found the leading lorry facing a squadron of French heavy cavalry, cuirassiers, resplendent even in those conditions in breastplates – 'tin bellies' to the Tommies – and magnificent helmets with horse-hair trimmings. In command was a large and haughty French captain, who was waving his sword in the air.

Confronting him was a small Army Service Corps sergeant, soaked and fed up, but still managing to keep a cigarette alight. Neither he nor the officer understood each other's language and it was obvious that neither was willing to leave the pave for the deeper mud alongside.

Captain Padstow was about the intervene when the sergeant, hands on hips, said, 'You can fermez your flamin' frog-face and ally off the perishing pave, you son of a knight in shinin' armour'.

The cuirassier bowed his head and without another word he led his men off the road.

EYEWITNESS OF THE CHRISTMAS TRUCE

ROUGES BANCS, WEST OF FROMELLES

Many accounts have been written about the fraternising between British and German troops on Christmas Day 1914. The official descriptions are less graphic than the stories of men present. One of these was Lieutenant Sir E. Hulse, 2nd Battalion Scots Guards, who wrote about the event in a letter.

We stood to arms as usual at 6.30 a.m. on the 25th, and I noticed that there was not much shooting; this gradually died down, and by 8 a.m. there was no shooting at all, except for a few shots on our left. At 8.30 a.m. I was looking out, and saw four Germans leave their trenches and come towards us; I told two of my men to go and meet them, unarmed as the Germans were unarmed, and to see that they did not pass the half-way line. We were 350–400 yards apart at this point. My fellows were not very keen, not knowing what was up, so I went out alone, and met Barry, one of our ensigns, also coming out from another part of the line.

By the time we got to them they were three-quarters of the way over, and much too near our barbed wire, so I moved them back. They were three private soldiers and a stretcher-bearer, and their spokesman started off by saying that he thought it only right to come over and wish us a happy Christmas, and trusted us implicitly to keep the truce. He came from Suffolk, where he had left his best girl and a 3½ h.p. motor-bike! He told me that he could not get a letter to the girl, and wanted to send one through me. I made him write out a postcard in front of me in English and I sent it off that night. I told him that she probably would not be a bit keen to see him again.

We then entered in a long discussion on every sort of thing. I was dressed in an old stocking-cap and a man's overcoat, and they took me for a corporal, a thing which I did not discourage, as I had an eye to going as near their lines as possible! They praised our aeroplanes up to the skies, and said that they hated them and could not get away from them. They would not say much about our artillery, but I gathered that it does good damage, and they don't care for it. The little fellow I was talking to was an undersized, pasty-faced student type, talked four languages well, and had a business in England, so I mistrusted him at once. I asked them what orders they had from their officers as to coming over to us, and they said none; that they had just come over out of good-will.

They protested that they had no feeling of enmity at all towards us, but that everything lay with their authorities, and that being soldiers they had to obey. I believe that they were speaking the truth when they said this, and that they never wished to fire a shot again. They said that unless directly ordered, they were not going to shoot again until we did. They were mostly 158th Regiment and Jaegers, and were the ones we attacked on the night of the 18th. Hence the feeling of temporary friendship, I suppose. We talked about the ghastly wounds made by rifle bullets, and we both agreed that neither of us used dum-dum bullets, and that the wounds were solely inflicted by the high velocity bullet with the sharp nose at short range. We both agreed that it would be far better if we used the old South African round-nosed bullet, which makes a clean hole.

They howled with laughter at a *Daily Telegraph* of the 10th which they had seen the day before, and told me that we are being absolutely misguided by our papers; that France is done, Russia has received a series of very big blows, and will

climb down shortly, and that the only thing which is keeping the war going at all is England! They firmly believe all this, I am sure. They think that our press is to blame in working up feeling against them by publishing false 'atrocity reports.' I told them of various sweet little cases which I have seen for myself, and they told me of English prisoners whom they have seen with soft-nosed bullets, and lead bullets with notches cut in the nose; we had a heated, and at the same time, a good-natured argument, and ended by hinting to each other that the other was lying!

I kept it up for half an hour, and then escorted them back as far as their barbed wire, having a jolly good look round all the time, and picking up various little bits of information, which I had not had an opportunity of doing under fire! I left instructions, that, if any of them came out later, they must not come over the half-way line, and appointed a ditch as the meeting place. We parted, after an exchange of Albany cigarettes and German cigars, and I went straight to Headquarters to report.

On my return at 10 a.m. I was surprised to hear a hell of a din going on, and not a single man left in my trenches; they were completely denuded against my orders. I heard strains of 'Tipperary' floating down the breeze, swiftly followed by a tremendous burst of 'Deutschland uber Alles,' and I saw, to my amazement, not only a crowd of about 150 British and Germans at the half-way house which I had appointed opposite my lines, but six or seven such crowds, all the way down our lines, extending towards the 8th Division on our right. I bustled out and asked if there were any German officers in my crowd, and the noise died down as this time I was myself in my cap and badges of rank.

I found two, but had to talk to them through an interpreter, as they could talk neither English nor French. They were podgy, fat bourgeois, looking very red and full of sausage and beer and wine, and were not over friendly. I explained to them that strict orders must be maintained as to meeting half-way, and everyone unarmed; and we both agreed not to fire until the other did, thereby creating a complete deadlock and armistice if strictly observed.

Meanwhile, Scots and Huns were fraternizing in the most genuine possible manner. Every sort of souvenir was exchanged, addresses given and received, photos of families shown, etc. one of our fellows offered a German a cigarette: the German said, 'Virginian?' Our fellow said 'Aye, straight-cut': the German said, 'No thanks, I only smoke Turkish!' It gave us all a good laugh.

A German N.C.O. with the Iron Cross, gained, he told us, for conspicuous skill in sniping – started his fellows off on some marching tune. When they had done I set the note for 'The Boys of Bonnie Scotland, where the heather and the bluebells grow', and so we went on,

FIGHTING FLEAS (?) IN FLANDERS

4TH DIVISION

FLIGHT OF FLEAS FROM FLANDERS

WITH BEST WISHES.

Xmas 1914

This postcard was sent from Flanders during the same period as the Christmas Truce. Soldiers' uniforms quickly became verminous with fleas and lice, and bath-houses, some of them mobile, were set up behind the lines. While the troops bathed their clothing was steam-fumigated. (Author's collection)

36

singing everything from 'Good King Wenceslas' down to the ordinary Tommies' song, and ended up with 'Auld Lang Syne', which we all, English, Scots, Irish, Prussian, Wurtembergers, etc., joined in. It was absolutely astounding, and if I had seen it on a cinematograph film I should have sworn that it was faked!

I talked to a lot more Huns and found many very young fellows, but a good, strong, and pretty healthy lot. Probably only the best of them had been allowed to leave their trenches; they included the Jaegers, 158th, 37th, and 15th Regiments.

Just after we had finished 'Auld Lang Syne' an old hare started up, and seeing so many of us about in an unwonted spot, did not know which way to go. I gave one loud 'view-halloo', and one and all, British and Germans, rushed about giving chase, slipping up on the frozen plough, falling about, and after a hot two minutes we killed it in the open; a German and one of our fellows falling together heavily upon the completely baffled hare. Shortly afterwards we saw four more hares, and killed one again; both were good heavy weight, and had evidently been out between the two rows of trenches for the last two months, well-fed on the cabbage patches, many of which are untouched on the 'No Man's Land'. The enemy kept one and we kept the other.

THE SONG OF THE TRENCH

As early as December 1914 the horror of trench warfare was occupying men's minds. This song, one of the first to be written about the war is also one of the least known. Composed by Captain C.W. Blackall, probably at Fromelles, it tells its own story.

This is the song of the blooming trench:
It's sung by us, and it's sung by the French,
It's probably sung by the German Huns;
But it isn't all beer, and skittles and buns.
It's a song of water, and mud, and slime,
And keeping our eyes skinned all the time.
Though the putrid 'bully' may kick up a stench,
Remember, you've got to stick to your trench –
Yes, stick like glue to your trench.

1915

The two sides became deadlocked and large-scale bloody battles were fought for no gain whatever. The generals demanded more and more guns and shells; they did not understand that heavy bombardments would so churn up the ground that the infantry advance would be slower than ever. For the first time, the Germans used poison gas at Ypres on 22 April. At the Battle of Neuve Chapelle, 10–14 March, the British infantry broke the German line for the only time in the war. The generals waited for reinforcements – and by then the Germans had plugged the hole. Those British generals who prolonged the slaughter of 1915 kept their posts and were promoted; any who protested ran the risk of dismissal. General Haig reported that, 'The machine-gun is a much over-rated weapon and two per battalion are more than sufficient.' The Germans had 60 per battalion.

A NIGHT OF ADVENTURE

WYTSCHAETE, FLANDERS

Between the first battle of Ypres at the end of 1914, and that of Neuve Chapelle, March 1915, the war on the Western Front is a chronicle of small events; a trench or two won here, a farm-house there, a wood somewhere else. Fighting was often fierce and stubborn even though the incidents generally had no influence on the campaign. The British attack on Petit Bois, a wood a little to the east of Wytschaete, is a case in point.

The Germans had been harassing the British from the higher ground of Petit Bois and the Lincolns, holding the trenches opposite the wood, were ordered to capture it on the night of 12 December supported by the Liverpool Scottish.

Four volunteers from the Royal Engineers were needed to cut the enemy barbed wire; Corporal John Williams and three sappers volunteered. The Lincolns gave Corporal Williams a sergeant and 12 men as protection. Williams divided the party into two groups, took a sapper and six Lincolns himself and chose the longest route to the wire,

about 120 yards on the right. They were fired on climbing over the parapet but nobody was hit, then passed a machine-gun emplacement and a sniper but reached the wire which Williams cut.

As he had stationed men at intervals the corporal now had only two with him and he left them to reconnoitre while he went off alone; they would rendezvous later. Here and there he cut gaps in the wire and found saps – of which he could see short lengths of trench – running out of the woods from some of which he could see snipers potting at the British lines. While he was investigating one sap the base of a three-inch shell was thrown at him. He put it in his pocket. Then a clod of earth hit his face. He guessed that a German must have taken him for a prowling dog.

Crawling along, he came to the enemy's main front trench, half full of water which the Germans were baling out with much muttering and swearing. Reaching the woods, his trained engineer's fingers found

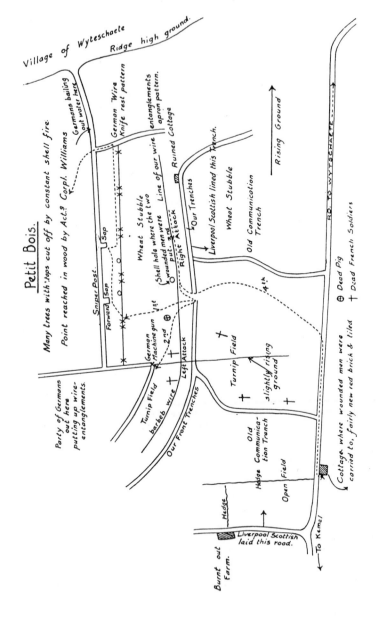

Petit Bois.

Many trees with tops cut off by constant shell fire.

Point reached in wood by Act.^g Corpl. Williams.

Village of Wyteschaete   Ridge high ground.

Germans bailing out water here.

German Wire Knife rest pattern

German Wire entanglements apron pattern.

Ruined Cottage

Line of our wire

Wheat Stubble

Shell hole where the two wounded men were put. 3rd

Right Attack

Our Trenches

Liverpool Scottish lined this Trench.

Wheat Stubble

Old Communication Trench

Rising Ground

RD. TO WYTSCHAETE

Snipers Post.

Sap

Forward Sap

German Machine gun

2nd

1st

4th.

Left Attack

barbed wire

Turnip Field

Our Front Trenches

Turnip Field

slightly rising ground

⊕ Dead Pig

† Dead French Soldiers

Party of Germans out here putting up wire-entanglements.

Old Communication Trench

Open Field

Hedge

Burnt out Farm.

Liverpool Scottish laid this road.

To Kemmel

Cottage where wounded men were carried to, fairly new red brick & tiled

After Corporal Williams' successful patrol this sketch was made to show his movements. It is reasonably easy even now to trace his route in the open country between Wytschaete and Kemmel.

several telephone wires which he cut. After this he returned to the two-men outpost and then to the Lincolns.

The other party which had gone to the left had long since returned but their report was unclear. Corporal Williams was asked to investigate. He found and traced the enemy trenches and also located a camouflaged machine-gun post, so he went again and cut gaps in the British wire so that the infantry, which were about to attack, could deploy from several places. The attack started prematurely because of the noise which the Lincolns made and Williams found himself in the middle of it, armed only with wire cutters. A sergeant by his side was hit and fell and the corporal carried him to a shell-hole; soon he carried a wounded private there too. After that, still under fire, he returned to the lines for stretcher-bearers for the wounded men. When he got them to a dressing station about 250 yards behind the lines, he met several staff-officers who complimented him on his courage and ability. The Lincolns' attack was successful.

He was awarded the D.C.M., promoted sergeant and placed in charge of several bridges of the Yser Canal, which were frequently shelled and needed repair. He was 34 in 1914 and lived in Tonbridge, Kent.

BEATING THE SYSTEM

ESTAIRES

Early in 1915 Colonel David Robie commanded the 1/2nd Highland Field Ambulance, in which capacity he learned how to overcome all the difficulties posed by Army bureaucracy. At one time he indented for 241 tins of iron rations – the units total allotment. This began a correspondence with H.Q.:

'Reference your indent for 241 iron rations. It is not understood how all your iron rations have disappeared. Please explain'.

To which Robie and his Quartermaster responded: 'These rations have been lost mainly through the action of rats'.

What they meant was that in many cases the rats had eaten through the linen bags in which the iron rations were carried and that the tins had fallen out through the holes while the men were on the march.

H.Q. sent another curt note: 'Please explain how rats can eat through tin'.

Robie replied: 'It is pointed out for your information that the rat prevalent in this district is not the small black rat but the large, grey Hanoverian rat'. (He meant the German soldiers.)

H.Q.'s reply was prompt: 'Thank you for information. Will suggest heavier metal. Your requisition is approved'.

THE QUICK OR THE DEAD

ARMENTIERES SECTOR

There was much patrol action by both sides during the winter months of 1914–15 preceding the spring battle of Neuve Chapelle. It was easier for the men to move when the ground was firm. Private Frank Richards had a narrow escape on the dangerous Armentieres front when he was one of a three-man scouting party in No Man's Land. A large patrol of Germans, not scouting but looking for trouble, could be seen approaching in the darkness. As the enemy patrol was well spread out the three Tommies scattered. Richards slid into a shellhole, broke through the ice and wriggled into the mud so that only his head and shoulders showed. From the lip of the hole he seemed to be dead and the Germans gave him only a passing glance.

CRACKING THE LICE

BOIS GRENIER, NEAR FLEURBAIX

In January 1915, the British took over trenches about 650 yards to the east of Bois Grenier. When the ground and water froze hard conditions were more bearable than when it was just cold, wet and

44

muddy. One advantage was that the men would take off their shirts and hang them out so that the lice would freeze to death when the shirts froze stiff. Even so, by midday a man's body warmth would hatch out more of the pests. Some soldiers reckoned, quite seriously, that the lice became not only helpless but visible in the ice and could then be cracked with a hammer or a piece of shell.

TO THE LAST MAN

CUINCHY

On the night of 24/25 January 1915 the Scots Guards held a position known as 'the Keep' because of its fortress-like appearance. It had been formed by linking up four brickstacks with walls of loose bricks so as to form a square fort with the brickstacks as the corners. The Keep was almost surrounded during heavy fighting and the defenders suffered many casualties but they held on. In front of the fort other Scots Guardsmen held a line of trenches, which the Germans had mined. When the mines exploded the German infantry rushed the position and stopped on the edge of the trench to shoot down into it. The Guardsmen fought desperately but in the end only one officer and three men were left and the men were picked off one by one. The officer, Major Morrison-Bell, now alone, surrendered. The most upleasant hour of all, he said later, was the final one when British artillery opened up on the trench to destroy the Germans.

So confused was this fighting that after the action no fewer than 235 men were posted missing. In fact, most were dead. At the time the officially dead numbered 27, with 120 wounded.

ONE-MAN STAND

LE BASSÉE CANAL

During an action at Cuinchy on the night of 31 January – 1 February 1915 a trench held by the 2nd Battalion Coldstream Guards was rushed and taken by the enemy and orders were given for its immediate recapture.

Company Sergeant-Major Seaman leading his men to the attack along the La Bassée canal. The towpath was the only possible way in which he could reach the British trench which the Germans had captured.
(*From a painting by M. Dovaston for* Deeds That Thrill the Empire)

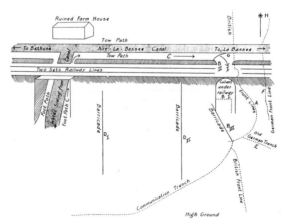

Plan of C.S.M. Seaman's exploit. A: Trench lost at 2.20 a.m., 1 February. B-I, B-II, B-III: Barricades put up by the Germans. C: Route taken by C.S.M. Seaman's party. D-I, D-II: British barricades. E: Old German trench along which the Germans advanced. F: Frontline German trench captured by the British counter-attack. G: Position of the Seaman party. H: Seaman later went to this position and kept up a continuous fire on B-I.

Lance Corporal O'Leary won the V.C. in the action at La Bassée Canal. First he killed the five Germans manning a barricade. Then, single-handed, he attacked an enemy machine-gun post, killing three Germans and capturing two. (*From a painting by J. Mantania for* Deeds That Thrill the Empire)

The job fell to C.S.M. Fred Seaman's company – or what was left of it, as only 20 men were still fit. At about 2 a.m. on February 1 C.S.M. Seaman was told to rush the trench along the towpath of the canal. A second party would attack from the other side of the railway embankment, which ran parallel to the canal.

Seaman led his party at the double until they reached a culvert under the railway. The Germans had barricaded it so that only one man could squeeze through at a time. To 'rush' it, therefore, was impossible. A runner arrived with a message from the C.O. asking if it was possible to get through the culvert. Seaman sent word that he proposed to do just that, by himself.

He squeezed through and remained there alone, picking off at close range every German who tried to reach him. In an hour and a half he built up a pile of German dead, though he himself was wounded by a bomb splinter. Eventually the trench was retaken by the other party, among whom was Lance Corporal Michael O'Leary of the Irish Guards, who charged an enemy machine gun and killed its crew. He won the V.C. and C.S.M. Seaman won the D.C.M.

FAIR PLAY

YPRES SALIENT

In a dawn attack early in 1915 British infantry reached a crater caused by a mine and now occupied by the Germans. It had to be taken and into it a captain, wielding a rifle and fixed bayonet snatched from a wounded man, led his company. Gradually the British mastered the enemy and the last fight was between a burly German and the British captain. Exhausted, but still with a sense of fair play, the troops watched the hand-to-hand struggle. At last the German went down and the captain, with one foot on him, raised his bayonet to deliver the killing thrust. Then he threw the rifle aside. 'I can't do it', he murmured, 'Hang it all, he was a sport!' Kneeling by the side of the panting German, he gave the enemy a drink from his own water bottle.

*The story was told by the journalist Levorno Sabatini, who added
'The incident shows that Britons conquer but do not crush'.
Several similar stories are told but most come from the early years
of the war.*

Once the fighting was over British troops could be generous. Here a Tommy distributes cigarettes to prisoners, some of whom seem glad to be out of action. Tommies were always immensely curious about captured Jerries, as this photograph shows. (*Author's collection and copyright*)

IN HOT WATER

POPERINGE

The brewery vats in Poperinge had been taken over by the Army and were used as soldiers' baths; they were very popular with the men down from the front line of the Ypres Salient. After a bath they generally were able to change some of their clothes and feel more human.

But the enemy often gave Poperinge brief but violent shellings. On

49

one such occasion it seemed that the old brewery was the target. A battalion of the King's Royal Rifle Corps was using the baths at the time and like any soldiers they had the wind up when caught in a strafe without their uniforms and weapons.

Above the din of explosions and falling bricks the crowd of men scrambling into their uniforms heard the voice of Sammy Wilkes, who was still in the vat. 'Lumme', he said plaintively, 'and I only asked for a little drop more hot water!'

The story was told by Corporal Albert Girardot, also of the K.R.R.C., when he lived in Cornwall Road, Ladbroke Grove, London W11.

NO TIME FOR CEREMONY

POELCAPELLE, YPRES

Before World War I, White City, London, was a great place of entertainment and one of its best known showmen was Alec Lancaster, who in 1915 became a sergeant in the Rifle Brigade. A short man, he had a big heart and an easy way with people; he got things done by sheer personality.

In front of Poelcapelle at a time when the British battalions were under immense strain, Alec exhibited his sangfroid in an unusual way. The brigade commander had been on a visit to the front line to inspect new belts of wire and passing the H.Q. of Alec's battalion he stopped for an impromptu call. At that moment shells started to come over and the experienced Alex, who was standing nearby, realised that a strafe was beginning.

He grabbed the brigadier by his collar and arm and propelled him violently into a dug-out. 'Nah then, nah then!' he said with showman's familiarity and style. 'We don't want any dead brigadiers rahnd 'ere'.

50

PARTING SHOT

NEAR HOHENZOLLERN REDOUBT, LOOS

On one of his Intelligence trips through the front lines Paul Maze,[*] in March 1915, came across a group of men bending over an officer who lay dead, shot through the head by a sniper. Standing dejectedly nearby was his batman, holding the valise of the officer, whom he was accompanying on leave to England; they had, in fact, been on their way out of the line. As they came to a sniper's post, the young officer had said, 'Just a moment, Bates, I think I'll fire a goodbye shot'.

It was just that; as he took aim a German sniper killed him. The batman looked helplessly at Maze and said, 'He was only going to have the one shot, just in fun like'.

[*] See story entitled 'Firing Squad' (p. 20)

TURNING SPACE

PLOEGSTEERT (PLUG STREET)

A soldier named Dave Coutts, a member of an infantry battalion, was famous for his quite enormous feet. His mates said that when he marked time during marching it sounded like a horse stamping on a concrete floor. At roll-call one morning the Company Sergeant-Major called his name – 'Private Coutts!' When there was no answer the C.S.M. tried again. Still no response. A voice said quietly from the ranks, 'Please Sergeant-Major, he's gone up to the cross-roads to turn around'.

Many soldiers said sourly that their feet grew large because of the great weights they were expected to carry. Here a fatigue party unloads ammunition under the eye of a sergeant of the Army Service Corps.

(Author's collection and copyright)

HOLDING FIRM

SPANBROEKMOLEN, NEAR WITSCHAETE, YPRES

The battle of Neuve Chapelle began, on the morning of 10 March 1915, with perhaps the heaviest artillery preparation in the history of warfare, to that time. A number of actions took place all along the British front to prevent any sudden massing of German reinforcements. One of these attacks was made against the German position at Spanbroek-

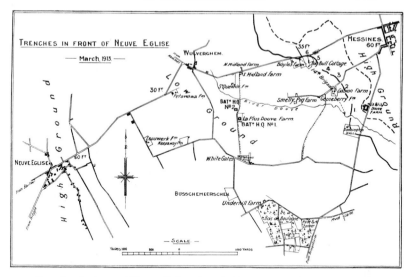

Trenches in front of Neuve Eglise, March 1915. Hundreds of maps of this type were drawn to show battalion battle movements. This map concerns a 'push' in Flanders from Neuve Eglise towards Messines Ridge, which, though only 60 feet high dominated the surrounding country.

molen. Though already wounded, Lieutenant Cyril Martin of the Royal Engineers volunteered to lead a small party of bombers against a section of the enemy's trenches.

They drove out the Germans, occupied the trench themselves and hurriedly piled up sandbags for the inevitable German counter-attack. During the next two and a half hours the Germans made one attack after another but the small party repulsed all of them. Finally a runner got through with orders to abandon the post and retire. Lieutenant Martin was awarded the V.C.

Martin already held the D.S.O., awarded during the retreat from Mons. Twice wounded, he had spent several months at home and had returned to the front only just before the Neuve Chapelle battle. The site of his exploit is not far from the 'Pool of Peace' at Lone Tree Hill.

53

THROUGH THE WIRE

NEUVE CHAPELLE

On 12 March 1915 the 2nd Battalion Rifle Brigade was sent in to attack German lines at Neuve Chapelle, on the extreme right flank of the British line in Flanders, and found that the wire entanglements protecting them were practically intact.

The battalion had expected the wire to be cut by British artillery fire; to proceed now would mean appalling loss of life. Under withering fire the troops went to ground but C.S.M. Daniels and Acting-Corporal Noble ran to the wire and began to cut paths through it. They were hit and hit again but before both fell with

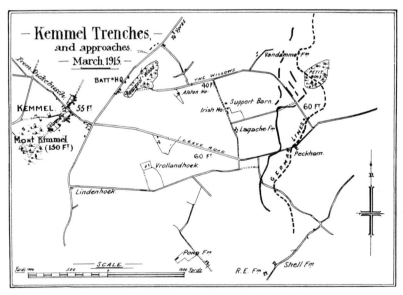

Kemmel, in Flanders, was held by the British for much of the war and Mount Kemmel (Kimmel on the map) was an important command and observation point. Several British war cemeteries were established in the immediate locality, including one at Irish House; the cemetery is known today by that title.

multiple wounds they had cleared a way through. The Riflemen rushed through the breach and in a bayonet charge routed the Germans.

Corporal Noble died of his wounds soon after this episode; C.S.M. Daniel recovered months later. Both were awarded the V.C.

'FRUIT SALAD M'LORD?'

FESTUBERT

The sangfroid of the Coldstream Guards has been illustrated many times but rarely more piquantly than by an incident on 10 May 1915, during the battle of Festubert.

The 9th had been a day of heavy shelling by both sides and on 10 May a gunner subaltern named Shadbolt was sent forward to observe from a captured German trench. Taking with him his batman, Gunner Langmead, and two signallers he threaded his way through the maze of battered trenches. Sandbags and dead bodies lay jumbled in wild confusion and finally they arrived at a trench so choked with dead that it had been left unoccupied by the British troops.

Shadbolt and the signallers settled down to work while Langmead went off looking for souvenirs. The enemy then began a tremendous bombardment and Shadbolt's major telephoned to ask what was happening and whether a counter attack was imminent. The matter certainly interested Shadbolt because between him and the enemy, only a few hundred yards away, was just one tired company of Coldstream Guards in hastily thrown up breastworks. The major said, 'Go and ask the infantry O.C. what's happening and see how we can help'.

The subaltern did a 150-yard sprint across the deadly ground and arrived panting and splashed with mud. 'Where's your O.C.?' he asked a bored sentry.

'The officers are having lunch two bays down the trench', the man said.

As Shadbolt rounded the next traverse he heard a voice say, 'Would you care for fruit salad, m'lord?'

Quite unmoved by the proximity and hostility of the enemy the aristocratic Coldstream officers invited Shadbolt for lunch but he wasn't sure that he would live long enough to finish it. 'Oh do stay, old chap', the captain said. 'Then you can go and shoot up a machine-gun that is rather disturbing us'.

Shadbolt declined the friendly invitation, stayed long enough to locate the offending machine-gun and ran back to his telephone to call the major. Fifteen minutes later, as the bombardment eased, in stag-gered his batman, Langmead, festooned with German helmets, sword-bayonets and other trophies of war. 'Please sir,' he said, 'I'm sorry I've been away such a long time, but I've brought you this ring which I got orf a dead German officer's finger'.

'You should join the Coldstream Guards', Shadbolt replied.

LOVE AND KISSES

YPRES SALIENT

In the support trenches of 13 March 1915, Lieutenant A.D. Gillespie of the Argyll and Sutherland Highlanders was writing home to his parents.

'I have been censoring the men's letters again and it's often very amusing, but they write so many that it takes up quite a lot of time. They send so many kisses, often to three different girls by the same post, and they are fond of quoting poetry copied from cigarette cards, or sometimes their own composition. And there are the usual Scottish phrases, "lang may your lum reek", and so forth, though as a rule it's only "hoping this finds you well as it leaves me".'

Gillespie led a charge of Highlanders at La Bassée on 25 September 1915. In the face of heavy fire he reached the German trenches, the only officer to get through, and was there seen to fall. His remains were never found.

VETERAN IN COMMAND

ST ELOI, YPRES

The British attack at Neuve Chapelle in March 1915 advanced the British line one mile on a three-mile front and the Germans then made furious counter-attacks. The heaviest of these struck British positions at St Eloi, a village on the southern ridge of Ypres. On March 14 the Germans massed their artillery and on that misty afternoon opened such heavy barrage fire against the 27th Division that wire defences and parapets were swept away. At the same time two mines were exploded at 'the Mound of Death', part of the front to the south-east of Eloi.

The brunt of the German infantry attack which followed was borne by the 2nd Royal Irish Fusiliers, whose C.O. and many other officers were killed. Command on the spot fell to C.S.M. Stanley Glover, a cool veteran. Holding his fire until a wave of enemy bombers were quite close, Glover gave the command 'Fire!' and the Germans died on the spot or as they ran back.

But because the line on either side of him had been forced back, Glover's post and its garrison of 50 men was practically surrounded. The din was so great that he could give commands only by hand. As he had to station men on both sides of his trench and at the ends his hand could not always be seen, so he tapped men on the shoulder to indicate in which way they should face and how many rounds they should fire. Movement was not easy as wounded men lay on the bottom of the trench.

Meanwhile a British counter-attack was planned, using Glover's central outpost as its 'peg', and it went in at 2 a.m. on the 15th. The C.S.M. was awarded the D.C.M. for 'conspicuous gallantry and marked ability' though many officers and men felt at the time that his exploit justified the V.C. The French showed their appreciation of Glover's courage with the supreme award of the Médaille Militaire. He was wounded in action on 4 May but survived the war.

HERO OF HILL 60

HILL 60, YPRES

About three miles south-east of Ypres and just east of the hamlet of Zwartelen – where dismounted Household Cavalry made a decisive charge on 6 November 1914 – lies an earth heap from the cutting of the Ypres-Lille railway. It is known to war history as Hill 60, since it is just 60 feet above sea level. Even this low height, in that flat land, afforded an artillery observation position which was worth fighting for. Hill 60 has countless stories to tell but what follows is one of the most heroic.

About 7 p.m. on the night of 17 April 1915 the British exploded seven mines under the hill. They created havoc in the German defences, blowing up the trench line and killing 150 of the enemy within. The 1st East Surreys then fought their way into the shell craters and established machine-guns. Throughout the 18th, 19th and 20th the Germans subjected Hill 60 to a tremendous bombardment, and followed with an infantry attack. The East Surreys were hard pressed and Lieutenant George Roupell won the V.C. for holding his post though suffering from several wounds.

Private Edward Dwyer, aged 19, had already shown much bravery in bandaging wounded men under fire. Now, late on the 20th, he found himself alone in a trench. He heard Germans talking in a trench about 15 yards away and knew another attack was imminent. Collecting all the grenades he could find he climbed onto his parapet and began to throw them at the enemy. They retaliated with bullet and bomb but by cool use of cover and bombs, Dwyer held the position until help arrived.

Dwyer was wounded on April 27 and sent to the military hospital at Etretat; a month later he learned that he had won the V.C.; he was decorated by King George V at Buckingham Palace on 28 June 1915. He reached the rank of lieutenant, a high rank at that time for a former greengrocer's boy from Fulham. The spot where he won his V.C. is at about the highest point of today's Hill 60.

SHOCK ON A SPRING EVENING

POPERINGE–YPRES ROAD

On Thursday evening, 22 April 1915, the men of the Queen Victoria Rifles of Canada were resting in a meadow off the Poperinge-Ypres road. They needed rest because they had just fought their first big action in the battle for Hill 60 and they had lost many comrades.

Some of the men were stretched out on the grass, others were washing and the cooks were getting a meal. Nearby, sappers were putting up huts to house the Q.V.R. It was all rather peaceful but as the sun was setting heavy shell-fire came from the north-west. The Canadians looked in the direction of the bombardment, which seemed to be where the British line joined the French, six miles away. Curiously, there was a low cloud of yellow-grey smoke and, most ominously, a dull murmuring which became louder.

Down the road from the Yser canal came galloping horses, singly and in teams, frenziedly ridden and whipped. The watching Canadians smelt something pungent and nauseating that tickled their throats and made their eyes smart.

Horses and men now poured along the road, often two and even three men to a horse. Over the fields came mobs of French colonial troops, throwing away rifles, equipment and even tunics. One man stumbled through the Canadian lines and an officer held him up with levelled revolver. 'What's the matter, you bloody lot of cowards?' he shouted. The African soldier, his eyes starting from their sockets, frothed at the mouth and fell writhing at the officer's feet. The Canadians were witnessing the effects of the first German gas attack.

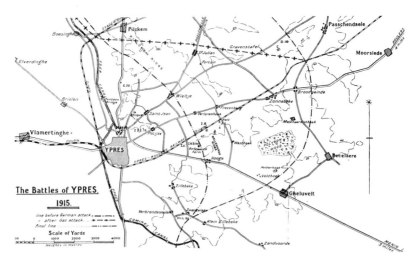

This map clearly shows the advantage gained by the Germans after their gas attack on 22 April 1915.

(See *'Shock on a Spring Evening'* and *'One-Man Action'*)

The 2nd Lancashire Fusiliers had no experience of gas before the attack at Ypres, so when they saw the green wall of what seemed like smoke approaching their trenches they underestimated the danger. Many of them were suffocated before the order to retire was given and in a few minutes the trench was empty except for the dead and dying – and Private Lynn.

(From a painting by H.J. Valda for Deeds That Thrill the Empire)

ONE-MAN ACTION

YPRES

On 2 May 1915, men of the 2nd Battalion Lancashire Fusiliers were peacefully making their tea in their trenches about 600 yards from the enemy line. Suddenly sentries called attention to a greenish yellow smoke which was rising from the German trenches. Puzzled by the smoky cloud, the men watched curiously. The Germans were seen retiring from their front trench and Private John Lynn hit many with bullets from his Vickers machine-gun.

Then the vapour reached the Fusiliers. It was poison gas and in seconds the men, choked and blinded, fell to the ground. Almost at once the order came to retire to the reserve trenches. Within a few seconds the front trench was left to the dead, the dying – and Private Lynn. He realised that behind the cloud of gas the enemy were advancing and though his eyes and lungs were full of poisonous fumes he waited for them behind his machine-gun.

The Germans came on confidently and upright, expecting no opposition. When Lynn opened fire they fell in swathes. None reached the trench. British troops in gas masks, making a counter-attack, were amazed to find the trench still held by one badly gassed man. They carried him to a dug-out but when the alarm was given for a second attack Lynn made a desperate effort to reach his gun. He died from gas poisoning 24 hours later.

Lancashire Fusiliers had been issued with primitive respirators the day before the attack but they had had neither experience nor training about gas. Private Lynn had already won the D.C.M. for courage on the Aisne River in September 1914. For his superlative bravery during the gas attack he was awarded the V.C.

BREAKING POINT

POPERINGE

On 4 May 1915, at a Field Ambulance post near Poperinge, Corporal Harold Chapin was on duty waiting for casualties to arrive from fighting taking place at Ypres, during the second great battle for that town. A man galloped up, reined in and said urgently, 'There's a man gone mad! They've got him in a little room by the railway station'.

Chapin took a motor ambulance and three bearers and hurried to the Poperinge station where he found the patient not raving but apparently asleep and wrapped in blankets. His mates were gathered round anx-

A soldier gives water to a shocked and wounded mate. Corporal Chapin (see 'Breaking Point') saw many soldiers in this condition, as did all members of Field Ambulance teams.

iously and Chapin joined in the discussion about what to do with him. One of his friends touched him compassionately. The soldier at once raved and struck out with his fists and feet, snarled savagely like a dog and tried to bite the men around him.

They overpowered him and lashed him firmly, but as gently as possible, onto a stretcher. As he bent across his patient Chapin's sleeve brushed his face. The man instantly seized it with his teeth, dog-fashion and tore at it. It took a dozen men to hold him down by arms and legs and even his hair and then they muffled him in blankets and got him into the ambulance which took him to hospital.

In the midst of this commotion in the dark a battalion of men passed the station, singing as they went up to the trenches. None of them noticed the episode outside the station.

The story was recorded by Corporal Chapin himself, an actor and playwright in civil life. An American by birth but educated in London, he enlisted in the R.A.M.C. from a 'sense of humanity'. He was killed on 26 September 1915, at the battle of Loos.

'SO MUCH PLEASURE AND EXCITEMENT'

PLOEGSTEERT (PLUG STREET) WOOD, FLANDERS

In May 1915, a very young subaltern, Gavin Greenwell, reached his regiment which was in trenches and billets in and around Ploegsteert Wood. His feelings, described in a letter, form a 'story' which shows that to many a young officer at that time war was still a glorious adventure. Greenwell's experiences at Plug Street should be contrasted with those he had on the Somme a year later.

I am at last among all my friends. I am supremely happy and have had the most interesting day of my life. I can't believe it is true. At 11 o'clock our *horses* came round and Alan Gibson and I mounted in the most divine sunshine to *ride* up to the trenches! I felt most contented and told him that I could scarcely believe we were so near the war. It was a glorious ride. In a few minutes we came to the village and then I first saw what war meant. It was shelled to pieces and almost every house had a hole in it, although the women and children, poor wretches, were still there!

We dismounted just behind the wood in which our regiment is, and walked through it along specially raised wooden platforms made by the Engineers. They all have names: the main road through to the trenches is called Regent Street. Hyde Park Corner, the Strand and Piccadilly are all official names, so I feel quite at home. I lunched with Hermon and his Company officers – six of them – in a beautiful wooden cabin: we had fresh meat, peas and fried potatoes, then tinned fruits and cheese and coffee.

Conny took me round this afternoon and I went through all our trenches with him. I kept meeting all my old friends round different corners. We had tea in a little dug-out with six other officers in the trenches, cakes galore and jam; very pleasant. Conny had three or four potshots with a rifle through a peep-hole. I had an excellent dinner, a beautifully cooked beef-steak pudding and rhubarb tart with cream; your present of a ham arrived to our great joy.

I have had a most ripping day: I can't remember ever having had so much pleasure and excitement. It is all so delightfully fresh after England that the unpleasant side of it does not strike me. I have been made Mess President and I am told that as long as things are packed *very securely* all is well. Good cheeses of the small Dutch variety and chocolates are welcome but Harrods will make suggestions. In Hermon's company they have a hamper from Harrods weekly.

THE C.S.M.'S VOLUNTEERS

FESTUBERT

At daybreak on 16 May 1915, after devastating shellfire, British infantry attacked German positions east of Festubert. The most successful attack was on the British right, against the Rue d'Overt trenches. The 1st Battalion Royal Welsh Fusiliers reached the first line of German

64

Having gone 'over the top', Tommies pass through some barbed wire in an attack. One man is already down and others will be hit. The gain in ground was rarely commensurate with the loss.   (Author's collection and copyright)

trenches and Company Sergeant-Major Frederick Barter called for volunteer bombers. With the eight volunteers who responded he cleared no less than 500 yards of trenches, captured three officers and 102 men and cut 11 mine leads; had they been exploded the attack could have failed. For this exploit, which became famous, C.S.M. Barter won the V.C.

However, there was more to the episode than the winning of a V.C. Among the eight men who assisted C.S.M. Barter was a private of the Queen's Regiment named Thomas Hardy, who had been temporarily attached to the R.W.F. for training in bomb-throwing. A man of splendid physique, Hardy was so pro-ficient in his military duties that Barter surmised that he had once been an officer. In fact, Hardy's real name was Smart and he had been a captain in the 53rd Sikhs, Indian Army. Being on leave in England when war broke out, he had decided not to return to India but to join a British regiment as a private to make sure of getting to the front. He was greatly respected in the Queen's.

He showed great courage in the bomb attack. Barter saw him hit by a bullet in the right shoulder and shouted at him to go back. He called, 'It's all right, I'm left handed!' While bombing the Germans he was shot through the head. Had he lived, Barter said, he would have received the D.C.M.

CIVILIAN VICTIMS

NEAR ARMENTIERES

It is often forgotten that French civilians were frequently the victims of German shelling but the Tommies frequently saw the effects of gunfire in still inhabited villages. Lieutenant A.D. Gillespie, billeted in a village, tells what happened before dawn one May day in 1915.

The next shell hit the roof of my friends' farm and sent most of it up in a cloud of red smoke and brick dust. I remember running up the road, with the doctor's pyjamas twinkling in front of me, shouting to the people to come out. The man came out, and three of the little girls, wounded and crying, and after them, the poor old woman, who was also badly hurt. We guided them along the road as best we could, back to our own farm, but the shells were still coming, and several times we

Soldiers had real feeling for the French and Flemish families with whom they were billeted. Here a farmer's wife indicates the swear box. The penalty for swearing during meals was one half-penny for each offence.

(*Author's collection*)

had to take shelter in the ditch.

Then I came away to rouse my own platoon, and get them down into the cellars, and while I was away, the Germans scored four direct hits on our own farm, and brought most of the wall onto my bed. In twenty minutes it was all over; we had seen nothing of Sophie and her mother, and were very much afraid they had been killed; but that plucky girl had stayed beside her mother, who is an invalid, dressed her, and guided her down to the cellar, where they were both safe.

Clemence, Amelie, and Simone had their wounds dressed, and were taken off in our ambulance; they will all recover in a few days I think, but the old lady is more serious. It does seem cruel that those little girls, who were so bright and jolly, and favourites with all the regiment,

should have to suffer for this war too; but, of course, I think they should never have been allowed to stay so near the firing line. Even now Sophie and her father are determined to stay here beside their cows, although they seem to have friends a few miles away. . . .

It took some time to clear up the wreckage in our room; luckily nothing had been set on fire, and there was great cheering when we discovered that a bottle of whisky which had been swept on to the floor was still unbroken! The doctor must have been very cold by the time his work was done, in a cold north wind, with only a thin pair of pyjamas. He is a first-rate man, and very good to all the French people round about, so that they all love him. His French is even worse than mine, but still he rattles along, and they enjoy his mistakes.

GRENADE ATTACK

GIVENCHY

The 24th Battalion London Regiment, a territorial unit, had attacked part of the German line on the night of 24 May 1915 and it was necessary to exploit its success. The following night 75 bombers assembled in a trench on a slight hill, about 40 yards from strongly manned German trenches. Their orders were to bomb the enemy out of his position.

The distance was short but the ground was cut up by shellfire and enemy fire was incessant; before the bombers were half-way across the open space half had fallen. Leadership of the attack fell to Lance-Corporal Keyworth, who commenced to throw his bombs when only a few yards from the enemy parapet. Then he jumped onto the parapet itself and threw his grenades with quick and deadly aim. When his own supply ran out he picked up the bomb-bags of dead or wounded comrades.

He maintained this attack for no less than two hours at various parts of the German line and threw at least 150 grenades. In this time 58 of his comrades were killed or wounded and others, having done their job, had retired. Keyworth, though often close enough to the Germans to be touched by their rifle muzzles, was not wounded. Not surprisingly his action, observed by many from the British trenches, won him the V.C.

BEST FOOT FORWARD

YPRES

In May 1915 heavy fighting took place in the Salient and the battalions of the King's Royal Rifle Corps had many casualties. One of the more seriously wounded was 'Topper' Brown, who had a bad reputation for losing items of his kit. He always seemed to be in trouble with the Company Quarter Master Sergeant.

Topper was carried to a dressing station where his mangled foot was amputated. He recovered consciousness on a stretcher and saw the C.Q.M.S standing nearby. The C.Q.M.S. had his own problems and did not then know the extent of Rifleman Brown's injuries, so he said in a kindly way, 'What's the trouble, Brown?'

Topper gave him a lopsided apologetic grin and said weakly, 'Sorry Quarter, lost one boot and one sock again'.

ON STAGE, GENTLEMEN

ELVERDINGHE, YPRES

Soldiers will get into any pool of water whenever the weather is warm enough and in the summer of 1915 it was sometimes very warm. One day some men of the Rifle Brigade were happily bathing in the lake at Elverdinghe Chateau, about a mile behind the line. Their chatter was cut short by enemy shells which landed too close for comfort and kept on falling. The swimmers hurried out of the water, stopped only to put on their boots, and stark naked dashed for the cellar of the chateau.

A sergeant on duty there bellowed, 'Now then, beauty chorus! Double up and change for the next act!'

The sergeant's words were heard by Captain G.E. Roberts M.C., a Signals officer of 21st Division who was supervising a wiring job at the time. He said he thought he heard the sergeant add in a grumble as he followed the naked troops, 'Gawd! I'd sooner look at girls any time!'

NOT AT HOME

MESSINES

Most frontline soldiers became fatalists and it was commonly said that you would not be hit unless a bullet had your name on it. A New Zealand unit was carrying gas cylinders to Messines on 5 June 1915, the night before the big attack. The ground was being sprayed by machine-guns and a bullet went through the ear lobe of a soldier known as Slabby. Having felt the clean, though bloody, wound and heard descriptions of it by his friends, he said, 'Cripes, that one had my name on it all right, but not quite the right address'.

During the warmer months soldiers were eager to get into any pool of water. These men are bathing in Lake Dickebusch – known to the troops as Dickie Bush – well within enemy artillery range in the Ypres Salient and not far from Elverdinghe Chateau lake.

INSPIRED NAME

HOOGE, YPRES

Lieutenant Gilbert Talbot of the 7th Battalion the Rifle Brigade was ordered to take his platoon and hold one of the craters which British shells had carved out in front of Hooge, just out of Ypres on the Menin Road. Having held it for a time, Talbot and his men were relieved. Later the Germans recaptured it with what was then called 'Liquid fire' – flame-throwers.

Talbot's platoon meanwhile had marched eight miles towards the rear and after only two hours sleep was turned around to be ready for a counter-attack on the captured trench. They were given nothing to eat or drink beyond a cup of tea but they marched back, worked their way along a communication trench through a wood that was being heavily shelled and then learned that they were to lead the attack. This meant a rush of 150 yards across open ground.

Talbot deployed his men on the edge of the wood and ordered them to lie down until the British artillery preparation was over. At the sound of five whistle blasts they were to go over the top. The whistle blew. Talbot was first up, shouting, 'Come along lads, now's your time!'

His platoon had already lost so heavily that only 12 men remained to follow him. He ran forward, pointing the way with his arm, only to be hit by a bullet in the neck. That one bullet probably killed him but another pierced his heart. Talbot's brother, Neville, recovered his body a week later.

The name Talbot is one of the most enduring on the Western Front because Gilbert Talbot was the inspiration for Talbot House, established in Poperinge by Padre P.B.H. ('Tubby') Clayton as a place of rest for all servicemen, regardless of rank.

RAISING THE WIND

FLEURBAIX

During 1915 the 11th Battalion of Rifle Brigade was in the line at Fleurbaix and sometimes it was quiet enough for a game of nap, even in the front line. Five mates, named Deer, Cullinson, Chapman, White and Bones, were enjoying just such a game one day in October.

Private Deer, flat broke, dropped out. A fanatical lover of the game, he offered various articles for sale – cigarette case, pipe, a mirror – but nobody else was interested.

'All right, you bastards', he said, 'I'll go and find a Jerry. Will somebody buy him for a franc?'

'It's a deal!' the others said, laughing, and Deer went off muttering.

He was absent for more than an hour and then turned up with a scared German soldier with his hands above his head. 'Now I'll have that franc!' Deer said grimly. 'From all three of you – you can have shares in Jerry'.

With his new capital he cleaned the others out and after that they turned the German over to a signal party going to the rear. All five riflemen survived the war.

A Tommy proudly brings his wounded captive along the fire-trench. It can be identified as such by the fire-step at left; the troops stood here when standing-to in order to repel an attack. (*Author's collection and copyright*)

ROYAL SALUTE

GORRE, FESTUBERT

On a morning towards the end of May 1915 just before the battle of Festubert, Privates J.F. Davis and Bill Cornish were returning from the village bakery on the Festubert road to their billets in Gorre. They had bought a loaf of bread each and were without rifles.

Turning the corner into the village they saw marching towards them a company of the Grenadier Guards in battle order. At their head was a slim, short young officer carrying a stick and behind him was a big guardsman playing 'Tipperary' on a concertina.

Davis and Cornish tucked their loaves of bread under their left arms, stood to attention and saluted smartly. The young officer glanced at the bread, smiled at the two soldiers and returned the salute. They at once recognised the Prince of Wales.

'Lummy!' Bill Cornish said as the company passed by. 'There goes the Prince of Wales himself a-taking the guard to the Bank of England!'

At that time and for many years. afterwards the Guards did mount a guard over the Bank of England. The story came from Mr Davis, who many years ago lived on the Old Kent Road. The Prince was certainly in the Festubert area at the time and he usually had an escort of Guardsmen.

Private Davies and Cornish would have seen something like this. The Prince of Wales joined the colours on 8 August 1914, only a few days after war was declared. In this photograph he is shown marching with a squad of Grenadier Guardsmen. He was 20 years of age at the time. (*Author's collection*)

SPECULATION

BARBURE

On 28 June 1915, a wet and miserable day, Captain Rowland Feilding of the 3rd Battalion Coldstream Guards was marching in front of his company and overheard a brief exchange from behind him. He recorded it in a letter to his wife.

One of the men, feeling very miserable, was holding forth on the hardships of a soldier's life. 'I wish my father had never met my mother,' he said.

After a moment's silence a voice came softly from behind, 'Perhaps he didn't.'

THE FIRST LIQUID FIRE

HOOGE, YPRES

On 30 July 1915, British troops in the front trenches at Hooge heard sounds as of splashing in front of them. Then there was a peculiar smoky smell like coal-tar. At one point a corporal cried out that he had been hit by a shell but those who looked at him found that he had a huge burn-like blister on his forehead while the back of his cap was smouldering.

The Germans had squirted their first 'liquid fire' at the British. Seconds later it poured in streams all over the earthworks, while star shells ignited the black liquid. Sandbags, blankets, tunics – anything that would burn smouldered and smoked. Where the stuff settled on the men ghastly wounds appeared. They were choked by the smoke and half scorched by the heat. Whistles shrilled and N.C.O.s yelled 'Stand to!'

The German infantry, led by the élite 126th and 132nd Prussian Regiments were following up the liquid fire, confident that the British were virtually wiped out. Behind the Prussians came a rabble of Land-

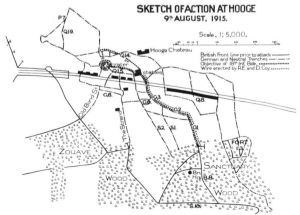

The 2nd Battalion Durham Light Infantry was one of many British battalions which distinguished themselves at the long-running battle of Hooge. The painting by Gerald Hudson shows the ferocity of the fighting. The map indicates the position of the Sherwood Foresters on 9 August 1915. The crater is now a beautifully landscaped cemetery of the Commonwealth War Graves Commission. More than three-quarters of the 6,000 soldiers buried there could never be identified.

sturm reserves, poor quality, over-age and under-trained troops.

Resenting the 'dirty trick' of liquid fire, the British troops kept down and then rose right along the trench and opened rapid fire. The Prussians went down almost to a man and the Landsturmers turned and ran, to be picked off in their hundreds. Had the British leaders left the affair at that it would have been a victory; but a charge was ordered and as barbed wire hundreds of yards deep and protected by machine-guns had to be crossed, British casualties were heavy.

FLIERS STICKING THEIR NOSE INTO ARMY BUSINESS

ZILLIBEKE, YPRES

The first big engagement of the 6th Battalion Duke of Cornwall's Light Infantry in the Ypres Salient was to mount a counter-attack to recapture trenches lost by the King's Royal Rifle Corps and Rifle Brigade on 30 July 1915. The Germans had used flame-throwers and had literally burnt the riflemen out of their positions.

To get into action on 1 August the D.C.L.I. had to cross open country in full view of the enemy and they caught his full fury as they reached Hell Fire Corner on their way to Zillibeke Lake. Casualties from shellfire were heavy and others were caused by a German airman who fired on the troops with a machine-gun.

Private Wally Robbins, his company's humorist, was looking up at the plane when a shell exploded and killed several men in front of him. As Robbins fell, his mate, Private E.W. Fellows, thought that he too had caught it and rushing up anxiously he said, 'Are you hurt?'

'I should think I am,' Robbins said indignantly. 'I wish they'd keep their bloomin' aeroplanes out of the way. If I hadn't been looking up at that damn thing I wouldn't have fallen over that bleedin' barbed wire stake.' Robbins was later promoted corporal and won the M.M. but was killed at

Lens. Fellows also became a corporal and was awarded the M.M. and survived the war. It should be remembered that aeroplanes were new in war and the soldiers were intensely curious about them.

From general to private there was a feeling in 1915 that they were intruders in the bloody game being played out below and that they should confine their activities to observation.

"IF EVER I CAN GET BACK THERE . . ."

STEENVOORDE, NORTHERN FRANCE

Flanders is so very flat that most British soldiers found it dull and drab and many longed for hilly country. Indeed, there are seven 'mountains' in south-west Flanders, though the highest of them is only a few hundred feet high. This area was behind the firing line until April 1918 and was much used for rest and billeting. Lieutenant A.D. Gillespie, Argyll and Sutherland Highlanders, fresh out of the firing line of Ypres and billeted in the French Flemish town of Steenvoorde, took a walk on 18 August 1915 and next day wrote about the experience.

I had a walk and a wonderful view, for after six months I was able to find a hill to climb – the Cats' Mountain – and from the monastery at the top I could look down on the whole plain. To the south and east it was rather hazy, so that I could hardly make out Lille and La Bassée, but to north and west I could see almost as far as Calais and Dunkirk – and Ypres lay below, across some miles of wooded hills and hop-fields, as pretty a stretch of country with its hops and corn-fields and woods and red roofs and church spires as you could wish to see, and although the trenches are so close in front, it seemed wonderfully unspoilt. A moving war tramples the country underfoot, but, except for the belt round the two lines of trenches, this waiting game does not do so much damage. I could see the ruined Cloth Hall at Ypres quite distinctly, and the ruined

Cathedral Tower, and I could even see the shells bursting over Hooge – where we captured some trenches the other day – in puffs of white and black smoke.

It was a marvellous sight; you might go there day after day for a week, and not get tired of it, and if ever I can get back there, I shall go – for on a clear day you could see beyond Arras to the south. The monastery has been turned into a convalescent hospital, a pleasant breezy place to lie, looking down across those miles of level country, with its villages and churches. I thought I heard the sound of monks chanting Mass, but when I came round the corner by the church, it was only six Tommies, dressed as pierrots, singing 'We pushed him through the window' to a large and happy audience of the patients. But some of the monks were there still, and I saw them bringing in their harvest, working in their long white robes, with cords round their waists. Some officers from the Indian Medical Corps gave me a 'hurl' down in their ambulance – which was lucky, for it was a good long walk, so long that, when I started, the others derided me and said I should never get there. But in spite of six months in the trenches, I can still walk.

Mont des Cats had been the scene of fighting earlier in the war and the Prince of Hesse was killed there by a British bullet. Later in the war the monastery was damaged by German long-range shelling. During 1940, in World War II, it was for a time a British military hospital. Lieutenant Gillespie did not return to enjoy more views; he was killed in action in September 1915.

THE BALL AND THE BATTLE

LOOS

When the 1/18th London Irish of the 47th Division went into the bloody shambles of the battle of Loos, 25 September 1915, a football went with them, swinging by its lace from a bayonet standard. At some time during the advance across No Man's Land some men on the right of the regiment's line began to dribble the ball towards the German trenches even though this caused some confusion and irregularity in the line.

78

At the German barbed wire the attacking British were seen by the Germans for the first time that morning; up till then the enemy had merely fired into the curtain of smoke which was supposed to give the British some concealment. As they got through the wire the Irish ran into aimed rifle fire, grenades and petrol bombs.

It was here that Patrick Macgill, a stretcher-bearer, saw the bullet-riddled limp lump of pliable leather which had been the football kicked across the field. It had not, after all, been the subject of such a romantic episode of war. With the ball he came across 'dead, dying and sorely wounded'. The ball mattered little against lives maimed and finished, all the romance that makes up the life of a soldier had gone for ever.

Much was later written about that famous football, most of it erroneous. Macgill, who already had a growing reputation as an author, wrote his impressions of the football incident at the time. The football could never have inspired a whole battalion; the line of men was too harassed by murderous fire to take any notice of it.

HOLDING ON

ST JEAN, YPRES SALIENT

The plank road outside St Jean was one of those many avenues in the Salient along which passed the dead, the dying and the badly wounded on their way back from the front trenches and shellholes. At one period some stretcher-bearers were bringing back a man whose left leg had been blown away below the knee. Another soldier, on his way forward, recognised the casualty and said, 'Hello Bill. Blimey, mate, you ain't 'alf copped it'.

Bill gave him a faint smile and pointed to his left sleeve which bore six gold stripes, one for every wound he had suffered. 'This makes seven', he said feebly, 'and that's me lucky number'.

This classic story was recorded by S.G. Wallis Norton, of Peaks Hill, Purley, Surrey. He was unable to give any further details about identity and unit of the 'lucky' soldier.

DYING HARD

HOOGE, YPRES

The astonishing courage of young officers, filled with *esprit de corps* and intensely aware of their obligation as leaders was never better exemplified than by 2nd Lieutenant R.P. Hallowes of the 4th Battalion Middlesex Regiment during the fierce fighting at Hooge in the period 25–30 September 1915. On four separate occasions the trenches held by him and his men were subjected to prolonged and powerful bombardment. It was terrifying but the young lieutenant clambered onto the parapet amid bursting shells and the crumbling trenches and by his reckless bravery calmed the fears of the men. When the enemy infantry attacked and the platoon ran short of bombs, Lieutenant Hallowes went back to the dump, under fire, for fresh supplies. After five days of almost incessant fighting he was hit, but he still continued to cheer and inspire his men. His last words were, 'Men, we can only die once. If we have to die let us die like men, like Die-Hards!' And he did die, just like that.

The Middlesex Regiment gained its nickname the Die-hards, during the Battle of Albuhera, Spain, in 1811. The regiment was standing under fire from the French attackers and their C.O., Colonel Inglis, rode along the front of the line calling, 'Die hard men! Die hard!' Like Lieutenant Hallowes, he too died.

CORPORAL'S CRATER

ZILLEBEKE, YPRES

On 30 September 1915 a British trench at Zillebeke was mined by the Germans and almost destroyed in the subsequent explosion. At the time Lance-Corporal C. Leadbetter, 1/5th Battalion Lincolnshire Regiment, was in charge of the listening-post at the end of the trench. The mine explosion was so great that it blew him over the parapet and inflicted serious injuries. Crawling back into the trench, the corporal collected the surviving men and ordered rapid fire on the Germans who were advancing to capture the mine crater. This prompt action saved the situation, for the German attack faltered and fell away. Leadbetter remained with his men until ordered to go to a dressing station and later he was awarded the D.C.M.

It was always important to capture mine craters and hold them; they could be quickly turned into mini-fortresses and were immensely costly to recapture. Many of the V.C. exploits of the war concern the storming and capture of fortified craters.

SEEING THE LIGHT

WIELTJE, ON THE ST JEAN ROAD, YPRES

During the winter of 1915 Corporal E.W. Fellows, M.M. of the 6th Battalion Duke of Cornwall's Light Infantry was in an isolated listening post in No Man's Land. Suddenly, the man with him, 'Nobby' to his mates, threw a grenade towards the German trenches. At once the enemy sent up flares by the dozen, turning No Man's Land into a ghostly daylight and alerting tens of thousands of men. 'What is it?' the corporal said tensely. 'Did you spot something?'

'I wanted to know the time', Nobby explained patiently, 'and I couldn't see my blinkin' watch in the dark'.

A famous encounter battle in November 1915 between the 2nd Battalion of the Ox. and Bucks. Light Infantry and a German battalion in Nonneboschen Wood, Ypres Salient. The painting is by W.R. Wollen.

BRIEF RESPITE

DIXMUIDE–VEURNE ROAD

Six doctors, a major and a colonel, all Belgian, a stray English officer and several British First Aid Nursing Yeomanry (F.A.N.Y.) nurses were celebrating in a Belgian regimental aid post one day late in 1915. One of the doctors had been decorated for gallant service and the group, for once not busy with wounded, was relaxing with champagne, biscuits and coffee and even speeches in a house by the side of the road, which had been made into the R.A.P.

In the midst of their merriment there was a loud knocking at the door. It flew open and a rain-drenched soldier stumbled in, dazed and white, clinging to a rifle with one hand – the other was tied up with blood-stained rags. After him came bearers with a stretcher and on it was a soldier with an ugly leg wound.

Another stretcher was carried in, this time with a lad who had half his head shot away.

'Ah well', the recently decorated doctor said with a sigh as he set to work, 'I am being reminded why I was given a medal – and why I should not celebrate with champagne. Blood and champagne do not mix'.

TALBOT HOUSE

POPERINGE

One of the best known places on the Western Front was Talbot House (Toc H in Army signal jargon) and it is the only World War I establishment which continues to function to the present day. The senior Church of England chaplain, Neville Talbot, assigned Padre P.B. ('Tubby') Clayton to run this rest and recreation house in Gasthuistrasse, Poperinge. It was to have been called Church House but the Army thought that this label might keep soldiers away from it. It was therefore called Talbot House, not so much to commemorate Neville Talbot as Gilbert Talbot, who had been killed in action at Hooge. Clayton's letter of 6 December 1915 is a story in itself.

Talbot has given me the job of opening a kind of Church House here in a town full of troops, some permanent like police, Signal Cos., R.E.s, R.A.M.C., A.S.C., etc., others coming in and out on their way up. True the Boche are less than ten miles away on three sides of us, and don't let us forget it from time to time. But, if they shell this place, one or other of their own billets gets a return of the compliment with interest from our 'heavies'. So that the game is, on the whole, unprofitable from their point of view. . . .

It is a beautiful house with a lovely garden, full of standard roses, pergolas, wall-fruit and a chicken run.

I'm going to get together a little batch of amateur gardeners to run the garden in spare time – it will be a peaceful recreation, much appreciated, and I'm anxious to have the place in apple-pie order. After the voluntary service last night (held in a music hall) about forty men came round with me and went over the house, which was great fun and made them quite keen on it all. We have an inaugural concert on Saturday night, and on Sunday morning at

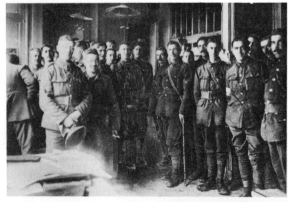

(a) *Talbot House, Poperinge, the rest house and sanctuary established by Padre P.B. ('Tubby') Clayton.*
(b) *British guardsmen and Canadian soldiers in the Talbot House tea room in 1916.*
(c) *Padre Clayton, centre front, with his staff in the garden at the back of the house. Operated by Toc H, the organisation founded by Clayton, Talbot House still functions as a guest house and the walls carry Clayton's famous instructions to his soldier guests, such as PESSIMISTS, THIS WAY OUT. – pointing to the door.*

84

11.15 the first Celebration in our Chapel (a big landing on the second floor). There is room for fifty or sixty, and I hope we shall have it full. . . .

Meanwhile, as I write, a stream of traffic like that of Fleet Street passes slowly – staff cars, motor cyclists, lorries, waggons, horsemen, ambulances, soldiers of all sorts and descriptions, carts with furniture of refugees who can stand it no longer tied on precariously. I covet these chairs and tables greatly. Meanwhile papers and books from time to time will be a great help. The men here are grateful for the simplest kindness shown to them personally, a cup of cocoa and a Belgian bun do not lack their reward.

FRENCH VALUES

VILLERS-BOCAGE

Villers-Bocage was on the direct route to the Somme front and in it many a battalion had its first glimpse of the human effects of the war; a motor ambulance unit used the village as a depot and the *Mairie* was a hospital. It was more dilapidated than villages further back and troops were lodged in derelict property. The 15th Highland Light Infantry was in residence there between 28 November and 1 December 1915. The short stay taught them much about the high value the French put on their ramshackle buildings and about the ways of French officialdom.

Some soldiers were frying bacon in a barn when it caught fire and someone made the mistake of throwing water on it. The fat spluttered, lit some hanging straw and in a minute the whole place was burning. The alarm was sounded and soldiers formed a bucket brigade to the pond 100 yards away. Some of the H.L.I. men had been Glasgow firemen and they isolated the blaze. With noisy ceremony the local fire brigade turned up and applied the traditional local method – they pushed a long pronged pole through holes in the barn and dragged down the gables. There was no great loss beyond the old mud and rush hut.

The owner put in a claim next day so high it would have paid for a chateau. The Gendarmerie and the Battalion court of inquiry sat simultaneously the next day. The battalion's inquiry finished at 1.30. The Gendarmerie was still sitting at 4.30 p.m.

Fortunately for the H.L.I. a

French-speaking Scottish officer made a few inquiries of his own and discovered that an insurance policy existed, so that a reasonable estimate of the barn's worth was established. By 2.30 p.m. the whole matter had been resolved.

The Gendarmerie inquiry adjourned at 8 p.m. for refreshments only to be told that the matter had been settled.

'So quickly!' the chief gendarme exclaimed.

The French-speaking Scottish officer said, 'Well, there's a war on, you know'.

FRONTLINE PIPERS

LOOS

On the afternoon of Christmas Day, 1915, Piper Donald Marshall, 1st Battalion London Scottish, with two comrades, piped Battalion H.Q. for a while and then went to the frontline, where they gave a rousing performance for the Germans, who were in trenches very close by. At first the enemy was startled and appeared to think an attack was imminent and sent up a flurry of flares. When the British showed no hostile intent the Germans joined in with some singing and mouth-organ music.

Marshall and his friend finished their playing and moved back down the trenches. As they passed the men of another regiment one of them said, 'Was that you Jocks playing them bloomin' toobs?'

'Aye', Marshall said. 'We have to admit it'.

'Hear that, Joe?' the soldier said to a mate. 'These blokes have been giving the Huns a bagpipe tune at close range'.

'Serve the bastards right,' Joe said sourly. 'They started the blinkin' war'.

Whatever Joe thought of the bagpipes, the fact is that the Scottish regiments, and often enough British regiments as well, found them inspiring. Some units attacked to the skirl of the pipes and on more than one occasion a wounded piper showed great gallantry by continuing to pipe his comrades forward. One German nickname for the kilted regiments was 'the ladies from hell'.
(Author's collection and copyright)

THE LONELY ARM

YPRES

Soon after Christmas 1915, Corporal Arthur Fairhurst of 129th Field Company, 24th Division Royal Engineers, was billeted in cellars close to the ruined Cloth Hall of Ypres. He had been 'up the line' during the night and after a few hours sleep he had a mug of tea and a bully beef sandwich before returning to duty. It was his regular

87

Ypres, wrecked by German artillery fire, as Corporal Fairhurst would have seen it. On the right are the remains of the famous and beautiful Cloth Hall and at left St Martin's Cathedral. Both were largely rebuilt with bricks and stone from the debris.

task to cross the town and report the night's activities of his section to Royal Engineers H.Q. some distance away.

The battered city was empty and Fairhurst had a lonely trip down Rue de Hearn and past the Cloth Hall ruins. He came to the ruins of a shop which looked like a carpenter's business, or perhaps that of a wood carver, and as he was a joiner by trade he went in.

The shop was devastated and all tools had been removed from the work bench but he found a brown paper parcel which contained two arms beautifully carved in boxwood; each was about six inches long and they were apparently for a crucifix figure of Christ.

Fairhurst knew that the carver would not want them destroyed so he wrapped one of the arms and took it with him. Later Fairhurst was wounded at Ploegesteert (Plug Street) but he managed to keep the wooden arm, which he felt brought him luck.

In 1982 Mr Fairhurst returned the arm to the city of Ypres (Ieper) and it is on display in the Salient Museum, which is part of the Cloth Hall. The house whose cellars sheltered Fairhurst and his comrades had been owned by a banker and it was between the post office and the prison.

'IT WAS A HORRIBLE NIGHTMARE'

YPRES SALIENT

This story, told by a soldier of the King's Royal Rifle Corps, vividly describes a man's first experience of battle. The battle he described took place in the Ypres Salient in 1915. His account is signed merely by his intitials, J.C.

The fatal day here! Received instructions just before dawn. Told to take opposite trench and hold until No 2 party arrived to consolidate, then to go forward to second line and hold until further instructed. Artillery going like mad, never heard anything like it. Got order and went over top. Could see shells pounding the enemy trench to atoms. Felt better by the sight. Suddenly noise lifted and a queer silence prevailed. My heart seemed to stand still. Could not see trench ahead, owing to smoke and dust. Then the order came and we went forward at the double with the bayonet. Everyone yelled like mad, and the sound was extraordinarily comforting. Soon lost all sense of surroundings, and doubled like one in a dream. I shall never forget the next quarter of an hour. It was a horrible nightmare that will always cling. Men were going down like ninepins, maxims crackling, and amid all the strange, rare sounds of battle nothing seemed so penetrating as the human voice. A man laughed idiotically, and it seemed to ring right above the din of guns, and yet as far away as the sounds that come when one is under the anaesthetic, just on the brim of unconsciousness.

We took that trench and held it – how, I don't know. But there I found myself amid the rubbish and dead men, muttering a word again and again in a ridiculous fashion.

Then I felt terribly sick and faint, and a cold sweat came out all over me. This I utterly failed to understand till a Corporal came up and put his arm round my shoulder. I saw him look at something on my chest, and, astonished, I turned my eyes down – a bullet had gone clean through me, and two of my fingers were missing – and I never knew a thing about it until then!

Home again in glorious Blighty and waiting for my discharge. I'm glad I've done my bit – small though it be.

Soldiers wounded in a battle which is still raging make their way along a communication trench. Treated at a regimental aid post or field ambulance and classified as walking wounded, they are on their way to a casualty clearing station. The soldier on the right wears the brassard S.B. – Stretcher-bearer.
(Author's collection and copyright)

DIRECT QUESTION
DIRECT ANSWER

BOULOGNE

Brigadier-General F. Hackett Thompson, commanding 117th Brigade of the 39th Division of the 5th New Army was a fearsome personality. Known as 'Hacking' because of his ferocity on parade, the brigadier had under his command the 15th, 16th and 17th

Highland Light Infantry and 15th Royal Scots and he visited these units in turn to make clear what he would – or mostly would not – tolerate.

As always, the new recruits were in E Company and were paraded on the flank. One day late in 1915 Hacking made a fateful inspection of 16th H.L.I.'s E Company. Stopping in front of a trembling subaltern, he said in a loud growl, 'What's wrong with that man?' and pointed to a private soldier. When the young officer stayed speechless, not knowing what he was supposed to have noticed, Hacking reached out and knocked off the man's hat to expose a mop of hair. 'See that!' he said. 'You see that? Look at his hair!' To the startled soldier he added, 'If we were on active service you would be shot!' This was rather unfair, as the brigadier himself had locks which curled luxuriously around his cap at the base of his neck.

'As for you,' he barked at the subaltern, 'well, I don't know what would happen to you!' And he moved on to another subaltern who was wearing a scarf. 'Anything wrong with your neck?' he demanded.

'No, sir, no', the officer mumbled.

'Then why in God's name have you got it muffled and bandaged?' the brigadier bellowed.

So he paraded on, reducing one officer and soldier after another to trembling fear. He came to a hard-bitten, recently joined Glaswegian whose blotched skin showed beneath an unmilitary stubble of hair. 'What's the matter with your face?' the brigadier demanded in harsh tones.

The reply came out in broad Glasgow dialect which Hacking did not at first comprehend, though the officers, who did, blanched. 'Repeat!' Hacking ordered.

The private soldier said loudly, 'It's the booze comin' oot sir'.

Time stood still as Hacking glared at him. Then he nodded approvingly and turned to his escorting officers. 'That's the frankest answer I've ever had in my career,' he said. 'Keep an eye on this man'.

And they did – right up to Loos. He was blown to pieces there in 1916.

CLEAN SWEEP

ARMENTIERES

Many troops from various parts of the British Empire were in billets in and around Armentieres late in 1915. It was not a safe place because the Germans shelled it intermittently but the soldiers preferred billets to trenches.

One afternoon a shell landed in the

street leading to the Institut St Jude. It exploded at a safe distance but with an alarming noise behind a brewer's dray, one of those four-wheeled carts typical of French Flanders with the beer barrels lying on two parallel rails. The horses went off at full gallop, the driver fell from his perch, and after him, in ones and two and threes, rolled the barrels.

The driver ran shouting and gesticulating after the horses while from their billets appeared Australians, Scots and various other British troops. Somebody who saw them swarm into the street said that it was like watching bees come out of a hive. The driver was not long capturing his runaway team and in turning them around but by then every barrel had disappeared and the street was deserted. The same witness said that the Australians won the event in the number of barrels gained but that the Scots showed the greatest strength, actually heaving barrels from man to man into open doorways.

'MY OLD MAN'

BAILLEUL

Outside an army transport office in Bailleul a party of Australian soldiers waiting for transport to take them on the first part of a trip to Blighty were showing one another their family photographs. A Guards officer passing by was interested and joined the group. One Digger showed him a photograph of his wife and family, another produced a portrait of his mother, and so on. The young officer said that he was sorry he had no portraits of his own family.

As he began to turn away, he said suddenly, 'Yes, I *do* have something'. He produced a florin from his pocket, pointed to King George's head, and said, 'That is my old man.'

Then the Diggers knew they had been speaking to the Prince of Wales.

It is difficult to date this incident precisely. It more likely took place in 1916 than 1915 but the Digger who recounted it was certain it was 1915. The A.I.F. as a body did not reach France until 1916, after service in Egypt and Gallipoli.

1916

Haig had become Commander-in-Chief of the British forces in France and Belgium and was convinced that offensive action could succeed. By July, with the arrival of Kitchener's New Army of volunteers, the British had 57 divisions on the Western Front (to the French 100 and the Belgian 6). After the French suffered 315,000 casualties during the battle of Verdun, Haig launched his great Somme offensive, with brave but largely ill-trained men. Sixty thousand British Empire soldiers became casualties on the first day, including 20,000 killed. Total British casualties for the Somme offensive were 420,000. After the Somme the British troops were sure that the war would last forever. Many of the stories in this section concern this most futile of battles.

DRAIN AND DIVE

NEUVE CHAPELLE

In the low-lying country of the Neuve Chapelle sector one of the most arduous and difficult tasks was trying to keep the trenches free from water. There were even platoons known as 'Divisional Drainers' who were supposed to be specialists in disposing of water. The job was not only exhausting but dangerous since the drainers were often exposed to enemy fire.

One day in the winter of 1915–16 men of the 19th Battalion Northumberland Fusiliers were repeatedly shelled off their draining work by whizzbangs. Over and over the men would dive for cover, such as it was. Generally they reached dry cover but in one emergency a soldier named Johnson flung himself into a drain with about three feet of weedy water.

Just as he reappeared, festooned with weeds and muck, an officer came to see if the men were safe. Noticing Johnson he said, 'What's the matter, Johnson? Got the wind up?'

'No sir,' Johnson said in an offended tone. 'Camouflage. I'm a water-lily'.

EASIER TO GET IN THAN OUT

BOUZINCOURT

In January 1916 the 16th Highland Light Infantry was in muddy trenches near Bouzincourt, Somme, and the men were miserable. One morning the battalion padre on his tour of the trenches had a convers-

95

ation with a sentry. According to the padre, it went like this:

Padre: How are you this morning?
Sentry: No weel at a'.
Padre: What's the matter?
Sentry: Fed up! Fed up!
Padre: You shouldn't talk that way; you know you are here in a great cause.
Sentry: That's a' very weel, but if you were here on this post takin' the place o' a man what's been killed an' not knowin' the minute you

may be sniped, you'd be fed up too.

Padre: Are you married?
Sentry: Yes
Padre: Have you any children?
Sentry: Four.
Padre: You look rather above military age; how old may you be?
Sentry: I'm forty-five.
Padre: And how did you get in the army at that age?
Sentry: I told a big lie – but I would tell a damned sight bigger one to get out.

The oldest soldier to die on the Western Front was Lieutenant Henry Webber of the South Lancashire Regiment. He was killed on the Somme on 21 July 1916 at the age of 68.

THIEPVAL PATROL

ANCRE RIVER VALLEY, NEAR THIEPVAL

Patrol actions were such minor events in the vast activity of the war that relatively few descriptions of them survive. Many were designed to show the 'offensive spirit' so often demanded by high command. The reality of these small-group actions is well illustrated by a patrol of the 15th H.L.I., under Lieutenant G.D.A. Fletcher, on the night of 13 January 1916. The unit historian felt that it brought 'adventure and honour' to

the battalion. With Fletcher were Corporal J. Macfadyen, and Privates J. Davidson, J. White, L.G. Ross and M. Clark, all of A Company.

The patrol started at 12.45 a.m. from the Hammerhead Sap in C2 sub-sector to locate and destroy an advanced machine-gun reported by a patrol of the previous night. The path lay through a wood and seemed to bear in the direction of Thiepval Road. On reaching the far edge of the wood a hard metallic road was encountered. Lieutenant Fletcher, who was ahead of his men, emerged from the wood at a well-defined gap and saw, about 20 years to his right, a fallen tree lying across the road. Two men were observed behind the tree and, at the same time, the sound of bayonets being fixed was heard in the still night. The H.L.I. patrol lay down. A German officer dressed in military frock coat stepped coolly from a cross-roads towards the left and walked towards Lieutenant Fletcher until he was only five yards distant. Then, he turned and joined the two men behind the fallen tree. Not a shot had yet been fired.

Suddenly, the frock-coated German officer waved his hand as a sign for the Germans to scatter and surround the British. Five figures of German soldiers, obeying the command of their officer, became visible near the cross-roads about to pass behind the British patrol. It was time to go if this H.L.I. patrol of an officer and five men was not to be trapped. Lieutenant Fletcher decided to leave his sting before he went. He rose and walked to within ten yards of the fallen tree. Taking a Mills bomb he pulled the pin and allowed the fuse to burn three of its five seconds before he lobbed it over the tree. It landed among the group of Germans and burst instantly. The group had no time to scatter. At the same moment the German officer fired his revolver and wounded Davidson in the knee. A splinter from the bursting bomb also struck the same man.

Before he withdrew Lieutenant Fletcher saw the German officer lying huddled and quite still on the ground, another man who waved an arm feebly once or twice before collapsing, and heard a third screaming and moaning. Then, in good order, the patrol retired, taking the wounded man with them, under fire from the Germans near the cross-roads. They re-entered the British lines at 2.30 a.m., after being out for nearly two hours.

THE UNBEATABLE MUD

MARTINSART/SENLIS

These two towns, right behind the Somme front, were the sites of transit camps for soldiers going to and from the front. From a distance, as the soldiers marched towards the camps the bell tents in neat rows

97

looked comfortably appealing and the word was that even in winter blankets were plentiful.

Something else was plentiful – mud. The tents had been pitched in summer on a lovely green park. Successive battalions had come and gone in the rain and the tread of their feet had churned the place into a dismal quagmire. Mud could not be kept off boots and clothes, not even out of food, and certainly not out of the tents. Soldiers new to mud and not understanding that it was invincible tried to make footpaths; these were swallowed overnight. Even the horses had to go to veterinary hospital for treatment. With 15 men to each tent and water a mile away there was much coming and going so the mud had little time to harden.

The men gave up the struggle sooner or later and found refuge in Senlis, which had excellent bathhouses. More especially they went to the Empire theatre, an old barn with a hard clay floor and wooden benches. Sitting with their hats on, the men saw performances in which women's parts were played by soldiers of the line so successfully that French interpreters blew them kisses under the impression that they were girls.

Men of a very muddied and fed-up battalion were in the audience one evening when the resident comedian, at the end of a sketch, consigned the Kaiser to 'the fires of hell'.

'Send him to Senlis!' a soldier shouted. 'Send him to the bloody mud!'

And soon the Empire was rocking as if to a popular chorus, 'Send the Kaiser to Senlis – send him to the bloody mud!'

FRIENDLY GESTURE

ST ELOI, NEAR ARRAS

A young platoon officer took rifle inspection one morning and spent a few minutes criticising the rifle of No 1 in the ranks. He was out to find fault. The subaltern moved on to the next man beginning, as usual, by lifting the hinged backsight – and a spider ran out.

'Well!' he said in a tone of great menace. 'Well?'

'I wondered where that little bugger had got to', the soldier said. 'Thank you, sir'.

The subaltern choked, the platoon sergeant clamped his teeth together and the men waited, frozen. Still speechless, the subaltern handed over to the sergeant and marched away.

- Corp^l G.H. Baker's Squad Grenadier Guards Feb - 1916 -

The soldier of this story was obviously not from a Guards battalion with its strict discipline. In February 1916 Corporal G.H. Baker proudly presented his squad in a photograph to be sent home. Not long after the picture was taken most of the men were casualties. On the back of this photograph is just one word – Mother's.　　　　　(*Author's Collection*)

INNOCENCE AT WAR

MERRIS

Tim was the good boy of the Australian unit fresh to France in 1916. No matter the conditions of war or the circumstances of life he never said more than 'Bust it!'or 'What a nuisance!' And he had no vices at all. The battalion went into camp at Merris and no sooner had the men dumped their kit than most of them were off into town to explore 'the possibilities'. Tim went sightseeing and when he returned that night his mates in the tent asked him what he had been doing. 'Oh, I met such a nice girl', he said. 'She beckoned me into her house and asked me what I wanted and I said I'd like a lemonade. By Jove, she had to go to a lot of trouble to find me a glass of it. Poor girl, she has a nasty cough'.

'How do you mean?' one of his mates asked.

'Well, she seemed to choke a couple of times'.

'Maybe that was your fault!' somebody said.

'Oh no!' Tim said. 'I only remarked that she seemed to have a lot of sisters living at home'. When his mates were silent he added, 'I suppose women feel safer if they're living together, in a war I mean'.

'SHEER BUTCHERY'

GIVENCHY

During the spring of 1916, when patrolling in No Man's Land was particularly aggressive, Lieutenant Hugh Knyvett, an Australian Intelligence officer, and a patrol of five men captured eight Germans and started to herd them towards the Australian lines. Then the Germans came to a sudden stop; apparently they had discovered that their captors were Australians and they were terrified by their rough reputation. They would not budge and the Australians outnumbered, had no means of tying them together. The disturbance was attracting attention and Knyvett's sergeant said. 'Look out sir! We'll be seen in a minute. What will we do?'

'The contest was short and sharp', Knyvett wrote. 'They outnumbered us but we went to it with a will. It was sheer butchery but I'd rather send a thousand of the swine down to the fatherland than lose one of my boys. . . .'

All the armies killed enemy soldiers under circumstances such as these. Incidents of 'chivalry' were extremely rare.

THE PLUG STREET HUT

PLOEGSTEERT (PLUG STREET) WOOD, YPRES

One Saturday night in early spring, 1916, all was quiet and black but just before midnight a star shell was fired from the German trenches and lit up the countryside around. Others went up, soon to be followed by high explosive shells. One shell burst in front of the little Y.M.C.A. hut and the explosion roused the workers asleep inside. Within a few minutes they had raced for shelter in a dugout to the rear of the building. A second shell hit the hut and set fire to it. This fire attracted the Germans and they strafed the wood and ridge with thousands of shells. When morning came not a vestige of the hut remained. A Y.M.C.A. worker, searching amid the ruins found the shrivelled rims of his spectacles and a soldier came across a two-franc coin and a 20-centime piece welded together by the heat. Nothing else remained of a place beloved of the troops. Soldiers in that wood noted that, amazingly, whenever there was a lull in the booming of the guns nightingales sang in Plug Street Wood as if peace reigned on earth.

Winston Churchill was on duty in the trenches of Plug Street Wood as C.O. of the 6th Royal Scots Fusiliers from January to May 1916. His advance H.Q. was at Laurence Farm and his reserve H.Q. was at Maison 1875.

THE ONLY WAY OUT

ST ELOI, YPRES SALIENT

The 4th Royal Fusiliers, among other units, were due to make an attack on the 'Mound of Death', very strongly held by the Germans early in 1916. The brigadier himself paraded the battalion and stressed

St Eloi, like all of Flanders, was notorious for its mud. This photograph shows three sergeants of the Northumberland Fusiliers after they had come out of the battle of St Eloi on 27 March 1916.

the great importance of capturing the mound. 'I want to tell you a story', he said. 'It's about two mice who fell into a basin of milk. One was faint-hearted and he gave up and drowned. The other little fellow churned away with his legs until the milk turned into butter and he could walk away. I hope that you men will show the same determination in the attack'.

The British had mined part of the German front line and when the explosion occurred the Fusiliers attacked each side of the crater and took the position, though they had many casualties.

The following day a soldier fell into the muddy, sloppy crater. As he frantically ploughed about in the ooze he shouted to his mates who were watching his antics with interest, 'When I've churned this bloody mud to concrete I'm hopping out!'

In this action at St Eloi Chaplain Noel Mellish won the V.C. for 'most conspicuous bravery'. During heavy fighting on three consecutive days he repeatedly tended and brought in wounded men under fire; three men were killed while he was dressing their wounds. He saved 10 the first day, 12 on the second and on the third day he brought in all the remaining wounded.

CONSOLATION PRIZE

DOULLENS

Sergeant Peter Kemp of 183rd Battalion 41st Division, R.F.A. was acting Quarter-Master-Sergeant during the winter of 1916 and one night was enjoying his sleep in the shed which he used for his stores.

In the early hours somebody banged heavily on the door. Sergeant Kemp, from his bed, shouted, 'What's the matter?'

'Sorry, Quarter', a soldier said. 'But you issued me with some boots today and they're odd. One's too small'.

'Well, take them off and go to bed', Kemp said.

'Sorry, Quarter, can't do that. I'm on stable piquet and honest, I can hardly walk'.

'You'll have to put up with the boots until morning', Kemp said. 'I'm not going to be up all night changing boots – and when I do see you in the morning I'll have something to say to you'.

'All right, Quarter', said the invisible soldier. 'I'm sorry I woke you up – but could you give me a tot of rum to stop the pain?'

LAST LIMBER FROM ALBERT

ALBERT

German artillery pounded Albert remorselessly at certain periods. As the major British forward forming-up centre and supply town on the central Somme sector it had more than its fair share of punishment. Early in 1916 the German shelling became so heavy that inhabitants streamed from the town as refugees.

One evening the bombardment reached a fearful and frightening crescendo and all roads received special treatment. An old man was seen between the shafts of a rickety four-wheeled cart and perched on top of a jumble of belongings was a tiny, withered and aged lady.

The old man struggled to haul the cart but collapsed between the shafts. Some sheltering soldiers started towards the couple, who were in imminent danger of being blown to pieces, when a transport limber with driver and his sidekick thundered around a bend in the road and drew rein. The two soldiers got down and eyed the aged pair worriedly. 'What the hell are we going to do with Darby and Joan?' the driver said. 'We can't fit them and all their stuff in the limber'.

'And you can bet they won't be parted from it', said his mate. 'Tell you what, hook them on the back'.

As another shell burst nearby they lifted the old man into the limber and hitched the four-wheeler to the back. 'Hang on tight grandma!' the driver said as he leapt back into his seat.

He whipped his horses into a gallop and forced them through the din and flying debris. The cart careered along behind with the old lady crying out in distress, though she did as ordered and held on tightly. Many soldiers sheltering in holes and behind walls poked their heads up to watch the incongruous sight. Occasionally dust and smoke hid the galloping limber and it seemed that any minute it would disintegrate or be wrecked in a shellhole. Then, miraculously it seemed, it was out of town and safe.

This incident was witnessed by Sergeant N.E. Crawshaw of the 15th London Regiment, who likened the limber and cart to the Mauretania *dragging a canoe in its wake at high speed.*

THEIRS BUT TO DO – AND GRIPE

JUST BEHIND THE SOMME LINES

A battalion of the 18th Division had come out of the firing line in the winter of 1916 and was supposed to be resting a few miles to the rear. At half-past midnight in pouring rain, a motorcycle despatch rider – a Don R in army parlance – arrived with an urgent sealed message from brigade headquarters. 'What is it?' the Orderly Sergeant asked the soaked Don R.

'Dunno. I was just told to get it to you quick'.

The message read: MUST HAVE CHASSIS NUMBER OF YOUR WATER CART.

Out of what passed for beds were brought the regimental sergeant-major, the regimental quarter-master sergeant and the orderly room clerk. The only light available was the stump of a candle and the R.Q.M.S. crawled under the cart, in the mud, seeking the number and swearing horribly.

As he moved the candle spluttered. 'For heaven's sake stop that candle from flickering!' the R.S.M. said, 'or the blinking Staff will think we're signalling to Jerry!'

The look on the R.Q.M.S. face as he sat in the mud under the cart with the spluttering candle in his grimy hand made even the soaked and suffering Don R laugh.

'What's the number of your water cart?' became a catch-phrase in the battalion whenever the men were fed up with pointless orders.

Any veteran of any war will recognise the ring of truth of this story. In the mountains of Papua-New Guinea in 1942 my unit was in muddy foxholes facing the Japanese on the next ridge. One night a lantern was seen approaching from our own rear and a native policeman, acting as an army messenger, appeared with a sealed envelope marked TOP SECRET – URGENT. As it came from Divisional H.Q. it was thought to be important and the adjutant was awakened from an exhausted sleep. We looked anxiously at the paper he drew from the envelope; it was headed THE CARE AND PRESERVATION OF TYRES IN TROPICAL CLIMATE. We were foot soldiers on precipitous jungle tracks and the nearest vehicles were many miles in the rear.

COOKHOUSE COURTESY

ETAPLES

The 1st Kent Cyclists were stationed at Etaples before going up the line in 1916. One day the colonel complain-ed to the sergeant-major that he had heard some of the foulest language of his life coming from the cookhouse. The sergeant-major should take immediate action, the colonel said.

The R.S.M. did just that and, as angry as sergeant-majors can be when goaded by commanding officers, he paraded the cookhouse staff and said, 'Right, which of you jokers has been swearing horribly?'

'What, *me*, Lord Mayor?' the corporal cook said. 'Nobody's ever heard me, Lord Mayor'.

'Don't lie to me!' the R.S.M. snapped. 'The C.O. heard the language. What exactly happened here?'

'Well, nothing', the cook said. 'Except that I slopped a dixie full of hot tea down Corporal Glover's neck. I said, "Sorry, Bill", and Bill said, "Granted, Harry!" And that's all that's happened. Can we be excused now, Sergeant-Major?'

'SILLY IDEA'

BETHUNE AREA: PETIT SAINS, NOEUX-LES-MINES

Not all 'stories' from the Western Front are funny or sad or heroic. Some are simply routine. Private W. Higgins of the 1st Battalion South Wales Borderers kept a diary. Here are five daily entries for June 1916. They are full of incidental information and they reveal much about an ordinary soldier's feelings. Throughout I have kept to Higgins' English and spelling.

June 19th

Its very cold again today went up to work at 10 oclock last night, digging new trenches a new idea, same as they have at Vurdunc (Verdun) a row of trenches behind each other, about 6 yards apart, they are called *Cemertary trenches* (because they looked like graves). Returned at 2 this morning rifle inspection at 10, went up again at half past 10, to deepen a trench, boards (duckboards) down, did not carry on with that very long, before they started shelling us with Lydite Shells, silly idea, digging in day-light. Came away from there at 12, only 2 platoons here now, in these cellars others gone back up to F.L. (front line). The Bantams, R.W.F., are in F.L. now mixed up with our other two companies, they are losing a few men, allready, Bantams and ours.

June 20th

Went up to F.L. (A Coy) last night

Elsewhere in his diary Private Higgins refers to the British soldier's love of souvenirs. This photograph shows the Northumberland Fusiliers who survived the battle of St Eloi on 27 March 1916. They brought with them German helmets and gas masks. In the centre of the photograph a captain looks on approvingly.

carrying barbed wire, very awkward stuff to carry through trenches started at 9 finished about 12. This place is getting very *warm*, its lucky that we are in cellars, shelling very often, going back tonight just a little way in reserve trench, we are *promised*. A lot of fatigues, before we get there our men seem half dead for want of food and sleep.

June 21st

Its a fine day, lot of *straffing* going on over head, we were releived by the Mansters (Munsters) at half past 5, last night, got here, to reserve trench about an hour afterwards went up to F.L. about 9 working till half past 1 oclock this morning makeing new trenches with the R.E. Its really their work that we were doing but we does that while we are having a *rest*, we got back here at day light . . . there's still no sign of our month's rest, they keep on postpond it all the time rations very scarce. Since we have been in this time we are doing 20 days this time, not *half – rubbing it into us*, trench mortars shaking this

Food was a constant pre-occupation for the soldiers of the Great War. In the frontline trenches they were often hungry because ration parties were killed on the way up or they lost themselves in the dark and mud. When hot food was available, as in this photograph taken on the Somme front, the soldiers made the most of it.   (*Author's collection and copyright*)

row of houses, all dropping on, or near the slag heap, could do with a good meal and sleep.

June 22nd

Very fine to-day (this morning) many arroplanes about, while they are shelling our arroplane it makes it very dangerous for us we are liable to be hit, by the falling peices, the Germans are shelling our arroplanes all day long, and *every* day they must have a tremendous stock of those air craft shells useing thousands each day,

their arroplanes dont come over our lines very often, the French air-men and ours are very daring doing great work here continually flying over our trenches, and some times over the German lines, near enough for the Germans to fire with rifle and machine gun besides shells, some times they bring one down but not often.

June 23rd

We are now at a place called Pettit Sains, got releived by the Cumorons (Cameron Highlanders) at 6 oclock last night rather long march from trenches quite close to Neoux Les Mines dont think much of this village two platoons in one building I think it has been a school room, too crowded, 3 of us have to sleep in centre of room water very scarce, have to walk about a mile, to wash. The people here takes away the rope from their wells so that we cannot have water, its a very heavy day today.

The Bantams, to whom Higgins refers, were the battalions of undersized men which were formed when military manpower was becoming scarce. Sometimes under five feet in height, these men performed well but trenches had to be adapted so that they could see over the parapet to fire. Higgins' statement that his unit had been 20 days in the front line is interesting; High Command claimed that troops were rarely kept longer than seven days in the front trenches before being brought back to support and then reserve trenches.

SILVER LINING

IN FRONT OF ALBERT, SOMME

On the night before the big British offensive of 1 July 1916, eight men of the 6th Battalion, Royal Berkshire Regiment, were sharing a dug-out trying to rest. The Germans were strafing the British lines heavily. Two mates from Stratford, London, were on their hands and knees with some lighted grease and pieces of dry sandbag, trying to boil a mess-tin of water to make some tea.

Just as the water started to boil Jerry dropped a big shell right onto the side of the dug-out and the whole place was obscured by smoke and dust. One of the tea-makers noticed the overturned mess-tin. 'Blimey,' he said, 'that's done it – the waters spilled'.

His mate, lying on his back with his face covered with blood and dirt, triumphantly held up a clenched right hand. ''S'all right, Bill', he said, 'I ain't put the tea and sugar in'.

This story was told by Corporal J. Russ, who used to live in Ilford Lane, Ilford, Essex.

A remarkable photograph of troops being organised in the shelter of a ridge and near dugouts for the great Somme offensive. In the foreground are some German prisoners; at least two are wounded. On the left an officer wears a white patch on his back as an identification mark.

(Author's collection and copyright)

EAGER FOR NEWS

BETHUNE

A battalion of the 47th London Division was on the way to Givenchy for its first experience of the front trenches, in 1916. As they marched by the La Bassée Canal the new, fresh soldiers passed a column of soldiers, from the same division, who had just been relieved from the front line.

A good many anxious questions were asked about conditions at

Givenchy – and a good many pithy answers were given. The exchange which stuck in the mind of Major F.G. Newton of the Machine Gun Corps was this:

'What's it like, mate?'
'All right'.
'Had any casualties?'
'Yes mate; two wounded and a bloke lost his hat'.

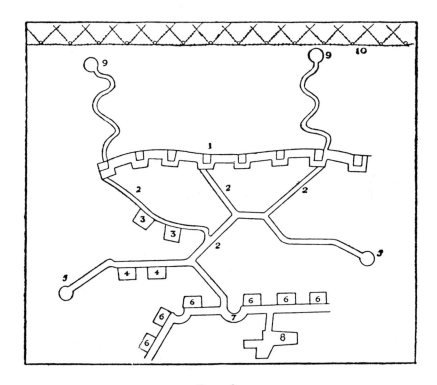

FIG. 8.

1. Fire trench.
2. Communication trenches.
3. Dugouts for medical staff and first-aid work.
4. Officers' dugouts.
5. Saps for machine guns.

6. Dugout quarters.
7. Supports trench.
8. Kitchen, water tank, stores, etc.
9. Saps for advanced lookouts.
10. Line of wire entanglements.

This diagram shows the way an ideal trench system was arranged. They did indeed start like this but after a while many other linking trenches were dug and men often lost themselves even in their own company area.

TIN HAT JAZZ

SAILLY-SALLISEL, FRICOURT

When tin hats were first issued to the Australians at Sailly, a Digger named Smithy tested one of them in his own original way. The soldiers were sitting around the cook's fire singing a rousing chorus while Smithy kept time on the 'tinnies' – as they were called then – with a poker. One of the soldiers, Darkie, received an extra hard crack and removed his lid to rub his head. Down came the poker again – and the stretcher-bearers took away another casualty.

Steel helmets came into being largely as a result of the immense number of shrapnel shells fired by the Germans. Mostly air-bursting, these shells showered thousands of shrapnel balls on soldiers who had no effective way of protecting themselves. High-explosive shells, such as that seen bursting here, also caused many casualties. A tin hat could stop an oblique bullet but one fired at short range and direct might well penetrate.

(Author's collection and copyright)

ORDERS FROM ON HIGH

BAVINCOURT, NORTH-EAST OF DOULLENS

One morning in the summer of 1916 a party of infantry from the Artists Rifles reported as ordered to an R.A.M.C. sergeant in the yard beside the local chateau, where G.H.Q. was situated. Private A.M. Burrage and another man were detailed to sweep the verandah and steps of the chateau.

The R.A.M.C. sergeant gave his instructions. 'Now don't go sweepin' this 'ere dust onto the drive. Sweep it up into a neat 'eap on the bottom step, see. And then when you've done that, see, go and find a tin and sweep it into the tin, see, and take it down to the incinerator, see'.

They swept the verandah and steps of the Commander-in-Chief's chateau efficiently and duly gathered the dust into the shape of a small beehive on the bottom step. Burrage said to his mate, 'Bugger off and find a tin somewhere and I'll wait here and keep the heap tidy'.

He hovered over the little pile of dust, tickling it with the broom from time to time when the breeze showed signs of scattering it. He was so engaged when the glass doors flew open and the Commander-in-Chief, Haig, strode out.

Burrage sprang to attention as well as a man can when he has a broom in his hand. Sir Douglas Haig spoke sharply, 'I don't want to see you stand to attention. I want you to get your work done, not standing about here doing nothing. Go on, man, sweep that dust away and then go'.

Burrage was already carrying out an order but he could hardly tell this to the Commander-in-Chief. He swept the dust broadcast onto the drive and ran for his life, privately hoping that Haig would later find his companion lurking on the steps with the dust tin. He reported back to the sergeant.

'Well,' the N.C.O. said, 'did you sweep that dust into a tin?'

'No sergeant, I swept it onto the drive'.

'What! Didn't I tell you —?'

'Yes, sergeant,' Burrage said, still more meekly, 'but I received another order'.

The sergeant's dignity was hurt. 'Hoh!' he said. ''Oo from?'

The Commander-in-Chief', Burrage murmured, and paused 'What shall I do now?'

'I think you've done enough for one day,' the sergeant said. ''Op it.'

The story was all over the unit by mid-day and Private Burrage was not popular. 'You bloody fool, you'll get us sent up the line', he was told.

And up the line they went – but that was inevitable anyway.

A MATTER OF PRIORITIES

HÉBUTERNE

On the first day of the great British Somme offensive the task of the 56th (London) Division was to attack strong enemy positions at Hébuterne. Corporal William Smith was on duty as a signaller, trying to keep intact the telephone lines between Brigade H.Q. and one of the battalions. A flat piece of shell knocked him unconscious and he was tended by a stretcher-bearer on his way back to a dressing station. When the bearer saw that Smith had recovered he went on his way while Smith continued with his job.

As he traced the telephone wire forward he encountered a young soldier of the 12th London Regiment, the Rangers. He was cut and bleeding and one arm was hanging limp and grotesque, probably smashed in several places. Staggering, he said to Smith, 'Is there a dressing station beyond here, mate?'

'Straight on down the trench', Smith said, 'but it's a bit far. Tell you what, you stay here and I'll chase a stretcher-bearer I saw a few minutes ago. I'll bring him back for you'.

'I don't want him for *me*', the young soldier said, wiping blood out of his eyes. 'I want someone to come back with me to get my mate. *He's hurt!*'

Mr Smith, who lived at Manor Park after the war, said that he never heard anything more selfless throughout the war.

114

Stretcher-bearers of the Royal Berkshire Regiment with a soldier wounded near Potijze, Ypres. He is beyond saving and one bearer is taking down particulars for the dying man's family.

RAT HUNTING

SOMME

Rat-hunting was one of the favourite sports of Australian soldiers in 1916. But first they had to find a way of getting them into the open. Somebody found that about 10 or 12 sticks of cordite stuffed into a rat hole and set alight would produce fumes which would force out the rats; the Diggers then pot-shot at them and chased them with clubs.

Their hatred for the rodents was understandable because they often made trench life as unbearable as the mud did. The sport came to a stop when some cordite sticks came into contact with an unexploded German mine and about 20 men were wounded.

Bunches of cordite sticks were used as the propellant which fired shells from the guns.

UNDER NEW MANAGEMENT

SOMME

During the British offensive a company of Londoners was rushed up to captured German trenches to search the dug-outs and bring in prisoners in the wake of the first wave of advancing British troops.

A Cockney went into one dug-out after another singing happily:

'All I want is lo-ove,
All I want is you'.

Entering one dug-out he found three Germans and fiercely menaced them with his bayonet. His mates heard the singing give way to a hoarse shout: 'Nah then, aht of it! 'Op it! I'm lan'lord 'ere nah!'

NOT WHAT WAS ORDERED

YPRES SALIENT

In July 1916 a battalion headquarters near Pilkem was anxious to know what German regiment was facing them and a large, strong Yorkshire corporal, with a reputation for being good on patrol, was ordered to bring in a prisoner.

After a dark night spent in No

Man's Land he returned at dawn with an insignificant little German, bedraggled and trembling with fear.

The corporal dragged him into the trench and lifted him onto the firestep for his first good look. Then he gave a disgusted snort. 'You won't do for our ol' man. I'll have to take you back tonight and change you'.

This story came from Mr S. Back of Leeds, near Maidstone. I heard of a similar incident at Vimy Ridge where a patrol leader reported back with a prisoner to his company commander. 'Sorry, sir', he said, indicating a dull-looking enemy soldier, 'I could only get into the bargain basement'.

'WE ARE IN A VERY BAD STATE'

SOMME, SOMEWHERE IN FRONT OF ALBERT

A little over three weeks after the beginning of the Somme offensive of July 1916, Private W. Higgins, of the South Wales Borders was in the front line and, as he said, 'got messed about something awful from one trench to another and we dread to see the night coming on'. His diary for 25 July is not exactly a 'story' but it is so patently honest that it says much about conditions in the line.

Just as it was getting dark last night they bombarded us most terribly, but we were pretty lucky; partly buried a few times. After it was over we were moved out of that little trench to another where all the battalion were formed up for an attack. The idea was for our artillery to bombard for a few minutes, we were to crawl out under it and wait in shell-holes until it stopped. Then we were to rush the trench while the Germans were demoralised. We got out all right at 2 o'clock and laid down, our artillery opened fire, but somehow the Gs must have got wind of it, for their artillery opened out, and their machine-guns, there was much confusion among our men, the worst fire that many of us have been under, those who got back into our trench without being hit, was very lucky, it was an utter failure. A Company did well on our left, they

The Yorkshire corporal would have been pleased with the capture of a German as big as the one shown on this postcard sent from France. On the back a soldier named Ted has written: What do you think of this for Sunday afternoon sport? (*Author's collection*)

gave the Gs a severe bombing, we lost in killed and wounded between 90 and 100, and a few missing, one of our chums hasn't turned up yet, Baldwin, (Yorkshire). The Australians made a big attack on the left, at the same time. (Later) the Gs counterattacked very severe fighting all the morning we came away from F.L. (front line) about middle day, and here we are now, in an old G trench, a little way back, but we are not many left now, I don't suppose we 200 strong, tired, sleeply, hungry, etc. we are all in a very bad state indeed, we *had* bread today 8 men on a 2 lb loaf and a few biscuits, I told our young platoon officer, yesterday that the men were not in a fit state, to do what was expected of them, doing this attack and he had to admit it, I don't know what they intend doing with us, now, Gs shelling these batterys near here, there are times when we hardly care what happens to us, properly *fed up* with everything.

THE DIABOLICAL AT LA BOISELLE

OVILLERS, SOMME

In July 1916 Paul Maze* during the Somme battle, walked through the rubble which was La Boiselle and on to Ovillers. His description of his tramp through the battlefield on a hot summer's day is one of the most vivid to have come out of the Somme.

This place (the captured craters of Ovillers) is like a huge ravine and had been strongly fortified and the craters were linked by subterranean tunnels which subsequently joined onto a maze of trenches. It had cost hundreds of lives to capture . . . clusters of corpses grilled in the hot sun, khaki and grey uniforms indiscriminately mixed. . . .

I toiled on . . . the trenches were all shot in, dug-outs were destroyed, many of the entrances being blocked with bodies, mingled with earth and sandbags . . . there was no shade anywhere.

At the junction of two collapsed trenches the clean-shaven head of a stout German, his eyes open, was perched on a heap of earth, sticking out like a head out of a Turkish bath.

The protruding hands and feet of other insufficiently buried comrades appeared all to belong to him and gave him a peculiarly diabolical appearance. As I clambered past him, the earth, giving way, made him lean over to one side with a horrid semblance of life. For days I had to pass this place. I don't know whether it was worse in broad daylight or at night. . . . Once I thought my runner and I had successfully hidden him by shoving earth over him but days later his fair moustache was waving again in the breeze; with many others he had worked his way through again, the area having been constantly shelled.

*See story entitled 'Firing Squad' (p. 20)

HATE HAD ITS LIMIT

FLESQUIÉRES

In mid-1916 Lieutenant C.G. Welch of the Rifle Brigade led a patrol into No Man's Land and had the tense experience of finding himself between a German patrol and the enemy front line. As Welch was on a reconnaissance mission he kept his men low and eventually brought them back without fighting. He went along to the Lewis gun post to warn the gunners that the Germans had a patrol out and to watch for them.

The corporal gunner said, 'Actually, one German dropped in here last night – in full marching order he was, all dressed up on his way home'.

'Did you ask him in?' Welch said wryly.

'No', was the short answer. 'Told him to hop it'.

'What! Why on earth did you do that?'

'You can't turn a Lewis gun on a man going on leave', the corporal said.

Officers were often astonished by such examples of humanity. I know of an Australian soldier who left a revolver holding one round with a badly wounded German lying in No Man's Land – so that he could shoot himself if the pain became too great.

PROSPECTORS OF DEATH

POZIÉRES

During the ferocious battle in July 1916 for the ridge of Poziéres, Somme, Australian soldiers at times turned the war into a grim sport. It has been vividly described by Charles Bean, the A.I.F. official correspondent who was never far from the front.

Stung by the killing of mates . . . small parties of Australians, some specially detached, others 'pros-pecting' on their own account for adventure and souvenirs, made their way among the heaps of rubble on both sides of the (Albert-Bapaume) road. The artillery of both sides was by this time almost silent, the gunners being tired and the respective staffs as yet uncertain where their own or the opposing infantry were situated.

The adventurers could therefore wander through the ruins without fear of shellfire, searching for the openings of cellars and dugouts where snipers were suspected of hiding and rolling phosphorus bombs into them. Throughout the village isolated Australians could be seen 'ratting' occasional fugitives from rubble heaps, chasing terrified and shrieking Germans and killing them with the bayonet or shooting from the shoulder at those who got away. Then they sat down on the doorsteps to smoke and wait for others to bolt from the cellars. . . . This grim sport – for so in the fury of war it was regarded – was not without great risk to the hunters.

'A BLOODY FINE TIME'

HANGEST, SOMME

A young infantry officer describes the scene, in July 1916, near a railway embankment as his battalion waits to entrain for a station near the battle line. His company commander, Rowley, has seen battle in Ypres Salient and smiles grimly as he talks to his officers over a cold breakfast.

'All you buggers will be dead in a week. Three hours' bombardment and you'll break the bones of your legs with your knees knocking together. You're in for a bloody fine time, I can tell you. Cheerio! Let's have that whisky. *You*'ll want whisky when you get into those trenches. And by the way – no prisoners. If any of you come back with prisoners to me, you'll be for it. We're not taking any more prisoners in this regiment and the Hun knows it. Shoot the buggers. If you bring 'em to me, I'll shoot 'em – and you, too'.

Rowley was not as ruthless as his words and the unit did take prisoners. The officer who told this story and a few others in this book was Lieutenant Franklin Lushington, who as 'Mark Seven,' was the author of the classic A Subaltern on the Somme.

121

ON THE CROSS

DERNANCOURT, SOMME

Another story by Lieutenant Franklin Lushington, July 1916.

There is a boy from D Company doing Field Punishment No 1 down by the road this afternoon. His outstretched arms are tied to the wheel of a travelling field kitchen. The regimental sergeant-major tells me that the boy is there for falling out on a march. He defended himself before the C.O. by saying that he had splinters of glass in his feet but the M.O. decided against him. Quite possibly the boy is a liar, but wouldn't the army do well to avoid punishments which remind men of the crucifixion?

And two men are being marched up and down in the blazing heat, under the raucous voice of the provost-sergeant. They disturb all peace of mind. I do not know for what offences they are doing pack-drill but it is depressing to see them with rifles and full packs going to and fro over a piece of ground not more than 20 yards long . . . Volunteers going into battle! It is not a pleasant picture.

Orderly Room.

A soldier paraded under escort before his O.C. or C.O. on any charge had to remove his headgear. Overwhelmed by the occasion, he had little chance of adequately defending himself. This wartime postcard might be crude art but it truly catches the soldier's look of apprehension. (*Author's Collection*)

Pack-drill was a punishment for minor misdemeanors such as having a dirty rifle. It involved non-stop drill for a certain number of hours under the orders of the Orderly Sergeant.

CAKES AND SHRAPNEL

POZIÉRES

During the heavy fighting which occurred when the Australians were capturing the massive German post of 'Gibraltar' in July 1916 Private J Bourke of the 8th Battalion, found some boxes in a lower chamber which intrigued him.

He wrote to his mother: 'They were cake boxes of cardboard and sewn in with calico, just as the parcels come to us from Australia. The addresses were in a child's handwriting as were a few letters. In another corner was a coat rolled up. I opened it up and found it stained with blood. Right between the shoulders was a burnt shrapnel hole – shrapnel is very hot – The owner of the coat was a German and, some might say, not entitled to much sympathy. Perhaps he was not, but I couldn't help thinking sadly of the little girl or boy who sent the cakes'.

RULE OF THUMB

SOMME

After an advance during the Somme campaign of summer 1916 a party of soldiers was detailed to bury German dead. They went about this hard work in silence until one of the men called to the sergeant in charge. 'Hi, Sergeant! Here's a bloke who says he ain't dead. What shall I do with him?'

The sergeant spat contemptuously. 'You can't believe a word the Jerries say. They're all born liars. If he says he's dead you can bet he's alive. If he says he's alive you can take it he's dead. Better put him in the hole'.

*The story as I heard it stops here but undoubtedly badly
wounded men were accidentally buried alive. Men became
hardened to death and mangled bodies but I doubt if many enemy*

123

were deliberately buried alive. If an obviously dying man was found among the corpses he would be left to die and buried later. It must be said that if an enemy soldier had a chance of living – and infantry men became expert in such matters – he was carried to an aid post. It must also be remembered that immediately after an action in which a soldier had seen his close. friends killed he was not inclined to show mercy to a fallen enemy.

GETTING THE BIRD

SOMME

During the Somme battle a certain infantry brigade was to lead a divisional attack and the brigade commander disclosed that his forward troops would use carrier pigeons so that the brigadier would receive early news of his leading unit's progress.

On the day of the attack, 1 July 1916, the pigeon was given to a soldier to carry. He was to move with the leading sub-unit and he was told that at a certain moment an officer would write a message to be fastened to a pigeon's leg. He would then release the pigeon which would fly back to its loft at Brigade H.Q.

The guns boomed, the infantry went forward – but no pigeon came back. The brigadier walked feverishly around his H.Q. while soldiers anxiously searched the skies. After a long delay somebody shouted 'The pigeon!' and the bird alighted in the loft.

Soldiers rushed forward to retrieve the message capsule as the brigadier shouted, 'Give me the message!'

It was handed to him and rather self importantly he read aloud to his staff: 'I am absolutely fed up with carrying this bloody bird about France'.

This story was told by Field Marshal Lord Montgomery who took part in the Somme battle as a lieutenant of infantry.

PASTORAL VIEWS

PIERRE-AU-BEURE, NEAR CALONNE-SUR-LE-LYS

A sensitive French lady, living in a house by the canal bank, complained to the nearest British Army H.Q. that she could not look out of her back window. Why was this, Madame, she was courteously asked. Because, she said with much embarrassment, the canal was so often full of British soldiers bathing, and they were stark naked.

An officer with tact and discretion was sent to see the lady. 'May I suggest, Madame', he said, 'that it is not strictly necessary for you to look out of your back window. From the front you have beautiful pastoral views'. And then he added, 'Unless, of course, you would *prefer* to look through the back windows. . . . ' The lady withdrew her complaint.

FALSE IDEA OF SECURITY

DICKEBUS–YPRES ROAD

Private Edward Tracey of a transport unit was driving a lorry towards Ypres during 1916 when German shells – high explosive and shrapnel – began to drop around him in alarmingly large numbers. Tracey slammed on the brake, and ran for the shelter of a ruined cottage, with its smashed windows boarded up. He leaned against a wall and listened apprehensively to the angry whine of flying steel.

From behind a finger poked him on the shoulder and a voice said, 'Don't think you're safe there, mate. We're chock full of bombs in here'.

NO NEED FOR TEARS

SOMME

One day in August 1916 Sergeant E Rutson of the Royal Field Artillery, 47th London Division, was about to open fire with his 18-pounder gun when German guns opened up with a brisk barrage of 5.9 shells and tear-gas shells. With his men he took cover in a trench behind the guns.

When the strafing died away he found the gun with one wheel, shield and sights smashed by a direct 5.9 hit. He and his crew sat around unhappily, with tears in their eyes from the gas.

Smithy, a lad from Walworth, London said cheerfully, 'Don't cry, Sarg'nt – they're bahnd ter give us anuvver'.

Tear gas was used more frequently than the infinitely more dangerous gases which caused blindness, blisters and death from asphyxiation. It is seldom mentioned in the histories, probably because it seemed relatively unimportant in a war full of more hideous weapons.

A SENSE OF PRIORITIES

HELL FIRE CORNER, YPRES

Sometime in 1916 a party of the 6th Dorsets under a lance corporal was sent by night from Hooge down the Menin Road to draw rations. He would rendezvous at a certain corner, the corporal was told, with a ration party from Ypres itself. Shells dropped all around the section as they crouched for shelter amid wreckage and after a time a

126

Hell Fire Corner, the most famous spot in the Ypres Salient. This view looks east along Menin Road towards the German lines. On the left of the road a hessian screen conceals military movement from German spotters but many men and horses were killed on this road and particularly at this crossroads.
(Author's collection)

commanding voice shouted, 'Don't stay there, you men! That's Hell Fire Corner!'

'Can't help that, sir', the Dorsets corporal called back. 'Hell Fire Corner or Heaven's Delight, we've got to stop here till our rations come up'.

For much of the war Hell Fire Corner, marked today by a demarcation stone to indicate the limit of the German advance, was known as 'the hottest place on earth'. Because it was a crossroads it was an easy target for the German artillery to range onto but the British Army had to use the Menin Road as it was one of the main tracks by which they reached the front. Few men dawdled when passing Hell Fire Corner.

HEAVY RESPONSIBILITY

DELVILLE WOOD

During the Somme offensive of summer 1916 the East Surrey Regiment was holding the line at Delville Wood and reinforcements fresh to France were rushed up to replace the heavy casualties. One of these men was a Cockney corporal. An officer ordered the corporal to take charge of a very advanced post, then gave him detailed instructions about ammunition, rifle grenades, ordinary grenades, what to do in case of a gas attack, emergency rations, signal flares – and much else.

Finally, the officer said, 'Now, Corporal, have you understood all that? Can you manage?'

'Blimey, sir', the corporal said with a deep breath, ''as General 'Aig gone on leave?'

This exchange was heard by Sergeant Geary D.C.M. later wounded on the Somme. He once lived in Longley Road, Tooting.

SOUVENIR FROM FRICOURT

BOIS DES TAILLES, NEAR FRICOURT

Major Rowland Feilding* was commanding the 6th Battalion Connaught Rangers in July 1916 when the unit was pitched into the Somme offensive. During a lull, Feilding, hoping to find a friend, went off alone to visit Fricourt, now reduced by bombardment to fragments of walls.

As he entered from the west he

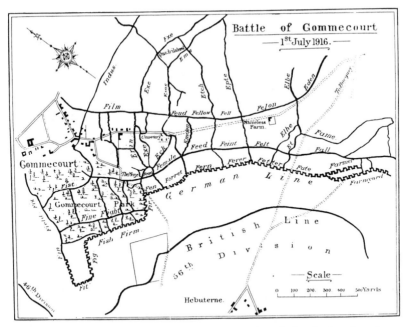

A map of one of the many actions which took place during the first day of the Battle of the Somme. It gives a clear idea of the way in which the British named enemy trenches and sections of trenches in order to lessen confusion about targets. No Man's Land was less than 200 yards wide at parts of this front.

passed the cemetery, in which all the tombstones had been shattered and scattered and coffins and human remains were exposed. Heavy fighting was in progress at Mametz Wood and the wounded were being carried back in streams, covered in mud from head to foot.

Feilding mentioned to a machine-gun officer that he would like a souvenir from Fricourt. 'I think I can help you then', the M.G. officer said and led Feilding to a place his men had discovered. Feilding had

seen many dug-outs but nothing quite like this. He was in what appeared to be an underground house of three floors, the deepest at about 60 feet.

It had two entrances, one of which could be recognised only from the inside, since the doorway had been blown in. The German occupants had abandoned the place in a hurry and left everything behind. The floors were littered with every kind of warlike object from heavy trench mortar bombs to grenades the size of

129

an egg and from steel helmets to underclothing. Many rifles hung from the wooden walls of the first flight of stairs. The nooks and corners of the rooms were occupied with sleeping bunks and from one of these Feilding picked up the illustrated book, *French Alphabet des Mademoiselle Lili*. He sent it home to his children as a *real* souvenir of the war.

' See story entitled 'Speculation' (p. 74)

RETURNED WITH THANKS

DELVILLE WOOD

In August 1916 the East Surrey Regiment was cut off for three days in the Delville Wood sector and suffered heavy losses. They remained cheerful enough and there was always somebody to draw a laugh. A young Cockney soldier was hit and rolled over, blood streaming from his neck and head. Struggling to a sitting position he said in tones of great astonishment, 'Strike me pink! One bleedin' wound on the top of me loaf of bread (head) and one in the bushel and peck (neck)'. Pulling the pin from a Mills grenade he heaved it at the nearby German trench. ''Ere Fritz!' he shouted. 'My thanks for a Blighty ticket'.

A RATHER SPECIAL PRESENT

HAMEL, ANCRE FRONT

Captain L.J. Morgan, Royal Sussex Regiment, was ordered on 26 August 1916 to command a guard over several big food dumps which had been established in the front line and the support trenches at Hamel.

130

The soldiers' fixed bayonets show that they are not far from the enemy trenches. The corporal leaning over (centre) is holding the barrel of a Stokes mortar; the soldier next to him has the bomv. Stokes bombs were notoriously unreliable and often failed to explode.   (Author's collection and copyright)

A major attack was about to go in and the food was for the troops making it.

Next night a corporal was detailed to take a party back for yet more rations and before he left he went to Morgan's dug-out and asked if he needed 'anything special'.

'Just a tin of cigarettes', he said. 'I'd be grateful for that, corporal'.

'You'll get them', the N.C.O. promised.

On the way back to the front the heavily-laden party had to cross a road which passed through a communicating trench and just as the men were squarely on the road a German shell hit it. Two men were killed outright and the corporal was fatally wounded.

One hand had been blown off but as he lay on the road he put the good hand into his pocket, produced a tin and said to an unhurt member of his party, 'You just get that to Captain Morgan, a present from me; he needs a fag, see.' And then he died.

Morgan got his smokes, which is why we know the story.

COMFORTABLE WORDS

ARMENTIERES

In the late summer of 1916 the Northumberland Fusiliers were in trenches in front of Armentieres. One quiet day, a company commander, Captain T.W.C. Curd, was convinced that in the German trenches opposite, a working party was busy strengthening a certain position during the lull. As he eyed the enemy line the mortar sergeant came along the trench with his Stokes mortar and crew, and Curd suggested that he try a round or two at the possible target. The sergeant ordered the mortar set up on the floor of the trench while Curd stood on the firestep, in front and a little to the side, to observe the shoot.

'Fire!' said the sergeant.

Curd heard a *plop*, then a faint hiss – and silence. There had been a misfire. He glanced around in alarm, fearing that the bomb would explode in the barrel and kill everybody nearby.

'Don't you worry, sir', one of the crew said cheerfully, 'if it don't go off while you count five you'll know it's a dud'.

Stokes mortar shells were often duds. The mechanism was relatively complicated and sometimes the lever which was supposed to allow the striker pin to hit the detonator did not fly off. When a bomb did explode it was not necessarily very dangerous as it was filled with black powder rather than high explosive.

PROUD REGULAR

ALBERT

Captain A.J. Dawson was on lines of communication duty near Albert a month or so after the Somme offensive began when he met a tall, fair-haired sergeant who came to attention and saluted, despite having

The soldiers on stretchers in this photograph probably had 'Blighty tickets' if they survived long enough. The officer (centre) is a doctor from an R.A.M.C. Field Ambulance unit. The wounded men had just come from the Somme battlefield. The stretcher support sling can be clearly seen on the bearer at right. *(Author's collection and copyright)*

his left arm in a sling. His ragged jacket was caked with blood-smeared mud. Despite his dreadful state he managed to look trim and smart.

Dawson said, 'Well Sergeant, how do you think the New Army is shaping?'

'Doing fine, I'd say, sir. The Boche finds them tough enough. I don't think there's much the matter with the New Army from the little I've seen of it'.

'Haven't you been out here long, Sergeant?'

The sergeant smiled. 'I was wounded in the retreat from Mons, sir. Hit again at Loos. This will be my third trip home wounded'.

'Then you're of the Old Army?'

'Fourteen years service sir'.

'When you come out of hospital this time you'll wear three gold stripes, sergeant'. (A reference to wound stripes.)

The sergeant smiled. 'We don't count wounds in my regiment sir'. He wore the badge of the King's Royal Rifle Corps.

133

GIVE US A HAND, MATE

GUILLEMONT, SOMME

In August 1916 the 12th Royal Fusiliers were moving forward in a communication trench when German artillery plastered them with shrapnel. Several of the lead balls hit Private Reynolds and messily severed his right hand at the wrist. His mates bound the stump as best they could and one of them said, 'You've got a sure Blighty one, old mate. When you get home don't forget to drop us a line and let's know how you're getting on in hospital'.

'All right, you can count on it', Reynolds said.

Then he pointed at his mangled arm. 'And the first thing I'll say to you is this – how the hell do you expect me to write a letter without a right hand to write with, you silly bastard?'

A TASTE FOR MUSIC

CORBIE, SOMME

When Corbie was captured in August 1916 one of the first officers into the town was the author 'Quex' of the Royal Field Artillery. Amid the debris of war, he came across a solitary Royal Engineer playing a grand piano in the open street with not a soul listening to him. The house from which the instrument had been dragged was smashed to rubble but except for some scratches on its varnish the piano had suffered no harm and the gunner officer found its tone pleasant. The pianist had no real technique but played with feeling. It seemed almost weird to hear Schumann's *Slumber Song* in such surroundings.

'BLOODY MURDER'

DELVILLE WOOD

Lieutenant Franklin Lushington was often asked what being shelled in trenches was like. He gave this description in August 1916, when at Delville Wood.

Dig a hole in the garden, fairly close to the house, a few yards long, six feet deep and four feet wide. At night go armed with a pop-gun and stand in this hole. Then ask the members of your family to throw into the hole from the upper window every utensil and article of furniture they can lay hands on: crockery, fire-irons, coal, chairs, tables, beds –

This photograph illustrates some of the 'bloody murder' the soldier spoke about. Many wounded men were being treated at the Durham Light Infantry R.A.P. when it was blown in by a shell. Their mates desperately try to dig them out before they suffocate. The incident occurred near Zillebeke, Ypres Salient.

let them heave the lot at you, not forgetting the grand piano, just to give you an idea of a nine-inch shell. You must not leave the hole but while the bombardment is going on you are at liberty to march up and down, eat, sleep, remove the debris that doesn't hit you, and generally to pretend that nothing unpleasant is happening.

Remain there a few days or you will evade the trench-dweller's worst enemy, boredom. And if you want to be realistic, add heat, shortage of water, stench, shortage of sleep, and give yourself the actual possibility of being killed every moment.

It would give you *some* idea. Of course you would miss the noise. But you would know the sense of futility which being shelled in a trench produces. At the end of your 'tour' I think you would understand how sage a comment on the experience was that made by a poor scared fellow I met in Pommiers Redoubt (near Mametz). He had just come out of trenches where most of his companions had been killed by shelling, and looking at me with wide, staring eyes, he said, 'Why, this isn't war at all! It's bloody murder!'

WEEKEND TOUR

SAUSAGE VALLEY, FRICOURT, SOMME

Lieutenant Pope Stamper of the 15th Durham Light Infantry was standing near his dug-out in Sausage Valley on a Saturday evening in 1916 when a draft of reinforcements from the Middlesex Regiment came up. They had to wait there for a guide to take them to the front line positions of their battalion. One new young soldier told Lieutenant Stamper that he had left England only the day before, Friday.

Not long after the draft had gone forward the British made a trench raid and the Germans retaliated with a raid of their own.

The casualties started to come back and soon stretchers littered the ground near the 1st C.C.S., which happened to be close to Lieutenant Stamper's dug-out. He saw that one of the casualties was the young soldier he had spoken to, so he gave him a cigarette and tried to cheer him up.

'Blimey, sir', he said, smiling faintly, 'this really *has* been a short weekend excursion on the Continent'.

*Officers of the Norfolk Regiment pose for the camera in a photograph
probably taken by Padre 'Tubby' Clayton. The officer in the centre wears the
ribbon of a recently awarded M.C.* (*Author's collection*)

FOUR-SECOND SACRIFICE

MORLANCOURT, SOMME

Major Rowland Feilding of the Connaught Rangers attended mass on Sunday 3 September 1916, and as he was leaving the church he met a fellow C.O., Cecil Trafford, who invited him to the mess of the Scots Guards, in a house with a small garden. Nearby in the Orderly Room the Scots Guards' bombing officer, Second Lieutenant G. de L. Leach, was priming grenades.

The safety pin of a grenade slipped out, the cap which ignited the fuse was struck, the fuse started to burn – and Leach had four seconds to get rid of the bomb. He shouted to the two men in the room to lie down and ran for the door. Outside in the mess garden he saw the two C.O.'s and other men and he knew that his last chance of safely disposing of the bomb was gone. Turning his back to the other officers and facing a wall, he held the bomb in both hands. When it exploded both his hands were blown off and he was wounded in the legs and stomach. He was taken to hospital at Corbie but died on the way. He was 22 years of age.

Many accidents were occurring at this time because grenade fuses were being shortened from five seconds to four and at times to three. Leach was awarded the Albert Medal but other soldiers who displayed the same kind of courage received the V.C., including a Scottish corporal who dropped a grenade in a trench and then lay on it to protect his comrades.

HATE AT FIRST SIGHT

SOMME

Two soldiers now known to history only as Darkie and Blue took an instant dislike to each other when they met in training camp and the animosity continued into the front line. One night Darkie was at work shovelling mud out of the trench and Blue was on sentry duty. Darkie's shovel handle dug Blue in the ribs and a moment later Darkie felt a blow on his shoulder like a kick from a mule. In a moment the two men were in a fierce all-in fight in the trench, which ended only when Darkie couldn't get up. He stayed down for so long that he was carried into a dug-out where it was found that the blow on his shoulder had been caused by a hurtling piece of German shell. He was away from the unit for three months and when he returned the two men became firm friends. They stayed friends until 1979 when Blue died.

The sketch to illustrate the fight between Blue and Darkie was drawn by an Australian artist in the 1920s. Australians commonly referred to a punch-up as a stoush; even an attack against the Germans was sometimes referred to in this way.

ASKING FOR IT

MESSINES, YPRES SALIENT

The 47th Division, a London formation, had seen hard service on the Somme in 1916 and in September it was moved to the Ypres Salient and a sector of the front which, at that time, was relatively peaceful. It was intended to give the survivors a rest and to allow the reinforcements a chance to settle into their units.

The 18th Battalion (London Irish) were told by their C.O. that Intelligence reports showed that directly opposite their part of the line was the German regiment which they had taken on and beaten at High Wood, on the Somme. The men were elated.

By dawn next morning they stood-to on the firestep but no attack came and the order was passed, 'Stand down!'

Moments later one rifleman mounted the firestep again and with his hands making a trumpet he bellowed insultingly, 'Hey, Fritz! Comprez High Wood?'

Crack! A sniper's bullet knocked off his steel helmet and he fell onto the duckboards, bleeding from a wound to the scalp. Despite the injury he picked himself up, gathered together his souvenirs of battle and addressed his startled mates. 'Cheerio, boys, I've got a Blighty one. But don't tell the colonel it was self-inflicted'.

VIVID PROSE

AUCHEL, PAS DE CALAIS

A certain Commanding Officer recommended one of his men for the Military Medal, the junior award for bravery. The recommendation was turned down by higher authority, because the act was not considered good enough for an award.

The C.O. was disappointed but since the case was a particularly deserving one he tried again. He rewrote the story, racking his brains for the most extravagant language he could muster. His success exceeded his wildest expectation. The man was this time awarded the Victoria Cross.

The story was told by Colonel Rowland Feilding, who hated the decoration system. He wrote to his wife: 'It seems to me that the most difficult place in which to win fighting distinction is the fighting line itself. Most of the awards that have been given, as well as very many that have not, have been earned several times over. The literary capacity of most C.O.s is inadequate for the task of writing up the specific acts in language vivid enough to tickle the imagination of the scrutineers'.

'IT REDUCES MEN TO SHIVERING BEASTS'

SOMME

In the 1915 section of this book there is a letter from Lieutenant Gavin Greenwell in which he speaks of having 'a ripping time'. In August 1916, six weeks after the beginning of the Somme offensive, he confesses that all the adventure and sense of great enterprise has gone.

You wouldn't be able to conceive the filthy and miserable surroundings in which I am writing this note – not even if you were accustomed to the filthiest slums in Europe.

I am sitting in the bottom of an old German dug-out about ten or twelve feet under the earth with three other officers and about ten men, orderlies and runners; the table is littered with food, equipment, candle grease and odds and ends. The floor is covered with German clothing and filth. The remains of the trench outside is blown to pieces and full of corpses from the different regiments which have been here lately, German and English. The ground is ploughed up

141

A remarkable photograph of men of the 1st Battalion Lancashire Fusiliers on their way to the front line on 1 July 1916, the opening day of the Somme offensive. The firing line arrow points in the opposite direction but everthing about these men indicates that they are going into action – not least the expression on the face of the soldier in the centre. The major (at right) wears a Tommy's tunic with the triangle of the 29th Division on his arm. An amber hackle is stencilled on his helmet. On his back is the pale cardboard triangle which denotes an officer; the lance-corporal at left wears a dark triangle which indicates an N.C.O. (Author's collection and copyright)

by enormous shell-holes; there isn't a single landmark to be seen for miles except a few gaunt sticks where trees once were. The stench is well-nigh intolerable. Everyone is absolutely worn out with fatigue and hunger.

Yesterday I wandered on round these awful remains of trenches with my bugler, simply sickened by the sights and smells until I found some poor devils cowering in the filth, where they had been for forty-eight hours. I moved them back.

I shall never look on warfare either as fine or sporting again. It reduces men to shivering beasts: there isn't a man who can stand shell-fire of the modern kind without getting the blues.

GOING FOR GOLD

SOMME

A brigadier of the 54th Infantry Brigade (18th Division) who had a glass eye, and his Cockney runner, were on their way up the line in 1916 when they noticed a dead German officer who had a prominent gold tooth in his death-grin skull.

The next day the pair passed the same spot and the brigadier noticed that the gold tooth was missing.

'I see that gold tooth has gone, Johnson', he said.

'Yessir.'

'I suppose if I'm knocked out someone will take my glass eye'.

'Yessir. I've put meself dahn for that, for a souvenir'.

SPORTING CHANCE

HAZEBROUCK

'Pat', who had been a shearer's cook in Australia, was really too old for the trenches so he was made an officer's batman, a job which was a little more comfortable than being a trench soldier. His officer was very surprised to see Pat one day with a German prisoner, and the officer surmised that he had borrowed the captive from some other Australian, so that he could boast about his captive.

'Pat, what on earth are you doing with Fritz?' he said.

'To tell the truth, sorr-r, I haven't yet made up my moind'.

'All right, so take him back to the cage'.

'Very well, sorr-r', Pat said agreeably.

About ten minutes later the officer saw Pat without his prisoner. 'What did you do with your prisoner?' he asked.

'Well, sir, he kept beggin' and beggin' to be let go, so oi just put a Mills (grenade) in his pocket with the pin out, and tould him to run for his loife'.

143

There is no reason to doubt this story. The Australian official correspondent and some unit historians record such incidents and my own father told me of them too. As a rule, it seems, the grenade was put in a rear pocket and the German held firmly for a count of two before being pushed away and told to run. An Australian veteran told me, 'It was a sporting chance. It was possible for Fritz to pull out the bomb and throw it away or even heave it at us. If he could get rid of it, good luck to him – we let him go'.

TROPHIES OF WAR

GEUDECOURT, SOMME

Lieutenant Keith Henderson, having fought his way to the smashed village of Geudecourt, at the end of September 1916, went on a search for souvenirs and made a list of his trophies:

1: A few buttons with double-tailed lions.
2: Four shoulder-straps with the figure 6 in red. This indicated a division which had been opposite us for some time and is exhausted, I think.
3: One haversack and one respirator haversack.
4: One rosary.
5: Five different sorts of bayonets from different regiments. These I thought we might hang up.
6: Four tassels. They are worn by Fritz in the same sort of way that lanyards are worn. Quite pretty, though rather soiled and worn.

7: A bit of a wing of a crushed aeroplane that is lying on the brown, feverish earth like a dead seagull.
8: A brass spring very beautifully made, that I am going to have made into a bracelet for you. (For Helen, his wife). Also from the aeroplane.
9: A cardboard box for signal flares. *Signal Patrolmen* they are labelled. I threw the flares away as they might go pop en route.
10: A jolly bit of gilded carving from a house.
11: A bit of embroidery . . . a vestment of sorts. It's white and there's heavy gold embroidery at the sides. Then '11A' is a piece of black and silver embroidery . . . Both these things are exceedingly beautiful.

There now, isn't that a good haul!

BATTLE - SCARRED BUT VICTORIOUS:
A Tank, mud-caked and slightly damaged, coming into Albert after the Battle of September 15th, 1916.

Lieutenant Henderson had taken part in the battle of 15 September, not far from Geudecourt, where the monstrous new tanks had been used for the first time in action. This contemporary postcard shows a male tank; that is, it has cannons. Female tanks were armed only with machine-guns.

(Author's collection)

'A TRULY AWFUL SIGHT'

GOMMECOURT, NEAR HÉBUTERNE

The outstanding feature of trench warfare (Lieutenant Franklin Lushington wrote in September 1916) is that practically speaking, one never sees the enemy. We know by his effects he is there but during more than half the day, if his trenches were empty and he himself a myth, 'twould be the same.

The exception proves the rule and I am reminded of this by two Germans I saw in the distance this afternoon digging and moving about on the slope behind their line. Their appearance was regarded as an impertinence asking for target practice, which prompty followed. It was probably off the mark but good enough to make them quickly disappear. They are the first living Germans I have seen beyond No Man's Land.

Looking over the top soon afterwards I saw what struck me as a truly awful sight. One of our guns was firing on the German front line. I happened to be standing in the direct line of fire so that I could actually see the shell in the air at the instant before it dived into the trench. To watch the actual devil of destruction on its way, hurtling through the air so that it appeared like a black cricket-ball seen in its flight for the thousandth part of a second, was to me the most awful sight I've seen. Instinctively one contrasted the force and velocity of the thing with the human bodies it was making for.

FACT AND FICTION

ST GEORGE'S HILL, SOMME

Troops in the trenches were often amused and sometimes enraged by battle reports which they read in the newspapers from home. Writing from the Somme in October 1916, Lieutenant Franklin Lushington spoke of an incident which he felt indicated the difficulty faced by anyone later trying to write a true history of the war.

The newspaper report says that on one of the nights when we happened to be in the line at St George's Hill, the Germans were seen leaving their trenches, but were driven back by the Allied barrage-fire before they could reach our line.

Now the true history of that little episode is this: There were strict orders at the time that S.O.S. signals were only to be used in extreme emergency. A certain company commander close to us became unnecessarily alarmed and sent up his S.O.S. rockets. The artillery gave concentrated fire and the Germans, apparently thinking that we were going to attack, replied in kind just in front of the British trenches. On neither side did the men attempt to leave their trenches. But the company commander had to save his face. Hence the report, received no doubt with enormous arm-chair satisfaction. Probably the German version was precisely similar.

SOLDIER TALK

BETHUNE–LA BASSÉE ROAD

In November 1916 men of the 483rd Field Company Royal Engineers were driving a double limber in pitch darkness, along the Bethune – La Bassée Road. From the village of Beavry onwards they ran into heavy German gunfire. The only passenger on the limber was a newly posted padre on his way to join an advance infantry battalion.

A shell burst only 50 yards ahead and the frightened mules reared and refused to go on. All was confusion as some animals lay down and kicked over the traces; the wheel pair even got their legs over the centre pole of the limber. There seemed to be no way of sorting out the mess and the padre, rather hesitantly but helpfully said to the lead driver, 'My man, can I do anything to assist you?'

'Well, yes, you can', the driver said. 'Sir, would you mind trekkin' off the road so that we can use language these blighters understand?'

'Perhaps *I* could say a few words', the padre suggested.

'Not the kind of words I've got in mind, sir', the driver said grimly. '*Please*, sir'.

So the padre trekked off. Five minutes later the team, now docile, caught up with him.

COMMAND LANGUAGE

AUCHONVILLERS

Corporal Charlie, a well-known character of 1/2nd Highland Field Ambulance, had general charge of the 100 or so German prisoners being used as auxiliaries during the battle for Beaumont-Hamel. That Field Ambulance was also running a Collecting Post at Auchonvillers and needed all the labour it could get.

On the evening of 13 November

the corporal was ordered to detail 12 men for wheeled stretcher work to go to Thurles Dump. He went to the shed where his command lay smoking, held up a hurricane lamp and shouted, 'Noo then, you Fritzes. A dizzen o' ye. Compree?'

.'Nein!' said a puzzled voice from among the huddle of Huns.

'Nein, ye gommeral! It's nae nine; it's twal' o' ye! C'wa' noo! Look slippy! *You*, Nosey! An' *you* Breeks;

– to a man whose trousers had been torn by barbed wire. He fitted Nosey between the front handles of a wheeled stretcher and Breeks at the tail end and with a firm shove sent them on their way. When his tally of six stretchers was complete he turned to the orderly in charge. 'Noo, laddie, there's your Fritzes! See ye dinna lose ony o' them! they onerstun' English if ye spek rill slo".

One Allied soldier was usually enough to guard 20 or even 30 German prisoners. Most were happy to be out of the war and it was rare for prisoners, once in the rear, to attempt escape.

DEFENCE OF THE FRANKFURT TRENCH

BEAUMONT-HAMEL

Most of the stories in this book are brief but this one deserves some detail if only because visitors to the Western Front can easily locate Frankfurt Trench where a grim and glorious action took place over a period of eight days beginning on 18 November 1916. The deed served no purpose in the scheme of battle which is probably why it gets little space in the histories.

On the snow covered battlefield, D Company and part of C Company, 16th H.L.I., had captured the Munich Trench. Three platoons of D

Company pushed on towards the second objective, the Frankfurt Trench, which a small party finally stormed and took prisoner the 50

A battlefield was inhabited by tens of thousands of men but they were rarely visible on the surface. They moved up to the front line, as at Beaumont-Hamel, through communication trenches which were sometimes like sunken roads. Not a single blade of grass survived on these battlefields. The troops shown here are Australian.

defenders. They were sent back under escort but on the way were rescued by superior German forces who shot the escort and retook Munich Trench. About 100 men, without officers, held Frankfurt Trench and in the vicinity little groups of H.L.I. sheltered in the shell holes. A runner was sent back to find company headquarters . This he did but the company commander was killed while giving the runner orders. The runner made a hazardous trip back to the Frankfurt Trench and his apparent confidence in the open encouraged several lost men to follow him; snipers shot them one by one as they bolted across the open. The runner, himself lost, stumbled on three Germans in a shell hole – and they surrendered to him. They not only guided him towards Frankfurt Trench but rescued him when he staggered into a shell-hole and embedded himself thigh-deep in mud.

By nightfall the Frankfurt Trench held 40 or 50 effective men and 50 wounded, under the command of a corporal. It was clear to the defenders that they were isolated and surrounded. Instead of holding the nose of a salient, as they had thought, they were a British strong point within the German lines. But the battle orders had been to hold the objective for 48 hours and this the senior British soldiers decided to do. They were an H.L.I. sergeant who assumed the duties of a sergeant-major and a lance corporal in charge of the machine-guns. A sergeant of the King's Own Scottish Borderers crept out that night to seek help.

The garrison replenished ammunition for the machine-guns from the bandoliers of the dead lying in the open. The infantry handed over their own ammunition to the gunners and armed themselves with abandoned German rifles. Food and water were scarce but water was skimmed from shellholes after dark and boiled with difficulty. The wounded were in a bad way since nobody had more than a rudimentary knowledge of first aid.

On the evening of the third day the Germans attacked and after hand-to-hand fighting were driven off, leaving many casualties. But the Scots had also suffered and the sergeant shortened his line. That night a heavy British artillery barrage boxed the trench to protect the garrison, an indication that the Borderers sergeant had got through. But there was no infantry follow up.

After four days the garrison was pitifully weak and many were suffering badly from thirst. The wounded were laid out on the floor of a gallery leading from the dug-out; it was quite dark there and men died silently without others being aware of it. Many wounds were gangrenous.

Little sleep was possible for the survivors because the sergeant ordered sentry relief every hour; he had to keep the men alert enough to fight. A married man and before the war a roads foreman with Glasgow Corporation, he was a natural leader with a robust cheerfulness and unflagging vigour. In the grim hour before dawn he even went around his position singing. The lance corporal of the guns was equally gallant. The son of a sergeant of the Scots Greys, he had been born in Ireland 'on the strength'.

The fifth day dawned. An aeroplane had dropped a message that relief was coming. But first the relief force would have to fight its way across the Munich Trench which lay between the outpost and the British lines, and it never did appear. On the afternoon of the sixth day the Germans launched a powerful attack from the front and flanks. The defenders responded to the alarm with painful, exhausted slowness and the Germans got close enough to bomb the entrance to one of the dugouts. Then vicious close-quarter fighting developed. The Germans with all the advantages, were beaten off and left eight prisoners in the Scots' hands. The machine-gunner lance corporal, standing in his emplacement when the fight was over, was sniped dead.

On the seventh wintry dawn the H.L.I. sentries saw fresh German troops entering the sector; a long procession of bucket-shaped helmets could be seen bobbing along a communication trench. The German commander sent in a message with a captured Inniskilling Fusilier: the garrison could surrender and be well treated or he would attack with great force and overwhelm them. The sergeant considered the proposition as a way out for his starving, frozen and exhausted men. When his reply was slow in coming the Germans shelled the Frankfurt Trench. The sergeant, expecting that the infantry attack was coming, jumped to the parapet, shouted 'Never surrender boys!' and was killed a second later by a shell splinter.

That night the exploring British patrols probed as far as the rim of the Munich Trench where they heard the Germans speaking and here a soldier found a pool of water. It was so foul that the corporal in charge of the wounded would not give it to his casualties. Those who drank it despite his warnings contracted a virulent typhoid.

The Germans attacked on the eighth day. The sentries and gunners were shot down before the garrison could properly come to arms. The eight German prisoners at last proved useful; their shouts prevented complete annihilation.

Fifteen of the original·100 were left unwounded but were so weak that they staggered dizzily; even so they were ordered to carry their wounded to the German lines. Two of the men taken prisoner died in captivity, another was shot by the Germans for accepting a piece of bread from a French civilian.

After the Armistice the H.L.I survivors were awarded 11 D.C.M.s and 22 M.M.s, an astounding number of decorations for a single action. That the episode was considered to have an epic quality was also shown by the granting of *any* award; it was rare to confer decorations on men who had become prisoners of war. The Fifth Army commander, General H.P. Gough, reported, 'I consider that these men deserve great recognition for the magnificent example of soldierly qualities they displayed'.

There was, unhappily, a sour note. The sergeant in command and the gunner lance corporal were both recommended for the Victoria Cross. The proposals were refused and they got nothing more than a Mention in Despatches. At that time it was not possible to get any decoration posthumously other than the V.C. General Gough was right about the 'magnificent example'. The defence of the Frankfurt Trench showed the Tommy's stubborn doggedness under extreme adversity, when boldly led.

'YOU REMEMBER BILL?'

AUTHUILLE, ANCRE VALLEY

An officer of the 15th H.L.I. for a time kept a collection of little gems from the soldiers' letters which he was called upon to censor. The collection was lost but he remembered some of the extracts.

Dear Mother, Please send me the *Christian Herald* and £1. Your loving son. Please do not forget the *Christian Herald*.

Dear Wife, We have a new chaplain. He is as hielan' (Highland) as peat.

Dear Wife, You will be glad to know that I am teetotal. The beer here is not fit to drink.

You remember Bill? Well, poor Bill has been killed. I am sorry. We were great pals. Before we went into the line we had a drink together. (This comment, the officer said, seemed sacramental in its tone.)

SUNDRIES

AMIENS

The Regimental Sergeant-Major of an Australian battalion in camp at Amiens in 1916 was preparing the men for Sunday church parade. Not particularly conversant with the various creeds, he announced: 'Church of England, fall in on the right, R.C.s on the left; all you other fancy religions parade in front of the Y.M.C.A. hut'.

152

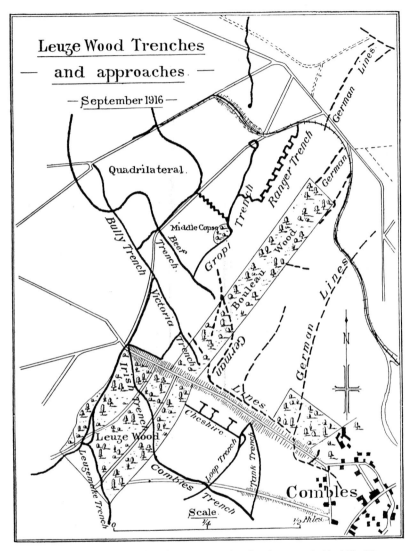

Leuze Wood Trenches
and approaches
September 1916

Quadrilateral

Bully Trench

Beef Trench

Middle Copse

Gropi Trench

Ranger Trench

German

Bouleau Wood

Victoria Trench

German Lines

German Lines

Irish Trench

Leuze Wood

Cheshire

Leuzenake Trench

Combles Trench

Loop Trench

Punch Trench

Combles

N

Scale
¼   ½ Miles
0

Combles shown on this frontline map, was in a bowl surrounded by hills. The Germans had made it into a fortress, with many gun emplacements, dugouts and tunnels. Hundreds of soldiers were killed here during the Somme battles in the woods shown on the map.

153

HEARTFELT

LE TRANSLOY, NEAR BAPAUME

In November 1916 the mud of the Somme was so thick and sticky that half an hour was needed to cover 50 yards in the trenches. Ration parties bringing food from the rear sometimes took all night to reach the front and then slept exhaustedly before returning the next night.

An officer at Le Transloy over-heard a man talking to himself as he struggled to move down the trench. Every word was punctuated by the prodigious effort of drawing a leg out of the mud.

'Lloyd George said – this – was a fight – to the finish – The bastard had better – come out here – and finish it.'

THE CORPSES ON THE WIRE

THIEPVAL

The British troops in the Ancre River Valley were exposed to the Germans on the formidable Thiepval Heights. From here they could observe everything and their artillery had flattened most landmarks. This made patrolling difficult because there were so few markers to give line or direction. A few existed, despite everything. Shrines still stood at crossroads that were never free of shell-fire, while some churches which had been destroyed still had uncracked windows. Occasionally in the deep rubble which was pounded over and over whole crockery pots could be found where peasant homes once stood.

For a long time the best landmarks well forward on the British lines were several French corpses in their scarlet and blue uniforms hanging on the barbed wire. They hung there despite massive machine-gun and

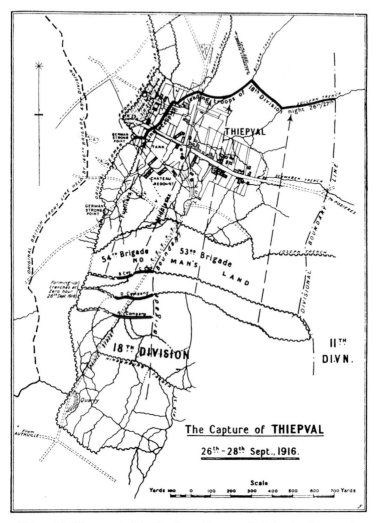

The Capture of **THIEPVAL**

26th - 28th Sept., 1916.

Thiepval heights, part of the Poziéres ridge, was held by the Germans in strength. Some of the positions, such as Zollern Trench and Schwaben Trench, became famous and tens of thousands of British Commonwealth and French troops died trying to capture the heights. This map shows the actual capture. Thiepval Memorial, to more than 73,000 men who have no known graves, is built on the site of the old chateau.

artillery fire and it was thought that the Germans never deliberately aimed at them.

It was common along the Ancre for one officer to say to another, 'Your old friend in the red coat was asking after you last night'. And both would laugh. They laughed because there were no human remains inside the uniforms – just roughly shaped pieces of wood and wire and stuffed sandbags. They had been put there as direction finders for patrols going in and out and, apparently, the German gunners never did discover the ruse.

UNFORGETTABLE

YPRES SALIENT

In December 1916 the platoon to which Bill and Jim belonged was ordered to occupy a section of trench and hold it until relieved. Snow had been falling for some days – except when it rained for a change – and on the way up the men found the communication trenches with about three feet of water in them. The sergeant, eyeing the place with gross distaste, said facetiously, 'Eh, lads, here's the crew, but where's the submarine?' A shell whistled over their heads, indicating the start of a strafe, and the sergeant, in the same dry tones, ordered 'Submerge!' Into slimy mud and water the platoon duly 'submerged'. As they surfaced and continued on Bill was lagging behind and Jim looked round to see him firmly stuck with one leg in the sticky clay at the bottom of the trench, while he poked the other around trying to find firm standing. 'Jim', he said, 'Do you call to mind them posters at home – "Remember Belgium"? Well, I shall bloody well never forget it. Come and pull me out!'

The REMEMBER BELGIUM posters were among the first propaganda displays of the war. The British public was exhorted to remember the way in which the Germans had invaded, raped and smashed 'poor little Belgium'.

British soldiers who served in the Ypres Salient developed a great affection for the Flemish people, even while hating the Flemish mud. This photograph of a Tommy with little Flemish girls occupies a prominent place in the Ypres (Ieper) museum with its many memories of British sacrifice.

157

'TICKLED ALL THE WAY'

RAILWAY WOOD, YPRES SALIENT

During the worst periods of 1916 the communication trenches from the rear areas to the front trenches were relentlessly pounded by German artillery. By reducing them to little more than shallow ditches the gunners were making it easier for their infantry to pick off reinforcements, messengers and working parties. British posts at Railway Wood were supplied via Muddy Lane, which had become very dangerous. At a score of places men going up or back were exposed to snipers and, as a sergeant put it, they were 'tickled all the way'.

In the support line one afternoon was Sergeant Vernon Sylvaine of the Somerset Light Infantry. He heard the *Crack! Crack! Crack!* which always heralded the arrival of a runner from the rear, and went to the trench junction to wait for the visitor. A soldier arrived with his tin hat dented in two places and blood trickling from a graze on the cheek. He looked reproachfully at the sergeant, who felt that some comment was called for, so he said, 'Jerry seems to be watching that bit'.

'Watching!' the soldier said. 'Not arf! 'Struth! I felt like I was walking darn Sarthend Pier naked!'

LEG BEFORE

SOMME, NEAR CURLU

In January 1916 Gunner 'Spider' Webb was with the Royal Artillery. He loved his guns almost as much as he loved cricket, which he played well as an all-rounder. No matter where a conversation started, Spider would turn it around to cricket. At this time the German and British guns were firing at one another rather than at the infantry and one day, for something like seven hours, the duel was intense. Then came a

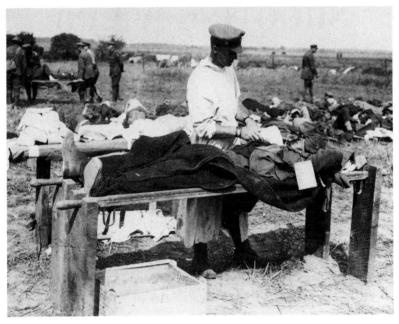

Unlike Gunner Webb, this wounded soldier has both legs intact, but he might well have been first treated in the open like this. Many other wounded men await their turn. This photograph was taken at a Field Dressing Station at Le Quesnel.

lull from the Germans and the British gunners also ceased firing.

Their nerves were just beginning to relax when the German gunners sent over five shells. They did no damage but after a brief pause a sixth exploded – next to Spider and two mates. When the smoke cleared Lieutenant George Franks M.C. ran to see what had happened. Spider's two friends were beyond help and he himself was on his back propping himself on his elbows to survey the scene. One of his legs was mangled.

'What's happened, Webb?' Lieutenant Franks said anxiously.

'What happened?' Spider said. 'Would you believe it! In one over Jerry has bowled two (he gestured at his dead mates) and I'm stumped (he nodded at his leg)'. Then he fainted.

'Spider' Webb survived the war and kept his love of cricket – as an umpire.

159

SHOOTING A LINE

BASE HOSPITAL

A wounded Irish soldier was relating his remarkable frontline adventures to a party of lady visitors at a base hospital. He vividly retold of the fight in which he knocked out 17 Huns and a machine-gun 'wid me wan hand along, begod'.

'That's the end of the shtory, lidies', he said. 'The surgeons took me and laid me for all as though I was dead in an ammunition wagon'.

'One of the women said, 'You mean an ambulance wagon, or course, not an ammunition wagon'.

'Sorra a bit', he said sadly. 'Shure, I was so filled with bullets they decided I ought to go in the ammunition wagon'.

THE WOMEN OF PERVYSE

DIXMUIDE

For much of the war two intrepid women – the Baroness T'Serclaes and Mairi Chisholm, a Scottish girl aged only 19 in 1916 – ran a 'private' nursing station not far behind the lines on the Belgian front.

At one time they returned to their quarters at two in the morning, desperately tired, and found the backdoor open and the glass panels smashed. Having searched the house, they fell into bed dead-beat. They were still in bed next morning when they heard a knock on the door. When Mairi opened it she saw a burly French soldier, looking embarrassed and uncomfortable. He explained that he wanted his revolver. 'I don't have your revolver', Mairi said. 'Gipsy (her name for the Baroness), here's a man who wants his revolver – at least I think that's what he wants'.

The poilu insisted to the two women, while unable to meet their eyes, that he must have his revolver.

'Well, where do you think it is?' they asked.

'C'est dans votre lit, mesdemoiselles', the soldier blurted out. He slipped past them, put his grimy hand under Mairi's pillow and drew out his heavy revolver. He confessed that he and other soldiers about the place who had no regular quarters were in the habit of sleeping in the beds during the day because they knew the ladies were always out until late. He was sorry about the broken door on this occasion.

The two women now had the answer to some little mysteries – not the least being where the fleas had come from.

The courage of these women was legendary and they became known as 'the women of Pervyse'. When their patients died they used to go through their pockets for articles to be sent home. On one occasion as Mairi was searching through the pockets of a greatcoat she came across the brains of a man, evidently blown there by the force of an explosion.

A RETORT TOO FAR

SHELTER WOOD, SOMME

While on guard at Shelter Wood, an Australian known as 'Baggie', the best known 'hard-doer' of the 19th Battalion, was having a Woodbine while leaning up against a post. His rifle was stuck by the bayonet in the ground in front of him.

Into Baggie's line of vision strode a British colonel, who eyed him severely. Baggie gave him a friendly nod, which Australian hard-doers generally reckoned was adequate recognition of senior rank.

'Look here, my man', the colonel said. 'Suppose a German appeared suddenly and grabbed your rifle. What steps would you take?'

The story was illustrated by an Australian artist in the 1920s. The men of the A.I.F. were reputed to have little use for spit-and-polish discipline and formality but everybody agreed that their fighting discipline was unsurpassed and British war correspondents continually sang their praises.

'Bloody long ones, sir', Baggie said cheerfully.

The next scene of the little drama took place in the guard tent where Baggie found out that British colonels had a bite as well as a bark.

ON THE TROT

DIRTY BUCKET CAMP, POPERINGE

Late in 1916 a British battalion stationed under canvas at Dirty Bucket Camp lost their old Medical Officer, who was himself evacuated sick. In a few days the word went round that his replacement, a new American M.O., believed everything you told him.

The Tommies were not slow to take advantage of this innocence, so that practically every man in the battalion – that is, those who had survived the Somme – paraded sick in the hope of getting light duty instead of the soul-destroying parades which the veteran troops hated.

All were a little loose in the bowels, so to a man they said they were suffering from diarrhoea. A doctor cannot tell a man has *not* got diarrhoea unless he follows him round all day.

Private A.M. Burrage had an unfortunate experience with this doctor; he was in the middle of a queue and he did not know what colossal lies the first men had been telling him. His friend Dave, who preceded him, entered the M.O.'s tent and told him that he had been compelled to visit the latrines 26 times in the previous 24 hours. 'Gee!' exclaimed the astonished doctor and gave him some medicine and three days' light duty.

Then Burrage went in. 'Waal', said the M.O., 'I suppose you've got diarrhoea too. I'm going to call this regiment the Charley's Aunts'. This was a delicate allusion to the fact that the famous play *Charley's Aunt* was still running. 'How many times have you responded to the call of nature in the last day and night?'

'Seven or eight times', Burrage said sadly.

The doctor gave him a look of blank astonishment; after the tall stories he had been hearing from the other men this did not seem excessive. 'Gee man', he said, 'you're bound!' If you come here telling me any more stories like that I shall have to give you some opening medicine'.

But he allowed Burrage one day's light duty and he went out mystified – until he heard what the other liars had been saying.

162

WITH SUCH FRIENDS . . .

FLEURBAIX

Men of an Australian infantry brigade were in trenches at Fleurbaix, in November 1916, when they realised one day that some of the shells landing among them were coming from behind. The angry officers called the artillery C.O. by telephone and said, 'We prefer to be killed by the Germans, thank you'.

British shells continued to land among the Australians and two officers were killed. The next Australian message said, 'If you fire on us again we will turn our machine-guns on you'. Lieutenant Hugh Knyvett was sent back with the message to make sure the artillery commander understood. He took with him as evidence one of the British dud shells.

The gunner officer insisted that his shells were landing two hundred yards in front of the Australians; German cross-fire had to be responsible. Producing the dud shell from his pack Knyvett said, 'Have you seen this before'.

'For God's sake bury it!' the horrified gunner exclaimed.

'It's on its way to Div. H.Q.', Knyvett said. 'It was your egg and you can bloody well hatch it!'

THE CHOICE OF WAYS

SOMME

It was a bitterly cold night near a small Somme village, probably Harponville, and the sentry was not in the best humour when an Australian Bluey approached him. Though the village was out of bounds Bluey decided to risk the sentry in order to see a girl who lived within the prohibited area.

'Halt, who goes there!' shouted the sentry.

Bluey walked up to him until the end of the bayonet touched the middle button of his tunic. 'Look here', he said. 'I've got a mother in heaven, a father in hell and a bonzer girl in this here village, and I'm going to see one of them tonight. Now, it is for you to say which one'.

Bluey saw his girl.

Many soldiers had a 'bonzer girl' in a French or Flemish village. The two Tommies shown in this photograph, taken in Flanders, had six between them. The sergeant is a member of the 10th (Service) battalion of the Notts. and Derbys. Regiment (Sherwood Foresters) in the 51st Infantry Brigade of the 17th (Northern) New Army Division. This was the only battalion to wear an identification 'patch' like that seen below the girl's hand. The Notts. & Derbys. were also the only regiment with the shoulder-strap titles of the type worn by the sergeant. The sergeant and his girl had a son who was born during the war and still lives on the Western Front. He and the author would like to identify the sergeant by name.

PERIL IN NO MAN'S LAND

FROMELLES

Patrols in No Man's Land were full of tension and danger although statistically it was one of the safest places because patrols did not take place during shellfire. One night during the winter of 1916 Lieutenant Hugh Knyvett, the Intelligence Officer of the Australian 15th Brigade, was crawling alongside a levee or raised path running across an irrigation farm. On the other side he heard a splash which he thought was made by a rat and put up his head and looked over. So did the enemy – not a yard away.

Australian and German stared blankly into each other's face for a second and then both turned and bolted. 'This was excusable for a German', Knyvett said, 'but I had no defence. I court-martialled by own conscience and went back to look for him but he was nowhere to be seen'.

The enemy got the better of him on another night in No Man's Land.

In his scouting Knyvett came across a path through the German barbed wire, evidently the place where enemy patrols went out. Knyvett planted some booby-trapped bombs and put a small Union Jack in the centre as bait. In the morning the Union Jack was gone and a German flag was in its place. Everybody from the brigadier down rubbed it into Knyvett that Fritz was too smart for him.

A similar incident had happened with the 1/7th Battalion Middlesex Regiment on 19 June 1915. The Germans planted a flag about 20 yards in front of a sap-head they held in No Man's Land. Sergeant Spencer crawled out through the long grass, in broad daylight, and brought the flag back. Three days later, at dawn, two German flags fluttered at the sap-head. Private Stinson ran out, under fire, and returned with the flags.

MOTHER'S GRIEF

MANSEL COPSE, BETWEEN CARNOY AND MAMETZ, SOMME

A company Commander, Captain Gilbert Rowley, received a pitiable letter signed by several influential people in Leeds, setting forth the case of Mrs Stream, nearly demented because she had lost two of her three sons killed in the trenches since July 1916. She was in mortal fear of what could happen to the sole surviving member of the family, Private Stephen Stream, of Rowley's company. They were petitioning the Prime Minister, the letter writers said, to ask for Stream's transfer to a less dangerous

job. In the meantime, could Captain Rowley do anything.

Rowley had no authority to release Stream but he showed the letter to the colonel, who promised to see what could be done next time the battalion was out of line on rest.

A few days later a big shell dropped into the company trenches blowing to pieces just one man, without injuring anybody else. The remains could not be identified but the man's paybook and identity disc were found – Private Stephen Stream.

FULL BELT FOR HOME

AMIENS – RIBEMONT-SUR-ANCRE

One black night in the winter of 1916, Bill and his assistant driver, Stan, were on their way from Amiens to the vehicle park at Ribemont in their Peerless truck.

The standard speed then was about 15 mph, fast enough to agitate the empty tins, chains and gear in the back and make a racket.

Shouts and the sight of striking

matches in the middle of the road pulled them up about five miles from home. They found another driver with his lorry stuck in a ditch and he needed help. Stan climbed down, hitched a tow chain's hook to the front of the disabled truck and they soon had it on the road again.

Disconnecting the chain from the rear lorry, Stan hooked it under his belt, called out 'Right away, Bill!' and jumped for the tailboard of his own truck. Unfortunately he *missed*.

Bill, with the engine roaring, couldn't hear Stan's frantic yells and Stan could neither get the hook out of his belt nor undo the buckle of his belt because of the pressure on it. He had to run or drop and be dragged five miles home. He ran and often stumbled but stayed upright. In about 15 minutes the truck reached the depot but Stan did not make his usual appearance to help Bill reverse the Peerless into place. Investigating, Bill found him sprawled on the muddy ground, gasping, the tow chain hook still in his belt. Several doses of S.R.D. (Special Ration Distribution or rum) were needed before Stan even began to recover. Bill was contrite but he found something to be pleased about. 'By God', he said, 'you've got to admit that these army belts are tough!'

Soldiers were not always tactful in their choice of postcards to send home. This one carries the caption, 'Into this battlefield grave two dead British soldiers have been reverently placed while the Padre reads the solemn words of the Burial Service.' A soldier named 'George' has sent it home with 'Love to all' and ten kisses. It is not too difficult to imagine the thoughts of his family when viewing the card. (*Author's collection*)

1917

During the Battle of Arras in April Canadian troops took the vital Vimy Ridge but 150,000 British Empire troops became casualties to the German 100,000. Following the disastrous Nivelle offensive 54 French divisions mutinied and more than 100,000 men were court-martialled. On 7 June 1917 Sir Herbert Plumer, having master-minded a tremendous mining operation, blew the Germans off Messines Ridge with a million pounds of explosive. Against the advice of his own Intelligence staff, Haig launched an offensive in the Ypres Salient – 'the battle of the mud' – which culminated in the battle of Passchendaele. The British Empire armies suffered 300,000 casualties for little gain. At Cambrai, in history's first great tank attack, 381 British tanks punched a big hole in the enemy lines but the Germans recovered. The Tommies did not find much to laugh at during 1917.

NATURE'S GENTLEMEN

ON THE ARRAS FRONT

At a Casualty Clearing Station in a farm shed a surgeon was exhausted from the work of dealing with one wound after another – and all bad wounds. There were no beds and the men lay close together on the floor.

After kneeling uncomfortably for some time while working on a dressing the surgeon stood to stretch his back and his foot hit another foot. There was a scream of agony, for that foot was attached to a badly mangled thigh. At once there was a chorus from the men lying around the floor. 'You *didn't* hurt him, sir. He often makes a noise like that'.

The surgeon, pulling himself together, found a hand taking his and looking down he saw his fingers gripped by a haggard soldier with three gaping wounds. 'It *wasn't* your fault, sir', he whispered hoarsely.

He realised then, as he said later, 'that every man in the room took it for granted that my mental anguish for my stupidity was greater than his own physical pain, and was doing his best to deaden it for me – and one of them was doing it at great cost to himself'.

'In whose ranks', the surgeon asked, 'are the world's great gentlemen?'

It is impossible to identify this surgeon because when he wrote his story in the 1920s he signed himself only 'The Clumsy Fool' and gave his address as Guy's Hospital, London.

*Medical officers and orderlies work on wounded men at an Advanced
Dressing Station close to the front. Many such stations were set up in farm
sheds or cellars vulnerable to shell fire. Shock is clearly discernible on the face
of the man whose head is being bandaged.*

SALIENT TRUCE

'DOCTOR'S HOUSE', KEMMEL, YPRES

On 19 Februray 1917 Colonel
Rowland Feilding led 9 officers and
190 other ranks of the 6th Connaught Rangers in an attack from
Shamus Farm towards Messines.

The morning was cold and foggy and
at 7.15 a.m. without preliminary
bombardment, the Connaughts were
over the top and running into No
Man's Land. At the same moment

Many British soldiers have vivid memories of Kemmel and its mountain, which received much attention from German guns. This photograph shows ground and trees torn apart by high explosive shells. Two British officers examine the German front towards the east.

the British artillery opened, putting a box barrage around the selected section of enemy trench to prevent the Germans from bringing in reinforcements.

The Connaughts had some wild fighting and suffered many casualties, especially when the Germans retaliated with high-explosive and shrapnel shells.

By 9.30 a.m all was quiet. An incident then took place, which for Feilding, was as remarkable as any that 'this most unchivalrous of wars' could have produced.

The dead and many Connaught wounded still lay out in No Man's Land when the fog lifted and the trench became clearly visible. As Feilding stood in the middle of his trench a soldier ran up to say that the Germans had allowed 'an armistice' for the purpose of collecting wounded. Hurrying along the trench, Feilding found that this was true; parties of British were out dressing the wounded and carrying them back to the British lines. One of the Connaught officers and a German were bending together over

173

a wounded man alongside the enemy wire. Large numbers of Germans were leaning over and even sitting on the parapet watching, and the Connaughts were doing the same.

'How did this happen?' Feilding demanded. He was told that the Germans had called out in English, 'Send out your stretchermen', and that a number of men had at once climbed over the parapet.

Feilding noticed Private Collins, on of the 'wild men' of the battalion. With a pipe in his mouth, he was sauntering about wearing a bomber's waistcoat, the pockets bulging with grenades. This was only asking for trouble under the circumstances for the Germans had insisted that the bearers be unarmed.

'Put down your bombs!' Feilding told him sharply and the soldier did so sheepishly. Then Feilding moved off up the trench to see how things were faring. He found that the 'armistice' had spread and was even more dramatic. By now, on the right, where only 40 yards separated the trenches, a German officer was shouting to the British to get their heads down or he would fire.

All the dead and wounded were now in and Feilding declared the 'armistice' ended. But the Germans had exacted a price – the British officer he had seen near the enemy wire was missing and as he was carrying two revolvers it was not surprising that the Germans had taken him prisoner.

A few days later Private Collins was awarded the D.C.M. but he was killed the day after he heard of the award. Truces such as that on the Connaughts' front were by no means as rare as is often imagined. The Christmas truce of 1914 is sometimes presented as the only one of the war. Feilding was billeted at the 'Doctor's House' Kemmel at the time of the Connaughts' attack.

STRAIGHT TALK

GAVRELLE, ARRAS

The British soldier's great delight was to talk to an officer in the dark and pretend not to know his rank. One black night in the early spring of 1917 a party of the Artists Rifles was waiting in the railway cutting near Ouse Alley, Gavrelle, with parties from many other units, for ration trucks to come up.

The Germans had the whole area

mapped and they knew the timing of ration arrivals so they put down their usual strafe and the men scattered for cover. When it was over, the Artists Rifles' officer tried to collect his men and going up to a soldier – who hap- pened to be in the Drake Battalion – he asked, 'Are you an Artist?'

The sailor turned soldier answered promptly, 'No, I'm a fucking com- edian'. And the darkness swallowed him up.

SOLDIERS AS NURSES

ETAPLES

Even at the big base hospitals, such as No 7 Canadian General Hospital at Etaples, the staff were so busy that lightly wounded men were given simple medical tasks to perform. In February 1917 Arthur Russell of the Machine-Gun Corps was directed by a nursing sister to one of these duties when he himself was suffering from sores on both hands.

He wrote of this experience, 'One afternoon the Ward Sister took me to a young soldier whose face and neck was pock-marked all over with countless pieces of grit and gravel. This youth had been caught by the blast from an exploding shell and the fine particles of sand and grit had left clear barely a finger- tip space. A nurse had already washed him clean of mud and dirt. I was now given a pair of tweezers, a pile of cotton-wool swabs, and a bowl of medicated water, and in- structed to remove as many of the foreign particles as possible. For two hours I probed with the tweezers taking out pieces of grip and stone, carefully wiping his face and neck with my cotton-wool swabs. Some pieces were too deeply embedded for me to attempt to move, and these I left for the nurses to attend to'.

THE LANCE CORPORAL AND THE GENERAL

HUBEMPRÉ, NORTH OF AMIENS

During the winter of 1916–17 the 16th H.L.I., after Beaumont-Hamel, was in billets in a village near Hubemprè. The hour was fast approaching for 'Lights Out' in farmhouse and barn. An order came through from Army H.Q which was typical of General Gough – the rigid disciplinarian, the commander who had a tough task to perform, and who was determined to perfect his machine to the last tooth on the smallest cog. The order was that every battalion, by a delegated scheme of command, should be prepared to carry out its purpose in action in spite of continuous casualties. Right down to sections men had to be ready to assume the duties of leadership when seniors were killed or disabled.

Since the hour was late and there was no immediate prospect of a quick return to the trenches it looked like excessive zeal to interpret the orders as meaning that this elaborate scheme should that night be inaugurated. But one company commander obeyed to the letter. With the assistance of his sergeant-major, he detailed his supernumaries on the spot, according to the exacting desires of the General.

Next day the battalion went on route march. As it plodded along the French country road, it was met by the General with his staff. The rear company of the battlion – that commanded by the efficient officer – by a lucky chance was the one ordered into a ploughed field at the roadside. The General got to business at once. With the Company officer at his side he called out, in declining order, for one subordinate after another, and closely questioned them as to their duties in the event of casualties among the higher ranks. The General was out to discover if his peremptory order of the previous night had been fulfilled without delay. At last he came to a lance-corporal, a former Glasgow policeman and a huge man, whom he put through his paces.

'You know your duties?'

'Yes, sir'.

'Very well. Advance your section at ten paces interval'.

The corporal exercised his men

176

with skill but as they moved across the rough terrain a trifle irregularly the temporary commander was sharply brought up. 'Are those men at ten paces interval?' demanded the General.

'Yes, sir, exactly'.

'All right,' said the General dryly, 'if you think so, pace it out'.

An uncomfortable interval followed for the watching Battalion; it was obvious that the spacing was scarcely uniform. The lance-corporal calmly paced the distances. Where the interval between the men was shorter than it ought to have been, he took almost mincing steps. Where the gap was greater than that laid down, he stretched his long legs in gargantuan strides. The result was that, as he shouted out the number of each pace, he always reached his man on the tenth.

'Come here', called out the General. 'What's the result?'

'Ten paces interval, sir'.

The General looked his man over keenly. then he turned to the C.O. 'Well, all I can say is that ploughed field is damned deceiving', he said. And then he added, 'Promote that man!'

It was very satisfactory for the 16th H.L.I., but other battalions which had suffered the same inquisition were not so fortunate.

NO MERCY

WARLENCOURT, SOUTH-EAST OF BAPAUME

One day early in 1917 a soldier, probably of a London Regiment, was wounded in a patrol skirmish and became detached from his comrades. He did not call out and could not be found before dawn; he was then seen about 20 yards from the British trench. Apparently unconscious for hours, he was in pain and shouting for help and many men volunteered to bring him in. It would need a party of four and the officers decided against a rescue attempt; there was no point in sacrificing four men to save one. All day the man's groans could be heard and after dusk an officer led four men in a rescue attempt.

The Germans had set a machine-gun on fixed lines during the day and when they suspected the rescue, or heard a noise, they opened fire. Two of the rescue party were killed and the rescued man died of his wounds as the survivors got him into the trench.

Next day a Tommy lying on the outside of the German wire was seen to be moving his arm as if calling for help. The company officers decided to bring him in that night, despite the losses sustained in the morning. During the afternoon the C.O. came to the forward trench with his telescope, fixed it between two sandbags on the parapet and took a long look. He was convinced that the man was dead and pondered on the arm movement. Then he saw that a string had been fixed to the Tommy's wrist and that it ran up over a barbed wire stake. By pulling occasionally the Germans produced the silent signal for help. The dead soldier was bait for an ambush.

'AS IT WERE!'

BAVINCOURT

Private A.M. Burrage, a senior soldier with an acute sense of humour, was given the job nearly every day of getting water for a Royal Engineers detachment in Bavincourt. The water was pumped from a well close by an estaminet. Then he had to march his party to the R.E's camp, at the bottom of the hill. Most days they met a little French general riding up the hill on horseback. Burrage thought he was probably a fine man but he was a rotten horseman and the charger he rode was extremely nervous.

As the water party approached the general, Burrage would scream at the top of his voice: 'Party will march at atten-shun! Party, 'she-hun! Heyes left!' At this the horse behaved like an unbroken bronco; the little Frenchman bounced like a pea dropped on a shovel and shouted angrily at Burrage. 'As it were! As it were!' What he meant was 'As you were!' the command to return to normal.

Many years later Burrage was still laughing over this incident, which was so often repeated. 'It was childish', he said, 'But you had to make fun where you found it, or you went mad'.

A RUM DO

DOULLENS

One spring day in 1917 two Australians on Doullens railway station were fascinated by a large pile of rum jars, stacked quite close to the office of the Railway Transport Officer. And guarding the rum were two British military police.

After a little discussion the Australians, who were on the station legitimately as they were going on leave, knocked on the R.T.O.'s door and one of them said politely, 'Excuse me, sir, what time does the Paris train leave?'

'Fifteen hundred hours', the R.T.O. said, looking up from his desk.

'Oh, three o'clock', the Aussie said. 'Thanks, sir'.

The two men walked up the platform, waited five minutes and then returned to the office. 'Sir', one said, 'you did say three o'clock for the Paris train?'

'That's right', the R.T.O. said curtly. 'Three o'clock'.

The Aussie saluted and withdrew. His mate made the next inquiry. 'I'd just like to check up, sir', he said. 'That train to Paris . . . Three, wasn't it?'

'Yes, dammit!' the R.T.O. said loudly. 'Three! That's what I said, three!'

'And from right here?' the Aussie said, gesturing at the rum jars, though the R.T.O. thought he meant that platform.

'Right there!' the R.T.O. practically shouted.

'Right you are, sir', said the Aussie. 'Three from here'. So each of them picked up a rum jar and hooked a finger through the loops of a third. Nodding agreeably to the M.P.s, they marched briskly off the station.

The story came from my father, who was in the region at the time,
though he never did admit any involvement in the incident.
He did say, though, that he remembered the same stunt
being worked at El Kantara, Egypt, in 1916.

POINT OF DEPARTURE

THE BULL RING, ETAPLES

On this famous training ground, a company of a raw Lancashire battalion was under the vocal fire of a fiery drill-sergeant. He roared for hours as he tried to instil some discipline into what he considered was a hopeless bunch. By the end of the afternoon the men were thoroughly cowed and the sergeant's commands grew more and more rapid and involved.

''Shun!'' he yelled, and the men froze. 'Left turn!' About fifty per cent turned indecisively and before the rest could follow. The sergeant followed up with, 'Right turn! About turn! Quick march! Halt!'

All this produced even greater confusion and the sergeant glared his disgust. He was astounded when one man left the ranks and headed for the barrack hut. 'Hi, you!' he bellowed. 'Where the hell do you think you're off to?'

The Lancashire lad turned a looked at him with pity and scorn. 'Aye, and it's real sick of it, I am', he said. 'Thou doesn't kna tha own mind for two minutes together'.

CLEARING UP THE MESS

GAVRELLE, ARRAS

The brief story which follows gives a vivid impression of the horror of life in the trenches. It was written by Private A.M. Burrage about an incident in 1917.

There came a series of terrific explosions quite close to us. There is no explosion which, for sheer gut-

stabbing ferocity, is quite like that of a *minenwerfer* . . . A minute or two later I was detailed for a job further on in the trench. The parapet was smashed to pieces and on the opposite wall was a great splash of blood. On the ground lay a man with a grey and witless face, one of his legs hanging by a string from just below the knee. Close to him lay a headless trunk with one leg attached to it. Stretcher-bearers were coming for the man who still lived; our job was to clear up the mess. We picked up unspeakable things with our hands and put them into sandbags . . . I derived an odd sort of comfort at finding that I could endure it. At least I knew the worst that my eyes could show me.

SOME SHOOTING?

POPERINGE

One pitch-black night in 1917 some Fusiliers were resting behind a wrecked wall when a party of the West Indian Labour Company came marching past. The Fusiliers knew who they were by their accents and their comments. A German gun fired just one round and a splinter of shell hit one of the West Indians.

A couple of Fusiliers went to help and one of them called back to his mate, 'Alf! Keep low, mate! Jerry has got his eye in – he's hit a nigger in the dark!'

Nearly all the British and Empire soldiers who served in Flanders reached the Ypres Salient through Poperinge, which the Germans often shelled. This magnificent sketch of a war-weary Tommy was drawn in Poperinge in 1917 and published in a Toc H booklet. (*Author's collection*)

SOMETHING TO BE THANKFUL FOR

PLACE UNKNOWN

Sergeant W. Blundell of the 2nd East Surrey Regiment had as a member of his platoon a man who was often in trouble, though his quick wit got him out of most difficulties. Known as 'Fast Stan', he was a man apparently without cares, though he never received a letter or parcel.

The battalion was ordered to the front, and before long, went over the top. Fast Stan was one of the first over the parapet and brandishing his rifle with fixed bayonet he shouted, 'Where are the blighters? Lead me to them!'

He was later brought into a trench riddled with bullets. Sergeant Blundell asked if he could do anything to help. 'No thanks, Sergeant', the soldier said. 'Did we have many blokes hurt?'

'Only a few', Blundell said.

'Thank Heaven for that,' Fast Stan said. 'Nobody'll worry over me – I'm only a blinkin' orphan'.

GOING TOO FAR

YPRES–POPERINGE ROAD

In the spring of 1917 a large shell hit the road, along which throughout the war so many soldiers moved towards the Salient. Among the wounded was a man noted for his addiction to a well-known song, 'Let the Great Big World Keep Turning'. He sang it on every possible occasion.

As he lay on the roadway, seriously hurt and helpless, one of his mates went to cheer him up. 'Hello, chum', he said. 'Why aren't you singing "Let the Great Big World Keep Turning", eh?'

The wounded soldier gave him a reproachful look. 'I *was* singing it, Bill, but I never thought it would fly up and hit me'.

This story came from private Albert Morsley of 85th Siege Battery Ammunition Column, who was passing at the time.

BATTLE PRACTICE

BLANGY-SUR-TERNOISE

Late in 1916 and early in 1917 the Heavy Machine-Gun Corps – the camouflage name for what was to become the Tank Corps – had its training depot near the French town of Blangy-sur-Ternoise. Few tanks were available for instruction and very little driving was possible. Those which were available could not, by order, be used for tactical training in the muddy fields; they were too precious. The solution was to use dummy tanks. Canvas was stretched over a wooden· frame, which had no top or bottom, about six feet high, eight feet long and five feet wide. Little slits were made in the canvas to represent the loophole of a tank. Six men carried and moved each dummy, lifting it by the cross-pieces of the framework. One officer, Major W.H.L. Watson D.C.M., described the contraptions as 'abortions' and reluctantly used them.

'We started with a crew of officers to encourage the men and the first dummy tank waddled out of the gate. It was immediately surrounded by a mob of cheering children who

The first tanks were massive and lumbering and travelled more slowly than a man could walk. However, they struck dread into the hearts of the Germans who first encountered them as they clanked menacingly across the battlefield.

thought it was an imitation dragon or something out of a circus. It was led away from the road to avoid hurting the feelings of the crew and to safeguard the ears and morals of the young. After colliding with the corner of a house it endeavoured to walk down the side of a railway cutting. Nobody was hurt but a fresh crew was necessary. It regained the road but then a small man in the middle who had been able to see nothing, stumbled and fell. The tank collapsed.

'We persevered with these dummy tanks; they were awkward and heavy and produced much childish laughter. In another company a crew walked over a cliff and a man broke his leg. They became less and less mobile because the manpower became less enthusiastic. One company commander mounted them on waggons drawn by mules. The crews were tucked in with their Lewis guns and each contraption, a cross between a fire-engine and a triumphal car in a Lord Mayor's Show would gallop past targets which the gunners would recklessly endeavour to hit.

'Finally these dummies reposed derelict in our courtyard until one by one they disappeared, as the canvas and wood were required for ignoble purposes'.

At this time the Heavy Machine-Gun Corps had six companies, four in France and two in England. The four had taken part in operations in the Flers sector of the Somme in September and October, 1916. The Staff were so impressed that they decided to enlarge each of the companies into a battalion. Colonel H.J. Elles had his H.Q. at Bermicourt, where officers were trained. On 20 November 1917 Elles, as a major-general, led the Corps into their first battle at Cambrai.

HOME BY UNDERGROUND

ARRAS–CAMBRIN

On a cold, wet night in 1917 a company of the 7th Battalion Middlesex Regiment was struggling along a communication trench off the Arras–Cambrin road. The mud was ghastly, waist deep in places, and the men were tired and irritable. Corporal Harold Bates was in front, next to the company commander, when word was passed forward that a soldier had fallen into the mud and could not be found.

Bates was sent back to investigate and on reaching the spot found that the soldier had fallen into the mouth of a very deep, old dugout. He tried to see into the darkness and shouted, 'Where are you?'

'You get on with the bloody war', came the reply. 'I've found the Channel Tunnel and I'm goin' 'ome'.

He was certainly well on his way – it took a team of diggers six hours to get him out.

PRESENCE OF MIND

SORREL LE GRAND, SOMME

The British had just taken the French village of Sorrel le Grand in 1917 and a Vickers machine-gun unit had established a position above a small dugout. Corporal Robert Fisher was cleaning his revolver on one of the steps when it went off. To his horror the heavy .45 bullet struck one of his squad, who was sitting on a step, in the centre of his steel helmet and made a big dent.

The gunner looked up and grinned. 'Lummy, Corp', he said, 'it was a jolly good job I was reading one of my girl's letters'. And he bent his head and went on reading.

ONE MAN'S BEST FRIEND

VERMELLES

Private Sandy Jones, pale, small and rather colourless in manner was the butt of many a joke from his more extrovert comrades in the Royal Berkshires, and he did not have a single close friend. One wintry night in 1917 his platoon was brought out of the line and billeted in a barn. In the farm lived its civilian owner and what was left of his livestock, including a goat in a shed. The platoon humorist, Happy Day, having discovered the goat's whereabouts, called to Jones, 'Hi, Sandy! There's some Maconochie rations in that shed. Fetch 'em in, mate, be a pal'.

Glad to be useful Sandy went off into the night but was quickly back with his face whiter than usual. ''Appy', he said shrilly, 'I *can't* fetch them. There's two awful eyes in that shed!'

They laughed at him but Sandy came to like the goat and in some strange way the animal seemed to like him. Soon after this incident German artillery obliterated the farm but the goat survived and Happy Day took it with him as the unit mascot. Sandy Jones was pleased about this for he would never have had the nerve to commandeer the goat himself.

Back in the front line the Berkshires cowered under the worst bombardment that many of the soldiers could remember. Sandy Jones and the goat suffered more than most and crouched together in terror and misery. Happy Day was one of many to be killed during the strafe.

Finally, the goat became so terrified that it clambered over the parapet and headed towards the German lines. Then, before anybody could stop him, Sandy went over the top after him into the shellbursts; he was trying to save his only real friend. Fascinated, several men took a chance and peered over the parapet to see the goat and his rescuer disappear behind evil black and yellow smoke. Neither came back.

The story was well attested by the Berkshire men and Private S.G. Bushell recorded it. He said that Sandy's courage in trying to save the goat made the men sorry for not having been kinder to him.

UNEXPECTED GUESTS

MONCHY-LE-PREUX, ARRAS

April 9 – Easter Monday – of 1917 had been a tough day. The battle of Arras was in progress during heavy snow and despite help from the gigantic British tanks the infantry was held up. The tanks themselves

186

had been savaged by field artillery and one of them was astride the German wire at least 300 yards from the British line.

That night Sergeant Denis Kelper was sent out with a few men to reconnoitre. It was a dangerous mission at that distance and the moon gave too much light for comfort. By now the Germans could be occupying the tank or a machine-gun crew could be dug in behind it. Kelper and his men crawled to the great machine but could see nobody. He tapped on one of the doors with a grenade. When there was no response he crawled to the other side

and tapped on another door. And again.

This time a voice answered, hoarsely and with apprehension. 'Who are you?'

'Fusiliers', Kelper said.

He heard some noises and then a tousled head appeared through the trapdoor in the roof.

'You're very welcome', the tank man said, 'but I'll have to come down and let you in myself. It's the skivvy's half day off'.

The process took a little time for the soldier had a smashed arm and other wounds and he was the sole survivor of the crew.

When I first heard this story the tank man was made out to be a Cockney, probably it was felt that slang made his remarks funnier. They are amusing – under those circumstances – with or without an accent.

JUST PART OF THE JOB

LOOS

In April 1917 two companies of the 11th Battalion Essex Regiment were ordered to raid and destroy German trenches near the sugar refineries close to Loos. Two lines of trenches had to be taken – a tall order – and when it was complete the survivors were to go to billets at Mazingarbe

while the Durhams took over their trenches.

Lieutenant L.W. Lees gave his batman, Private Beedles, orders to stay out of battle and go straight to the billets with the officer's kit and wait there for him. Then Lees, in command of the right half of the first attack, fought his way into the German trench.

He supervised the blowing up of concrete emplacements and dugouts and was waiting for the signal to return to his own line when he saw Pte Beedles picking his way through the German wire, now behind the Essex troops. A great deal of battle noise was going on but Beedles took no notice, though he had to shout to Lieutenant Lees to make himself heard. 'Sir, I hope yer don't mind me having come to this garden party without an invitation'.

Beedles had carried all his officer's kit the four miles to billets, returned, and had then come clear across No Man's Land to make sure that his officer returned safely. It was not the sort of action that warranted a decoration but Beedles had nevertheless risked his life out of loyalty.

The history of the war contains many instances of batmen going above and beyond the call of duty, in the interests of the officer they served. Many a batman died trying to protect his officer.

'LET'S ALL GO DOWN THE STRAND'

ARRAS

The 1st King's Own Royal Lancaster Regiment was waiting to go over the top in the Battle of Arras on 9 April 1917. They were gloomy and despondent as they waited for their rum issue so Tom Collins, one of two Cockneys in a platoon of A Company gave his mate a wink and started some morale building.

He bawled, 'Let's all go down the Strand . . . ' and after a few lines the Lancashire lads joined in.

When this was over, Tom said to his mate, Jimmy Pugh, who was hardly more cheerful than the others, 'Aw, come on Jimmy, you're all right, aren't you?'

'I suppose I'll see you in London Hospital next week', Jimmy said glumly.

'Shut up!' Tom said. 'If Jerry sends one over and it's got our names on it, why worry? And if we get a bad Blighty one, then I hope they bury us at Manor Park. Be a pal, Jim, and tie this disc around my neck'.

The rum ration came up soon after

When troops were withdrawn from the frontline trench and were safely back in reserve their mail was distributed. Here some survivors get parcels and letters from Blighty. Tom Collins, of the accompanying story, did not live to get his mail. (*Author's collection and copyright*)

this and Tom started the platoon on another song: 'Another little drink wouldn't do us any harm'.

Over the top went the platoon and ten minutes later Jimmy found that Tom had disappeared. His body was never identified, despite the identity disc.

The Battle of Arras was the same battle as that for Vimy Ridge, depending on where you stood on the line. Jimmy Pugh always believed that his friend was buried at Blany, Arras.

NEARLY LUCKY

ARRAS

In an action in 1917 a company of Canadians had reached their battle objective early in the afternoon and had nothing much to do but to wait for the inevitable German counter-attack. A corporal had taken an impressive Luger pistol from a German officer and was getting used to the way it worked. Accidentally he fired the weapon and a bullet made a mess of the boot heel of a friend at the parapet. The man surveyed the damage to his boot, and started a stream of fierce abuse. The corporal, rather surprised, said, 'Cool down, I didn't hit you'.

'That's the whole damn trouble! ' the aggrieved soldier said. 'If you had put the bullet into my foot I'd already be on a stretcher headed for Blighty. Next time you poop-off, aim'.

GETTING THE JOB DONE

BULLECOURT: VAUX VRAUCOURT

The 2/2nd Battalion of the London Regiment occupied the support trenches in front of Bullecourt on 14 May 1917. 'A' Company was furthest to the rear, about 1,000 yards behind the front line trenches. From 2 p.m. that day the Germans shelled the whole area for 13 hours non-stop; an Order of the Day later described it as 'the most intense bombardment British troops have had to withstand.' During this shelling No 3 platoon of 'A' Company – one officer and 31 N.C.O.s and men – was sent forward carrying grenades for the troops holding the front line.

With 40 boxes of bombs, the platoon moved along a communication trench nowhere deeper than two feet, tangled with barbed wire and telephone lines and broken up by shellholes.

The Allies had plenty of artillery of their own with which to pound the Germans. Here gunners drag a heavy howitzer from concealment to pound German lines on the Somme. Its great shells caused immense destruction. (Author's collection and copyright)

Machine-gun fire swept the trench, high explosive shells burst close by and overhead the shrapnel shells released their deadly balls. Man after man was hit and after giving what treatment they could the survivors pressed on with an even greater load of bombs per man. Ninety minutes later, the nine men of the platoon who survived reached the front trench with all 40 boxes of bombs.

In the front line a lance corporal of No 3 platoon was blown to pieces. The other eight stayed on and fought with the garrison. When relieved four days later the last eight men of No 3 platoon returned as a section under the only N.C.O., another lance corporal. Passing through Vaux Vraucourt they picked spring blossom which they stuck in their rifle barrels and twined in their equipment. So adorned, they marched whistling into their battalion lines.

A good many other bombardments could rival that at Bullecourt on 14 May 1917 as 'the most intense', but the shelling was

191

certainly extremely heavy. This story was told by a company commander of the London Regiment to illustrate the indomitable nature of the Tommy. It illustrates equally well the casualties sustained by troops caught in the open.

THE TOOL TO HAND

VIMY RIDGE

The area just behind Vimy Ridge was sprinkled with German shells which had failed to explode. Fatigue parties were frequently sent to mark each shell by a DANGER board nailed to a stake. On one occasion Lieutenant H.S. Anderson of the Suffolk Regiment saw at work a soldier who had been detailed to put up the warning notices. He stopped at a shell, selected a DANGER board – then picked up the shell and drove the stake into the ground.

This story has the ring of truth. Many soldiers became blasé about unexploded shells and others did not realise their potential danger. Vimy ridge is still liberally sprinkled with unexploded shells – and they are still dangerous. The soldier whom Lieutenant Anderson saw might well have blown himself up later.

A REGULAR'S RESENTMENT

YPRES SALIENT

At one point on the Ypres Salient, near Wytschaete, the British front-line trenches were about two hundred yards apart. No Man's Land in between was much fought over, mostly at dawn and dusk, and many soldiers died there. About the middle of 1917 a Regular Army soldier, a 1914 'Contemptible', was a member of an infantry section on duty in a front trench on this sector. Known as Dandy, he had no ambition for rank but as befitted a regular soldier of the pre-war army, he made great efforts to keep himself, his weapons and his equipment clean, complete and when possible, shiny. His New Army comrades, less meticulous, respected him but they often laughed at him for being so 'fussy'.

On several consecutive days an officer passed Dandy in the trench with a button missing – the third button of his tunic. 'It's not right', Dandy was heard saying. 'His batman ought to catch it hot and strong for not sewing it back on'.

The British made another night raid and again some of them didn't come back. Next day about noon Dandy was once more irritated to see an officer with a button missing. In fact, he stopped in front of Dandy and asked him how to get to Battalion Headquarters and where the nearest machine-gun post was situated. Dandy noticed that the tunic seemed to be the same, and the third button was missing – but it was not the same officer.

Dandy took his outraged Regular's pride to his sergeant. 'I want to ask you a particular question, Sergeant', he said. 'Why do officers always lose their third button?'

The sergeant took the question seriously, as a former policeman might be expected to. He made inquiries and found that the original owner of the tunic with the third button missing had been reported missing a few days before, believed killed in a trench raid.

Soon after this the battlion adjutant was seen in the frontline trench, the nearby saps and communication trenches and after a time he came across the officer with the uniform button missing and accosted him. Dandy, who witnessed this meeting, said, 'He did it real civil-like. He just said "I wonder if you would mind coming along to talk to the C.O. at H.Q.?" Of course, he stuck a revolver in the bloke's ribs'.

Soon after this there was a firing party at dawn for the apprehended German spy.

The news of the spy quickly reached the front line. Dandy said grimly, 'Once, when I was a rookie, I was crimed for having a button missing on parade. Now I've got even by having an officer crimed for the same thing. Pity he was only a bleedin' Hun'.

LAST WORDS

BULLECOURT

The men of an Australian company were at their posts wating to 'hop over'. Everything was in readiness for the big attack. All was quiet. The enemy had ceased shelling for the first time in three hours and the men's nerves were tense. A pin could have been heard dropping.

Suddenly the voice of the humorist of the company broke the silence. 'Well, for fear that I don't come back from this stunt, I want everybody to know that Captain ——— is a bloody bastard. If I come back, he's not'.

He didn't return.

DOWN TO EARTH

ST OMER – AMIENS

In June 1917 Brigadier-General R.J. Kentish shared a staff car with the Chaplain-General to the Forces, Bishop Gwynne, who was on his way from St Omer to Amiens. Kentish was en route to the Third Army School at Auxi-le-Chateau.

Bishop Gwynne asked the infantry officer if he thought the chaplains reaching France were right for the job; in particular did the regimental officers and men think they were the right men.

Kentish said: 'The chaplains differ very little from any other body of men in France. Some are men of the world and very human and they get on splendidly with the troops others find their job very difficult and make little impression.

'Let me tell you a story', General, the Bishop said. 'I knew a chaplain who was attached to a London regiment who always made a practice of living in the frontline trenches when he could have stayed with battalion headquarters. He even had his own dugout which was labelled "The Vicarage".

'One day a young soldier in the line for the first time was walking along a trench with an older soldier and turning a corner suddenly he noticed "The Vicarage".

"'Gorblimey, Bill!" he said to his mate. "Who'd have thought of seeing a bloody vicarage in the front line?"

'Immediately the padre popped out from behind the blanket covering the dugout entrance. "Yes!" he said. "And who'd have thought of seeing the bloody vicar too?"'

The Bishop winked at the General. 'That's the kind of chaplain I'm trying to get them to send out to France'.

Many chaplains distinguished themselves on the Western Front; three won the Victoria Cross.

THE REALITY OF WAR

SOMME

Digging trenches in the much fought-over Somme battlefield, or taking over a German trench, was often a vile experience. Nobody has better described it than Lieutenant A.D. Gristwood, writing in 1917.

Sometimes the Germans had buried their dead in the floor of the trench, where, baking in the sun, the earth had cracked into star-shaped fissures. A foot treading unwarily here sank downwards, disturbing hundreds of white maggots. In one place a hand with blue and swollen fingers projected helplessly from the ground. Close to the trench a man stood clearly upright, buried to the waist, his arms fast bound to his sides, his glassy eyes wide open to the sky, his face stained livid yellow from the fumes of an explosion. Who he was no one knew; doubtless his dear ones were still writing to him in hope and trust for his welfare; doubtless they had prayed that night for his safety. And all the time he stood there, glaring upwards as though mutely appealing from Earth to Heaven.

All the armies buried their dead in the trenches when it was too dangerous to carry the corpses to a safer place for burial. Often enough the dead were thrown forward onto the parapet to act as further protection for the men still living: equally frequently the bodies were heaved out to the rear of the trench. None of this indicated callousness; it simply made no sense to risk other men's lives to bury those who were beyond help.

195

READY FOR THE SLAUGHTER

VLAMERTINGHE

On his way up to the Ypres Salient front line one morning in July 1917 Paul Maze,* on a mission for General Gough, rode slowly alongside a marching battalion. He heard the sound of an engine at work in a yard and saw puffs of exhaust smoke rising from behind a wall. As he

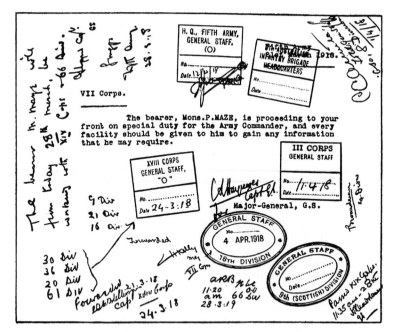

One of several passes issued to the Frenchman, Paul Maze, to enable him to move freely about the battle area. Even so, more than once Maze was suspected of being a spy. The gallant Frenchman did valuable work for the British Army.

reached the open gateway it was evident that Belgian carpenters were at work with a steam saw.

The yard was piled high with wooden crosses. It was an ominous sight and Maze wanted to spare the soldiers. He hurried in to have them removed but the Belgians threw up their arms in despair and pointed behind them; Maze saw a still bigger pile of crosses. The soldiers were now marching past and nothing could be done to conceal the crosses.

Maze watched the men as they passed by. Some smiled, some didn't look, some pretended not to look but peered from the corner of their eyes.

One man said, 'Naughts and bloody crosses . . . and we're on naughts'.

Somebody else, mistaking Maze on his horse for a staff officer, jerked his thumb at the crosses and said bitterly, 'Thank 'Aig for his vote of confidence'.

'See story entitled 'Firing Squad' (p. 20)

THE MAN FOR THE JOB

ALBERT

Known to the troops as 'Pepper Pot', the M.O. of an Australian unit was a fiery old fellow. It was before him that the Diggers were paraded when they were seeking an excuse to prolong their stay behind the lines.

To him came 'Homeless Hector', a soldier who had earned his nickname before the war when he had been 'humping his bluey', as the Australians say. He had been a tramp.

'Well, Homeless, what's wrong with you', enquired Pepper Pot.

'I can't eat, sir', said Homeless mournfully.

'Can't eat?' exclaimed Pepper Pot. 'Hell, I wish we had a battalion like you. You're just the sort of man we want. Up to the trenches with you lad; you'll get bloody little to eat up there'.

Sketches
of Tommy's life
Up the line — N° 3

We marched into the Trenches, late in the evening, going across fields on « duck boards ». There is nothing to be seen but shell-holes, and wintry looking tres.

A contemporary postcard, one of a series, showing life at the front. Many a soldier slipped off the duckboards while carrying a heavy weight and drowned in the liquid mud. (*Author's collection*)

STRIPPED FOR ACTION

MORY, FRANCE

The 12th London Regiment was in the line at Bullecourt in the summer of 1917 and had endured a lot of heat – turned on by the weather and by the Germans. The men were brought out on the night of 14/15 June for a rest at Mory and dossed down, exhausted,

in the dark. When they stumbled out onto parade next morning they were astounded and delighted to see a big hole in the ground lined with canvas and filled with water.

Their last bath had been at Achiet-le-Petit six weeks before so the men stripped off as a battalion for a turn in the bath, which accommodated 20 at a time. There was so much enjoyment, and anticipation of enjoyment, that nobody took any notice of an aeroplane approaching. Those who did sight it assumed, because it was flying low, that it was British. Then somebody shouted, 'It's a Jerry plane!'

Dripping wet, the men stampeded to get their rifles. The officers who saw the spectacle of naked men clad only in tin hats taking pot-shots at the plane said it was the funniest sight of the war. The German pilot was apparently surprised because he fluttered this way and that before turning round to open up with his machine-gun – fortunately without causing casualties.

The men watched in silence as the enemy flier made off and somebody said, 'What bloody fools we are! If we hadn't put on our tin hats how was he to know we aren't German? Jerry and us have the same bits and pieces, don't we?'

It has been suggested that the 12th London Regiment might well be the only one in the history of the British Army to attack the enemy while clad only in tin hats.

POINTED SARCASM

FESTUBERT

The Portuguese were holding part of the line to the left of Festubert and one day in the summer of 1917 a Portuguese officer rode up to the 29th Division artillery lines on a sadly emaciated and broken-down horse.

He dismounted and looked around for somewhere to tether the horse while the gunner drivers eyed both him and the mount critically. One of them, a Cockney, was a London hansom cab-driver in civvy street and the sight made him shake his head and spit. 'Don't worry abaht tyin' it up mate!' he shouted to the Portuguese officer. 'Lean it up agin this 'ere fence'.

THE RIGHT CARD

MESSINES

Soon after Messines Ridge was blown up by 19 great mine explosions on 7 June 1917 a young soldier was brought into the Advanced Dressing Station of 3/5th Field Ambulance with large gaps torn from both thighs by pieces of shell. He was in intense pain as a sergeant doused the wounds with sterilising iodine. The medical officer said, 'How are things going this morning, lad?'

The young soldier was wearing a red heart on his tunic as his battalion recognition sign and he said, 'O.K. sir. Hearts are trumps this morning'.

THE WAY BACK

MOUNT KEMMEL

As the battle of Passchendaele started on 31 July 1917, the troops who had captured Messines on 7 June were pushed forward in a feint attack to keep the enemy occupied. This aim was achieved, for German artillery pounded the back area around Kemmel. A soldier named Bill Causley who had been wounded in the arms during the infantry attack was sent to the rear for treatment. Passing Mount Kemmel on the road from Wulvergem he came across a stretcher party carrying a rifleman of the Rifle Brigade, bathed in bandages.

Causley dropped behind cover every time a shell burst and so did the bearers, though they left their casualty lying in the open. The wounded man called to Causley, 'Hey mate, keep with me. Two shells never busts in the same 'ole, right? And if I ain't a shell 'ole who is?' And he laughed at his joke.

Causley stayed with the rifleman, whom he called Smiley, until they both reached the War Hospital at Warrington, Cheshire. Here Smiley died.

'I HOLD FRITZ WITH ALL RESPECT'

WIELTZE, YPRES

The 55th Division, with others, took part in the push towards Passchendaele in August 1917 and among them was Signaller Randall Heffer, with two comrades. They finished up in a large German dugout at Rat Farm, near Wieltze. This is Heffer's story:

The arrangements for the wounded the first day were scandalous; they were being brought into the dressing station on oil sheets, blankets and even planks of wood; not a stretcher-bearer was to be seen anywhere. Of course it was very rough for the poor beggars who had been wounded and had to lie out in the open as the rain and mud made things very uncomfortable, but it didn't damp their spirits in the least.

People are always ready to speak ill of Fritz but I hold him with all respect and so would anybody else if they had seen the way the German prisoners worked. Directly stretchers were available, Fritzes offered to take them over and they kept it up all day taking our boys back to the dressing station.

A lance corporal of the Liverpool Scottish and a Fritz got wounded and as the Fritz was not so badly wounded as our boy he assisted him into a dugout to get a bit of shelter.

Days went by and nobody found the two but everyday the Fritz went out to get some water for them both, but as sure as he went out he got hit. For four consecutive days he went out and each time got hit, but the Scotty said nothing would stop him from going out. When they were found the Liverpool fellow said. 'Take him first as he has saved my life', but of course our stretcher-bearers wouldn't take him until our fellows had been taken back. Another case our stretcher-bearers found was an Englishman and a Fritz with their arms around each other's necks trying to comfort each other. They were lying in a shell-hole and were already waist deep in water.

Signaller Heffer was promoted corporal and awarded the M.M for his work in the Salient. He had many narrow escapes from death or injury as he worked under fire in the open but none was more dramatic than at Rat Farm. He left there on a Sunday evening; in the early morning the whole place was blown up by a mine.

A LOUSY WAY TO GO

BUGHT CAMP, NEAR BROEMBEEK, YPRES SALIENT

On 16 September 1917 Major M. Barne, D.S.O., returned from home leave to his duties as a second-in-command of the 1st Battalion Scots Guards. A popular officer, he had seen more continuous service than any other officer of the battalion. His duties on the morning of 17 September took him to the battalion's transport lines and while there he saw a British plane in difficulties. Major Barne and five Guardsmen watched the pilot lose height, then briefly regain it before falling again. He threw something out of the cockpit but the watching soldiers lost sight of the object.

It was a bomb and it exploded with a roar in the middle of the group. One man was killed instantly, the major was severely wounded and the other men were also wounded. Barne died of his wounds next day and was buried at Mendringhem cemetery, Proven, north of Poperinge.

WHEN THE LABEL FITS . . .

NIEPPE

When a unit was dismissed from parade the command 'All gentlemen fall out!' was occasionally used. This meant the officers – although in most units the order was, 'Officers fall out!'

A Canadian unit in Nieppe in 1917 had a new C.O. who had ordained that the command would be, 'All gentlemen fall out!'

On the first parade this order was given by the Adjutant, as the Colonel looked on. At once every man – all 600 of them – saluted smartly, turned right and marched off the parade ground.

The Regimental Sergeant-Major used his stentorian voice and rounded the other ranks up but never again was that particular command heard in that particular unit.

No Offence Intended

SIEGE CAMP, YPRES

The 5th Seaforth Highlanders were under canvas at Siege Camp, which was close to a battery of heavy guns. There was much friendship between the Highlanders and the gunners and they visited each other's camps regularly. In September 1917 German aeroplanes came over on bombing runs every hour, almost to the minute.

One day a gunner was writing a letter in the tent of some of his Seaforth friends when word came through that enemy aircraft were approaching. The Jocks scattered.

After the raid they returned to the tent to find the gunner calmly writing his letter and they learned that he had not moved during the air raid. 'That must be a bloody important letter', observed Corporal W.A. Bull M.M.

'Just ordinary', the gunner said. 'Listen, "As I write this letter Jerry is bombing the Jocks but although I am in their camp, being a Londoner I suppose the raid is not meant for me, and I feel quite safe."'

ASK A SILLY QUESTION

SOMME

Private Louis Foley of the Australian 23rd Battalion and renowned as a runner who would always get through with a message, had ploughed his way through mud and rain and shellfire to H.Q. The orderly on duty said, 'Do you want to see the C.O., mate?'

'No', Foley said sourly. 'Take me to the bloody harbour-master'. Not long after this he carried one message too many and went west.

Australian water carriers return from the front line to fill empty cans for the next issue. Getting water and rations to the forward trenches was a hazardous duty. Many soldiers considered it more dangerous than being at the front.

TRENCH FLEET

LAVENTIE

The 5th West Yorkshire Regiment held a section of the line in front of Laventie during the winter of 1917. It was a comparatively peaceful spot so it could be held by a series of posts well spaced out, sometimes 300 yards apart. This made the task of bringing up water arduous and difficult, especially as the communication trenches in the sector always held several feet of water.

One cold, wet November night a miserable ration party was sloshing through the thin slimy mud and the sentry at the top of the communication trench heard them coming. As ordered, he made the standard challenge – 'Halt! Who goes there?'

From the wet darkness a weary voice replied, 'Admiral Jellicoe and blinkin' fleet'.

CHANGE OF SERVICE

CAMBRAI

In November 1917 a battalion of the Rifle Brigade was moving in single file into the line in front of Cambrai. In the pitch-black night warning messages came down the line – 'Ware wire' or 'Ware shellhole' or 'Ware unexploded shell'.

In front of Rifleman John S. Brown was a Cockney, who suddenly disappeared. Brown heard a curse from a shellhole just off the track. He trod gently to the edge of the hole and peering down anxiously he saw his mate's face turned upwards.

'You all right?' he said.

'Blimey', the Cockney said, 'I'm drownded, so let the missus know I died like a sailor'.

Three days later, Rifleman Brown records, his comrade died like a soldier, in action.

205

TRADING INSULTS

ABBEVILLE

A good-natured but prolific source of argument between infantry and gunners concerned the merits of their respective arms as war winners. In No 3 Australian General Hospital at Abbeville a gunner and a foot soldier had this shouted conversation across the ward:

Artillery: Hey, infantry! How'd you get knocked?

Infantry: Dodging your drop-shorts. Why don't you land a few on Fritz for a change?

Artillery: Drop-shorts nothing! We had to lob then behind you footsloggers to stop you running away!

UNSUNG HEROISM

MESSINES

On 4 October 1917, after the storming of Abraham's Heights by the 4th New Zealand Brigade in the advance on Passchendaele, an enemy machine-gun in a pillbox harassed the 6th Hauraki Company. A Kiwi was hit by a bullet in his left arm, which shattered it. Mad with rage and pain he swore he would knock out that pillbox or die in the attempt.

Crawling out, careless of the heavy shellbursts, he flanked his objective, working his way on his stomach through the mud and slush. Wriggling round to the front of the concrete fort, he drew the pin from a Mills bomb with his teeth, released the spring, paused, and then stretched up and pushed the bomb through the loophole under the machine-gun muzzle, which was then firing.

He waited for the explosion, then he prepared another bomb and crawled around the back, to the entrance of the pillbox. He found that his effort had been rewarded with five dead Germans and eight wounded, and the machine-gun was wrecked. He returned to his lines with seven prisoners, two of whom were supporting him. They had no option but to do what he ordered or he would have let them have his other grenade.

Back in the line, the strain over, he collapsed and was taken away. His action went unrewarded, though it had been witnessed by several soldiers.

The New Zealand soldier's bravery was illustrated by an Australian. Nearly all pillboxes were of heavy rectangular constuction and were virtually indestructible; many still exist in Flanders. The most famous are in Tyne Cot cemetery, Passchendaele.

THE UTMOST GALLANTRY

PASSCHENDAELE

The third phase of the Third Battle of Ypres, the capture of Passchendaele, commenced on 31 July 1917, and raged continuously for three months. On 12 October, when the Australians were heavily committed, one of their battalions, the 34th, encountered two big concrete blockhouses east of Augustus Wood.

These strong-posts stopped the centre of the advance. A 23-year-old captain, Clarence Smith Jeffries, organised and led a bombing party which rushed and eliminated the obstacle, capturing four machine-guns and 35 prisoners. The 34th Battalion moved on, despite heavy losses, but were again harassed and critically held up by machine-guns in another blockhouse on the right flank. Jeffries gathered another party of a sergeant and 10 men and they succeeded in getting close to it. Picking a moment when the gunners were firing in another direction, Jeffries gave the signal and his men rushed the crew. Just then, however, the gun swung round, killing Jeffries immediately. Jeffries' example had so inspired the men that they took the post and captured the garrison.

The advance continued to the 'Blue Line', the second objective, but by then every 34th Battalion officer had been killed or wounded. Captain Jeffries was awarded the V.C.

Jeffries, who had already been severely wounded in the Battle of Messines, on June 9, is buried in Tyne Cot cemetery. The place of his heroism is particularly easy to find. He captured the blockhouse which forms the centre-piece of the cemetery, on which was erected the Cross of Sacrifice. The blockhouse near which he was killed is the one just behind his grave.

SHRAPNEL RAIN

YPRES

During the third battle of Ypres, late in 1917, a German field gun was trying to hit a British tank. Big and lumbering and travelling at its maximum of 3 mph in the mud it was almost a sitting target. The German gunners also had the advantage of directions from one of their observation balloons.

On top of the tank was an infantry man who was sick of struggling through mud and was getting a free ride. The German gunners' attempts to inflict a direct hit on the tank apparently didn't worry him. But then a shrapnel shell burst just behind and above the tank and the hundreds of steel balls thudded down.

Some British gunners nearby expected to see the infantryman roll off dead. But unhurt he cupped his hands around his mouth and yelled to the tank crew, 'Hi, conductor! Any room inside? It's raining!'

Gunner A.H. Boughton of B Battery, Honourable Artillery Company, was a witness to this episode and years later said that it was the most spontaneously funny thing he heard during the war.

BUSINESS AS USUAL

ARRAS

For much of the war the great Arras road leading in from the south and from St Pol was screened by canvas because the Germans held Vimy Ridge and had good visibility towards the Allied lines behind Arras. Before a big battle the road was busy but at more dangerous times it was almost deserted, just as

Arras was. The city had taken a lot of punishment from German artillery.

But the Commerce Hotel, in the main street close to the railway station, less than 2,500 yards from the German trenches, carried on under its gallant proprietress and staff. The windows of the restuarant had been broken, and upper storeys were

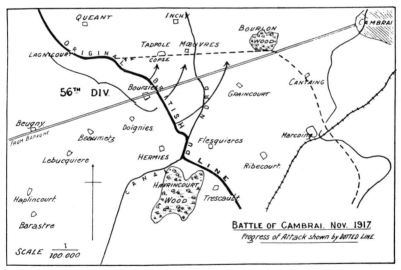

Major Watson, who liked the Hotel de Commerce so much, took part in the historic battle of Cambrai, 20 November 1917, when tanks were used on a large scale for the first time. The British tanks broke through the German lines and captured much territory, as this map shows, but the Commander-in-Chief, General Haig, had little confidence in the tanks and had not arranged for adequate infantry and cavalry support in the event of a breakthrough. In due course most of the British gains were lost.

badly damaged and the ceiling of the dining room was scarred by shell splinters. In 1917 the city was being shelled every night and often by day and German aeroplanes flew low over the town and machine-gunned the streets.

British officers, amazed to find it functioning, lunched there. Women dressed in black waited on them and the lunch was cheap, beautifully cooked and well served. The proprietress, pinched and drawn and with a scrap of fur always flung over her shoulders, occasionally left the cash desk to speak to a diner or remonstrate mildly with a waitress.

After the battle of Arras the Provost Marshal put the hotel out of bounds – for serving drink during forbidden hours. It re-opened later and continued to flourish until the German offensive of April 1918 when the shelling became too heavily insistent even for the staff of the Commerce Hotel.

A British officer who dined there more than once, Major W.H.L. Watson, wrote in 1919: 'I beseech all those who visit the battlefields of Arras to lunch at the Hotel de Commerce – in gratitude.'

WHY WORRY?

ANYWHERE ON THE WESTERN FRONT

This story may be apocryphal. It seems that a good many officers from adjutant to general used the same official notice shown below. It crops up in several memoirs of the war, which say that a certain Order of the Day was hung up in a dug-out or office or on a parade ground notice board.

When one is a soldier, it is one of two things. One is either in a dangerous place, or a cushy one. If in the latter, there is no need to worry. If one is in a dangerous place, it is one of two things. One is wounded, or one is not. If one is not, there is no need to worry. If the former, it is either dangerous or slight. If slight, there is no need to worry, but if dangerous it is one of two alternatives. One dies or one recovers. If the latter; why worry? If you die you cannot worry. In these circumstances the real Tommy never worries.

NOT GONE YET

WIMEREUX

For more than two years 56th General Hospital was stationed at Wimereux and on certain mornings there were clearances of men for Blighty. Nurses and orderlies would then be very busy getting the sick and wounded soldiers ready to travel.

One day two orderlies walked down a certain ward with a stretcher on which was fixed an open oblong box; the idea was to keep the patient steady while travelling by road, rail and ferry. They placed it beside the bed of a soldier from one of the Manchester regiments, dressed his stump of an arm and put him in clean pyjamas. Then they lifted him into the box. A nurse tucked blankets all around him and made sure his head was supported so that it wouldn't be banged against the box while travelling. 'There you are', she said. 'Feeling nice and comfortable?'

'Fine', the really ill soldier said weakly. 'But don't let them put the lid on it until I've kissed you goodbye'.

ENDLESS MISERY

DIRTY BUCKET CORNER, YPRES SALIENT

On the day before men of the 58th London Division were to return from what passed as rest at Dirty Bucket Corner the Christmas (1917) mail arrived. The men of a stretcher-bearer squad were particularly happy about the mail because one of their members, a school-teacher, received a letter telling him that he had become the father of a son.

He was depressed, though, because he could see no end to the war; for that matter, none of the men had any hope of its ending. Still, they congratulated their mate, the new father. The only man who was silent was a man from Seven Dials, known to the squad as 'Townie'. He was busy with a pencil and writing pad and after a while he handed the new father a piece of paper.

He looked at it without speaking while the others crowded round to look. They saw lines and circles and various symbols. The puzzled teacher said, 'What's this, Townie?'

'It's a map I've drawn for your kid'.

'Why would he want it?'

'Because when he's called up say in twenty years it'll tell him where his old pot and pan (man) is. But tell him to be careful of that ruddy shellhole' – he put his finger on the map – 'cos I've fallen into the perishing thing twice this week'.

The story is sad rather than funny. It indicates the hopeless despair of many soldiers at the end of 1917. Christmas was a time of despair for men at the front reminding them of what they might have been doing at home if only the war would end.

MIND OVER MUD

ARRAS

A company of New Zealanders was in the worst place possible in the Great War, a wet, slimy trench in winter with rain pouring down. When on sentry duty in the trenches many a man, while outwardly watching for enemy activity, inwardly imagined himself elsewhere. It was the job of the N.C.O.s to make sure that sentries were on their toes. Some were officious in this duty, as they went around to make sure that sentries remembered what they were supposed to be doing.

One night in 1917 a sergeant-major sneaked up to the rain-soaked, miserable sentry and barked, 'Give me your orders!'

'Steak and kidney pie and a beer', the half-dreaming sentry said promptly.

ILLUSION

ROUEN

Sergeant P. Webb of the East Surrey Regiment was in the American General Hospital at Rouen. His ward was for surgical cases and during a push it could be full of men coming out of anaesthetic, all either shouting, singing swearing or moaning. Webb had been in the ward for a few days and was worried about the man in the bed next to him because he had not stirred or made a sound since orderlies had brought him in from the operating theatre hours before.

But at last he sat up, looked around him in amazement and said to Webb, 'Strike! I've been lying here for about two hours afraid to open me peepers. I thought I was in hell with a lot of poor suffering bleeders'.

The American Hospital, like the British, Australian, Canadian and French hospitals, took all comers.

PERTINENT SUGGESTION

NEUVE EGLISE, FLANDERS

Next to Assistant Provost Marshals, Town Majors were most disliked by the Australians. At Neuve Eglise, Christmas 1917, a particularly dilapidated barn was allotted to a gun battery for billeting. In fact it was so bad that even the Town Major admitted it was below standard. He had the Diggers mustered and to calm things down a bit told them how sorry he was to see the troops so badly housed, particularly at the festive season. However, it could not be helped. Still, if anybody would suggest anything that he could do to improve the comfort of the boys he would be pleased.

He was about to leave when a big driver shouted, 'What about shuttin' the flamin' gate and keepin' the wind out of the paddock'.

APPEALING TO THE BEST IN MEN

POPERINGE

Padre 'Tubby' Clayton, who 'managed' Talbot House, the soldiers' rest house, relied heavily on humorous notices to get the discipline and manners he expected from his guests. Many of them can still be read in Talbot House; below is one, from 1917, which perished many years ago.

UNWELCOME VISITORS

Welcome yourself to Talbot House . . . You are surely not one of those who—

(1) Imagine the House has an off-licence for magazines, stationery, etc. – e.g., I put a current number of Nash's magazine in a cover, heavily stamped, on the first floor last week. In twenty-four hours the cover was empty. This is how misanthropes are made.

(2) Imagine we have the Y.M.C.A. or some unlimited funds at our back. At present we are trying hard (like my Sam Browne does) to make two ends meet. Three noble Divisions (55th, 39th, 38th) help us from their funds. But otherwise we are in a bad way. My tie-pin was in pawn long ago: and even the House is in Pop.

Writing materials for use in the House cost some £6 a month, so that he who departs with his pockets full of envelopes is guilty of what Mr. Punch calls 'Teuton conduct'.

(3) Woe betide the imbecile, who begins three letters one after another on three sheets of paper, with a fourth to try nibs and fancy spelling on; and with one large blot on a fifth sheet, and the other on a pad of blotting paper, splashed ink about like a cuttle-fish (is it?), and draws a picture (libellous, we hope) of 'my darling Aggie' on a sixth sheet, and then remembers that he really came in to play billiards.

The House aims at reminding you a

little tiny bit of 'your ain folk'. Hence pictures, flowers, and freedom, help to strengthen the illusion of being a Club-able spirit.

This is not a G.R.O. (General Routine Order) but just a G.R.O.U.S.E. by the poor old Chaplain.

By 1917 some of the best known war artists, such as R. Caton Woodville, were telling graphic stories of battle in their paintings. His caption 'Blinded for you!' was calculated to induce people to give money to help care for blinded soldiers. Woodville's soldier in this drawing has apparently been blinded by shell flash. Others were made blind by poisonous gas or head wounds.

1918

On 21 march 1918 the German army began their own Somme offensive and the entire British Fifth Army line crumbled. The Tommies suffered great losses but reinforcements and supplies were rushed into the breach and blocked the German advance by 5 April. On 9 April the Germans struck again, this time in Flanders against a weak Portuguese division, and smashed a hole 30 miles wide by 5 miles deep. On 12 May Haig issued an Order of the Day: 'With our backs to the wall and believing in the justice of our cause each one of us must fight to the end.' The exhortation became famous but what the troops said of it is unprintable. Somehow the line held and on 8 August, again on the Somme, the British forces counter-attacked. It was the beginning of the end for the Germans and they fell back steadily eastwards. For the British Empire troops the agony of the Western Front ended on 11 November.

'I COMMEND MY SPIRIT'

CAMBRAI

In the winter of 1917–18 Private A.M. Burrage of the Artists Rifles was a stretcher-bearer and was busy every day and night that his unit was in the line. He had many dangerous and horrible experiences and one in particular he found memorable.

There were yells for bearers and McCracken and I went to see what was the trouble. The first man we found seemed to be pretty badly smashed up but as we were quite close to the Aid Post we did not bandage him but carried him straight away. He was a great long lean loon and plaguey heavy. He had only just come out to us and we hardly knew him but I learned afterwards that he was the son of a Buckinghamshire parson. We carried him feet foremost, McCracken leading, so that his head was between my hands.

Neither McCracken nor I could keep our feet on the frozen surface. First McCracken would fall base over apex and the end of the stretcher would tilt down on him and I would curse him. Then I would do the same and the other end of the stretcher would cant down on me. We must have given hell to the poor devil on the stretcher and I kept saying to him, 'I'm awfully sorry, old dear, but we can't help it.'

After a while I heard a muttering come up from the head, which was more or less on the same level as my waist, and bent to listen. I thought I was going to hear something to this effect: 'You great big clumsy cow, why can't you stand up on your great big bloody feet?' I was used to hearing this kind of thing from tortured men whom I couldn't help shaking. Instead I heard: 'Into Thy hands, O Lord, I commend my spirit. Lord Jesus receive my soul'. He died not many minutes later.

NICE TOUCH

STRAZEELE

Early in 1918 a sergeant detailed a particular soldier to go out into No Man's Land as a one-man listening post. The soldier said, 'Gawd, you're hard, Sarge. I've been out for four nights in a row and that shell that landed near me last night deafened me and I can't hear'.

'You don't need to hear', the sergeant said. 'You just have to keep your eyes open for Jerry patrols'.

'Blimey, Sarge, you know I can't see in the dark after that time I was gassed'.

'It doesn't matter if you're deaf, dumb and blind', the sergeant said, 'you've got to go out tonight'.

'All right', the soldier said, 'I'll go out. But remember, if I'm not back in the morning I've been caught *feeling* for the flamin' Germans in No Man's bloody Land!'

UNDERSTANDABLE ANGER

CAMBRAI SALIENT

During the winter of 1917–18 many units had turns of duty in the Cambrai Salient or what had been the old Hindenburg Line. At one period the Artists Rifles were in close support near a dump area and they complained that they never could get any rest because of the ceaseless movement of ration parties, ammo parties, wiring parties and others.

The weather was icy and the bottom of the trench was as slippery as could be. One night men of the Drake Battalion, Royal Naval Division, crowded past the Artists Rifles as they went back to rear trenches to get their rations. As they returned the man in the lead, with two sandbags of rations around his neck and a can of water in either hand, kept falling over. To make

220

matters worse a large party of Royal Engineers laden with barbed wire was passing along the trench in the other direction and many collisions occurred. The accident-prone Drake man picked himself up yet again and said viciously, 'Gawd, if ever I catch that kid of mine playing soldiers, I won't half knock his block off!'

UNSUNG HERO

LEMPIRE

Early in January, 1918, there had been unfortunate cases of sentries mistaking wiring parties of the Divisional pioneer battalion for the enemy in No Man's Land and firing at them. Such a mistake was easy enough to make in the darkness, especially if the wiring parties had not notified the infantry in the front line that they were going out. A new brigadier made a great fuss of the incidents, though nobody had been hurt. Colonel Rowland Feilding's battalion, the 6th Connaught Rangers, was in the line at the time.

About 4 a.m. on the morning of 10 January, the Germans tried to raid one of Feilding's machine-gun posts, placed well out in No Man's Land about 150 yards in front of the firetrench. It was in a sunken road which crossed both the British and German trenches. The raiders, camouflaged in white overalls, attacked across the snow.

In such a dangerous post there were double sentries and the two men heard but did not see any movement in front of them. Hesitating to shoot because of the recent row over 'indiscriminate firing', they challenged – and the immediate reply was a shower of grenades. Private Mayne, in command of the Lewis gun, was hit in many places including the stomach and his left arm was reduced to pulp. Nevertheless, he struggled up and leaning against the parapet, with his uninjured hand he fired a full magazine of 47 rounds into the enemy now running in to the attack. They broke and not a German reached the British post. Then Mayne collapsed. A rescue party brought the men back to the trench where the second sentry's badly shattered foot was amputated. The M.O. performed this operation without chloroform – as the man was in a numbed condition; the wounded man, an Irishman, looked on smoking a cigarette.

Colonel Feilding, writing to his wife, said, 'Words cannot express my feelings of admiration for Private Mayne's magnificent act of bravery, which I consider well worthy of the

V.C. It is, however, improbable that he will live to enjoy any decoration that may be conferred upon him'.

Feilding expected high-level acknowledgement of the successful and heroic repulse of the German raiders by Private Mayne and his companion. Instead he received a memo which had been circulated through the division: *Another instance had occurred of an enemy patrol reaching within bombing distance of our line. This must not occur again. Our patrols must meet the enemy patrols boldly in No Man's Land.*

Feilding was very bitter and never forgave the staff officer who wrote 'this pompous admonition'. Private Mayne died of his wounds and received a posthumous Mention in Dispatches.

BENEFIT OF THE DOUBT

YPRES SALIENT

One Australian C.O. in particular had a very poor opinion of H.Q. staff officers. His forceful expressions of opinion on the subject led H.Q. to demand an explanation.

His report was duly forwarded. 'I did not say that all the staff officers were a bloody lot of fools', he wrote. 'How could I, seeing that I have not come into contact with *all* of them'.

NICKED KNICKERS

VIEUX BERQUIN, SOUTH OF BAILLEUL

An Australian battalion had been in billets at Vieux Berquin and when it was about to be moved to another part of the front the usual crop of claims from the villagers flooded in. One caused quite a commotion. It was 300 francs for four ducks, a petticoat and a pair of knickers.

The claims officer accepted the four ducks as a fair claim but he baulked at the petticoat and the knickers. 'If one of my men has a petticoat and knickers', he told the lady claimant, 'then some girl gave them to him as a . . . a souvenir'.

'Ah no, you don't understand!' the lady said. 'The petticoat and knickers were taken from my clothesline to carry away the ducks'.

The officer knew his men – and he passed the claim.

A DROP OF THE GOOD STUFF

BUS-LES-ARTOIS

Colonel David Robie of the Royal Army Medical Corps and two other officers were detailed to billets in Bus during foul weather. When they could get no answer to their knocking they entered the red-tiled kitchen, just as the landlady, Madeleine, came in through another door. She cut short Robie's introduction with a shriek of '*Trois* officiers? Jamais! Jamais! Jamais! Toujours *un* officier - un officier, seulement.' (*Three* officers? Never! Never! Never! Always one officer – one officer only.)

Robie explained that the mayor had detailed her home as a billet for three. Jacques, the lady's husband, came in and also shouted 'Jamais! Jamais!' Then he opened a table drawer, took out a carving knife and brandished it ferociously to defend his hearth.

One of Robie's companions, a Glasgow officer, always carried a large and sometimes full flask and Robie asked him to put it ostentatiously on the table, which he did with the profound solemnity a Scot always shows when handling whisky. Then Robie asked Madeleine for five glasses. The 'jamais' storm cleared magically. She produced the glasses, Jacques put away the knife and wiped his heavy moustache with the back of his hand in expectation of the delight to come, Robie used to say jokingly that it was for this exploit that he won his D.S.O.

223

FOOLING FRITZ

FROMELLES

At Fromelles the Australians enjoyed what they called 'great sport' through the use of a dummy trench. This was a ditch they dug about 75 yards behind their front line and running parallel to it. They would light fires in this at meal times, to indicate cooking, and occasionally during the day a file of men would move through the ditch with their bayonets exposed, as they would in a real trench. As the Germans used their second line as a living trench they probably thought the Australians did the same and it was very satisfying to see their shells exploding on the dummy trench.

Sometimes the Germans broke the unwritten law that there should be an armistice during meal-times. The Australians reminded them of this breach of the rules by systematically putting out their cook's fires with rifle grenades. Thereafter both sides were able to have their meals in peace, though the Australians took care to change their hour's lunch break from 1 p.m. to 2 p.m. instead of 12 noon to 1 p.m. – a change of schedule in case the Germans 'turned nasty'.

GUARANTEED LOUSE-FREE

HAVRINCOURT

Before a party of soldiers left the trenches on home leave the M.O. was required to examine each man and give him a certificate to the effect that he carried no lice. To soldiers with a sense of humour this was the funniest farce ever devised by the Army mind. As one soldier said, 'I for one carried on my person a large assortment of all the fauna on which Mr Keating (the maker of insecticide) wages war – with the single

For Christmas 1917 the Kite and Balloon Section of the Royal Flying Corps performed Cinderella *for the troops at Bapaume, Somme. Two airmen, while rehearsing, came across a group of soldiers in the snow. Life was grim on the Western Front and any form of clowning got a laugh.*

exception, perhaps, of beetles'.

At Havrincourt early in 1918 a leave party paraded for the M.O.'s inspection and being a decent and understanding man he just looked each soldier in the eye and nodded approval. But he frowned when he contemplated the last man in the row, plucked something from his tunic, cracked it between his nails and said, 'You're lousy, Private Stone'.

Private Stone nodded agreeably. 'And if you stop my leave, you'll be lousy too, Captain Barlow'.

'Off you go', the M.O. said.

MAROONED

BULLECOURT

A platoon of Royal Fusiliers was passing a mine crater between Ecoust and Bullecourt in January 1918, on what had been a quiet day, when the enemy sent over a heavy shell which wounded six of the fusiliers. The blast pitched another man into the crater, which was full of water. Struggling to his feet he staggered towards a pile of rubble that stood like a tiny island in the muddy water. He sat on it, drew up his feet, looked around and his mates heard him say, 'Blimey, Robinson bloody Crusoe!'

'NO BLOODY SUNSTROKE'

SOMME

In February 1918, on a bitterly cold and wet afternoon, a corporal and four privates were sheltering as best they could from the weather and from German shells. They were thoroughly miserable and none more so than a little Cockney who had served with the 10th Middlesex in the Far East. His main complaint was the sheer lunacy of fighting a war in winter.

'You and your grumbling!' the corporal said. 'You and your fancy tales of India! Any rate, there ain't no bloody mosquitoes here and no horrible malaria'.

A big shell came over and the party cowered as it exploded close by, badly wounding the little soldier. 'Corporal', he said faintly as the others gathered round him in their efforts to help, 'You forgot to mention there ain't no bloody sunstroke – nor any earfquakes neither!'

'Sorry son', the corporal said. But it was too late.

Mr Victor Meik, who recounted this story, was one of the party. He said that the Cockney died with a 'delightful whimsical smile' at his own humour.

226

'THE POSITION WILL BE HELD'

SPOIL BANK, YPRES SALIENT

One of the most famous orders of the war was given in writing by a young Australian machine-gun officer on 13 March 1918, at the position known as Spoil Bank; the spoil was the waste earth from the railway cutting running out of Ypres.

SPECIAL ORDERS No. 1 Section
13/3/18

(1) This position will be held, and the Section will remain here until relieved.

(2) The enemy cannot be allowed to interfere with this programme.

(3) If the Section cannot remain here alive, it will remain here dead, but in any case it will remain here.

(4) Should any man through shell shock or other cause attempt to surrender, he will remain here dead.

(5) Should all guns be blown out, the Section will use Mills Grenades and other novelties.

(6) Finally, the position as stated, will be held.

> F.P. Bethune, Lieut,
> C/C No 1 Section.

The story of this order is little known outside Australia – and even there it is no longer well known. Towards the end of February 1918 the 3rd Machine-Gun Company, A.I.F., was moving into the line and two officers were sent forward to reconnoitre the position where forward machine-guns were to be posted – by request of higher command. They reported to Lieutenant Bethune that the position was hopeless as it had a field of fire of no more than six yards. If the enemy attacked the crews would be killed before they could fire a shot. Lieutenant Bethune protested to his C.O. but the order stayed, so Bethune insisted as a matter of honour on being the officer in charge of the post. He called for volunteers – and every man of his section stepped forward; he selected three veterans and three new men.

In fact, as Bethune led his men to the suicide position he was overtaken by a runner who told him that orders had changed; he was to take up positions at Buff Bank. This was much more to the young officer's liking. He got his guns into position, loaded all spare belts and placed the 10,000 rounds per gun ready to hand. At that time British and Australian infantry were in strength near the guns but they were

227

Lieutenant Bethune used Vickers machine-guns of the type shown in this photograph. These gunners will soon be going into action and are filling the guns' ammunition belts with .303 rounds. Men of the Machine-Gun Corps were sometimes called, at least among Australian infantry, the 'shoot, shit and scatter boys'. This was a crude way of accusing the gunners of going on a job and then getting smartly out of the way before the enemy artillery opened up on them. The infantry was left to take the punishment. The expression persisted into the 1940s.   *(Author's collection and copyright)*

moved back to prepare for an attack and this left the guns dangerously exposed.

With the safety of that part of the front entirely in his hands, Lieutenant Bethune considered it only right that each man should have written orders. 'I wanted to make it absolutely clear to the men exactly what our job was', Bethune said in 1937, 'so that if a man had to die, he should die in his own light-hearted fashion, in goodly company'.

The position was held and the crew survived, though some of the men were later killed. Bethune's battle order was circulated by H.Q. 1 Div A.I.F. and later by other staffs. In the American forces copies of the order were mimeographed and distributed as 'an admirable model of all that a set of standing trench orders should be'.

It should be emphasised that Lieutenant Bethune did not seriously believe that his men might surrender. He himself said, 'They knew that I knew they could not consider such a possibility (of surrender) and so between us we enjoyed in silence the joke that to an outsider might have seemed a little grim . . . My name is connected with the orders that I wrote but it was the fighting men beside me who made those words come, for this was the spirit in which they fought throughout those years and I only translated into words the spirit of the fighting A.I.F.'

Lieutenant Bethune won the M.C. He had been a clergyman in Australia before the war and he went back to the cloth when it ended.

IN LIGHTER VEIN (VANE)

VIMY RIDGE

During February and March 1918 the 1/13th Battalion London Regiment, temporarily commanded by Major Frederick Heath, were on Vimy Ridge. A big German attack was expected and the men had been kept at stand-to for much longer each morning than the regulation hour. One of the company commanders was sorry for the men and their tension and for light relief he did his best to pull the legs of his battalion H.Q. One of his duties during this 'windy' period was to send in 'situation reports', so he wrote his report in verse. Sent over the wire to Battalion H.Q., it was taken down as prose and read with astonishment bordering on consternation by the adjutant and others. It was left to the C.O., Major Heath, to recognise the report for what it was.

C COMPANY SITUATION REPORT 19/3/1918

There is nothing I can tell you
That you really do not know –
Except that we are on the Ridge
And Fritz is down below.
I'm tired of 'situations'
And of 'wind' entirely 'vane',
The gas-guard yawns and tells me
'It's blowing up for rain'.
He's a human little fellow
With a thoughtful point of view,

And his report (uncensored)
I pass, please, on to you.
'When's old Fritzie coming over?
Does the General really know?
The colonel seems to think so,

The captain tells us "No".
When's someone going to tell us
We can Stand-to as before?
An hour at dawn and one at dusk,
Lor' blimey, who wants more?'

The Germans attacked two days later. The word 'vane' refers to the weather vane used in the trenches to indicate whether or not the wind was favourable for a gas attack by the enemy. The 1/13th Battalion was known more familiarly as 'the Kensingtons'.

MODIFIED FATALISM

CAMBRAI

In March 1918 a German sniper fixed his attention on a particular British trench and frequently took a shot. A young soldier was looking over the parapet while an older soldier – long enough in the army to be an 'old sweat' – eyed him curiously. Then he said casually, 'Are you a fatalist, son?'

'Yes, I am', the boy said.

'Me too', the older man said. 'But I believes in ducking'.

A sentry at an observation hole in a covered forward position. This is not a sniping position as the rifleman has nowhere to rest his elbows and the bayonet is fixed; it would be detached if he were sniping. However, the sentry would be in danger of being sniped because his peephole would show up as a white patch among the sandbags. A good observation hole had sacking hanging behind it.

OUT TO WIN

LE CROTOY

An infantry school was established at Le Crotoy and in March 1918 there was great interest in the final of the platoon competition between the Seaforth Highlanders and an Australian battalion. To give themselves an advantage the Australians filled their packs with straw – and there was no instruction which said they could not do this. The packs were not only lighter but they all looked neat and identical. The men of the demonstration platoon were even physically carried to the parade ground by their mates so that their brightly shone boots would not be muddied.

After failing to fault either platoon in a hundred drill tests the judges examined webbing puttees, boots and equipment. The Australians lost two points because one man was found to have diagonally crossed bootlaces while another was wearing a ring. But the Seaforths lost two points for showing more fatigue than the Australians after a long double-march.

The final test decided on by the judges – the shape and uniformity of packs – gave the contest to Australia. Both platoons were resting, lying or sitting on their packs, when the Australians were suddenly called to attention to receive the congratulations of the C.O. of the school, who had just ridden up. 'You Australians won', he said, 'because of the faultless uniformity of your packs. I shall now be pleased to examine them myself'.

Thirty six deep but inaudible groans came from the Diggers, whose packs now lay squashed out of shape by the weight of the sitters. Some even sprouted whiskers of straw. After pulling out several handfuls of straw the C.O. said, 'You won by two points but you should have won by 12 points for initiative. I can't allow you these points but I am going to award the Seaforth Highlanders two points for the extra weight they carried throughout the contest. The result is therefore a tie'.

EXCLUSIVE NEWS

VIMY RIDGE

A company of the Devon Regiment was making a forced march to part of the line on Vimy Ridge in March 1918. It was a foul night with rain and thick fog and when a halt was called several men were missing. Sergeant Greg Lidsell was ordered to round them up but he too became lost in that featureless landscape and foggy night. After much frustrated wandering he encountered a young London soldier, so they sat down and waited for the morning.

As the fog lifted the sergeant said, 'Right, soldier, you take a look from that hill on the right and I'll reconnoitre on the other side. Come back to this spot and tell me if you see anything'.

Lidsell was still moving to his flank when he heard a muffled shout and turned to see the young soldier running frantically towards him and breathless with excitement. 'Sergeant! Sergeant!' he said. 'Germans! Germans! Fahsands of 'em – and there's nobody but you and me knows anyfink abaht it!'

He had, in fact, seen the beginning of the German offensive which broke through the Allied line and nearly caused a fatal collapse.

THE CUCKOO GAME

STRAZEELE-MERRIS

During 1918 the Australians carried out a lot of aggressive patrolling on several parts of the front but nowhere more effectively than south of Armentieres. Wryly, they called their work 'peaceful penetration'. Infantry patrols went out each day to see how the Germans were getting on with their new trenches. When the enemy had dug themselves well down and were making themselves comfortable, a patrol N.C.O. reported to his company commander, 'I think it's deep enough now, sir'. A brisk raid was mounted and the Australians made themselves at home in the trench and dug-outs the Germans had sweated to make. This happened on several parts of the front.

232

A fatigue party, having carried supplies to the front, returns along a dusty road in the Arras sector, passing a group of soldiers on a low ridge. The white background is from the underlying chalk brought to the surface by years of shellfire and mining.　　　*(Author's collection and copyright)*

HIGH SPIRITS

MENIN ROAD

In March 1918 a North Country Regiment sent a wiring party along the Menin Road towards the front. The party contained two Cockney members and they were heard to have this conversation.

1st: I'm fed up with this stunt.

2nd: Same 'ere. 'Tain't 'arf a life, ain't it? No rest, no beer, blinkin' leave stopped. Got any fags?

1st: No mate.

2nd: No fags, no nuffink. It's only us keepin' so ruddy cheerful as pulls us through.

The authenticity of this exchange was vouched for by Corporal V. Marston, Surrey Regiment, when he lived in Worple Road, Wimbledon, London.

233

UNDERSTANDING ENGLISH

AMIENS

When the American troops first arrived on the Western Front it was necessary for them to work closely with veteran British and Australian soldiers and pick up some of their skills. For administrative purposes the US units were part of British divisions and corps and consequently operated according to British orders.

As all British soldiers knew, one word in particular dominated orders sent out from the 'Q' or administrative branch of the Army – the word *Return*. There was a Return of Personnel, a Casualty Return, Ammunition Return, Men on Leave Return. When in the course of time the American division was transferred away from a British Corps the Q branch sent a telegram after it. RETURN WANTED OF ALL TENTS AND TRENCH SHELTERS IN YOUR POSSESSION. Next day H.Q. American Division received a second message: RE MY 0546/8023 HASTEN RETURN OF TENTS AND TRENCH SHELTERS.

The day after this the Corps staff was startled by the steady arrival of hundreds of tents and trench shelters in a convoy of waggons The wires hummed furiously and the Corps staff captain shouted his hardest to American Div H.Q. that 'Hasten return' did *not* mean 'Send back as quickly as possible'.

The Americans were just a little peeved. 'We thought we had got a proper move on sending back those tents', said the American major who told the story. 'You English sure have a funny way of using your own language'.

STERN MEASURES

ARRAS SECTOR

In March 1918 a West Country battalion was billeted in a village near Arras. Some chickens were stolen from a nearby village and military police traced them to a West Country billet by following their feathers. The

234

O.C. could not find the culprits so he punished the entire company by stopping leave for six months. Theft from French civilians was a serious offence, he told the men.

A few days later the Germans broke through further south in the great spring offensive. One night the company orderly sergeant went around the billets and read out orders of the day, which concluded with Sir Douglas Haig's soon-to-be-famous despatch.

'All leave is now stopped throughout the army until further orders', the sergeant read.

The men were mostly under their blankets at the time but a tousled head appeared and its owner said in tones of awe, 'Blimey, Haig means to find out who pinched those blinking chickens!'

FINAL GAMBLE

VLAMERTINGHE

On 19 March 1918 a remarkable ceremony took place at what is now the New British Cemetery, Vlamertinghe. The occasion was just one more burial but it was made distinctive by the presence of six generals and the six Victoria Cross winners who carried the coffin. They were burying Company Sergeant-Major John Skinner, V.C., D.C.M., of the King's Own Scottish Borderers. He had won his V.C. in August 1917 for great courage when he knocked out three German blockhouses. The first he took single-handed; to clear the other two he led six men and captured 60 prisoners, three machine-guns and two trench-mortars.

He returned to England for the V.C. Investiture – and the usual 14 days leave granted on such occasions – and was then posted to the K.O.S.B. Reserve Battalion in Edinburgh. But he disobeyed orders and returned to the Front, where he felt more 'at home' than in Britain.

He had another reason to get back into battle – a bet. He and a friend, Quarter-Master Sergeant Victor Ross, had both been wounded eight times and they had a wager on which of them would first get a ninth wound. Skinner won but could not collect – a bullet hit him between the eyes as he was rescuing a wounded soldier.

The army made a spectacle of his burial, despite heavy rain; Skinner was most probably the only soldier carried to this last resting place on the Western Front on a gun carriage drawn by a carefully groomed team of horses.

The irony of Skinner's bet is that, according to records, he had already been wounded nine times – three times during the Boer War and six times between 1914 and 1917. He may have lost count. C.S.M. Skinner joined the army in 1900 at the age of 16 so when he died in 1917 he was a seasoned veteran with 17 years' service.

'I SHIVERED WITH PRIDE'

GREVILLERS, SOMME

On 23 March 1918 the Germans broke through the British line at Mory, near where Captain Arthur Behrend, an officer of Heavy Artillery, was on duty in his battery office trying vainly to discover how much ammunition remained to try to halt the German advance. Already the forward British infantry had retreated through their own artillery positions and the situation was critical. Suddenly he heard the sound of bagpipes and drums and ran outside to see what was happening.

It was magnificent (he wrote) and too moving for words. No music, not even the trumpets of the French cavalry which I heard screaming their wild song of triumph after the armistice, has stirred me as deeply as the sobbing, skirling pipes of the 51st Division playing their survivors back to battle, and I shivered with pride as I stood there watching those grim Highlanders swing by – every man in step, every man bronzed and resolute. Could these be the weary, dirty men who came limping past us yesterday in ragged twos and threes, asking pitifully how much further to Achiet-le-Grand? Who could behold such a spectacle and say that the pomp and circumstance of war is no more?

The Highlanders were making up for their ragged retreat under the fierce German assault.

236

KILLED BEFORE ACTION

GREVILLERS

Reinforcements, many of them with little training, were being rushed into the British line to stem the tremendous German assault of March 1918. Often large groups of men arrived without a nominal roll so that no officer knew exactly what men had arrived. On the night of 23 March infantry and artillery reinforcements arrived at a depot near Grevillers and a sergeant-major put them into a Nissen hut. While he was reporting to his adjutant, Captain Arthur Behrend, there was a tremendous explosion and huge shell splinters ripped through the hut while branches snapped off trees in the tempest-like blast.

The firing *pop* of a howitzer could be heard and there was generally time to take cover. Experienced troops could also hear the sharp, distinctive bark of a high-velocity gun several seconds ahead of its shell. On this occasion there had been no warning. 'My God!' the sergeant-major shouted. 'It hit the hut where I put the reinforcements!'

Casualties were heavy – 15 killed and wounded and others so completely blown to pieces that they could not be identified. It was not even possible to count the number so killed. Many weeks later the unit received a letter from a woman in England asking for news about her son, from whom she had not heard since he sailed for France. Royal Garrison Artillery Depot could tell her only that on 20 March, with 40 other men, he had been sent to a particular brigade, 9th Brigade, Royal Garrison Artillery. None of the officers knew how to write to tell her that her son was one of the many blown to pieces before he had really got into the war.

The brigade medical orderly, Bombardier White, reported that in the explosion he had seen the most horrible sight of his career. A shell splinter hit a bully beef tin held by a reinforcement soldier, burst it and scattered its repulsive contents over his bare stomach. Bombardier White was not joking; in that arena where flesh was torn and blood flowed so freely, what he saw seemed ghastly.

In fact, the depot had been hit by a 9.5 shell on a railway mounting, firing from the railtrack somewhere near Havrincourt, at a range of about 10 miles.

THE FRENCH LIEUTENANT

VILLERS BRETONNEUX

On 6 April 1918 two N.C.O.s of the Australian 54th Battalion, Regimental Sergeant-major Bramhall and Sergeant H.H. Kennedy, were standing in the sunken road just behind the town, on the Villers – Aubigny road. A lieutenant in the grey uniform of the French artillery – which was in Hangard Wood, to the right – came up and said he wished to speak to the C.O.

Bramhall asked him his business with the C.O., Lieutenant-Colonel Machonochie. His family had lived in Villers Bretonneux, the lieutenant said, and he wanted to visit his home and inspect the damage. 'O.K., sir', Bramhall said. 'You can go there'.

'Thank you', the lieutenant said, 'but I must have the C.O.'s permission'. Bramhall took him to the C.O.'s dugout, where the second in command, Captain Norman Lovett, and the Intelligence Officer, Lieutenant Staples, were also present. After a few minutes the French lieutenant came out and walked towards the town. 'That chap's accent seems more like German than French', Sergeant Kennedy said to the R.S.M.

About 3.30 that afternoon 30 yards of the sunken road where Battalion H.Q. was situated was heavily shelled. Machonochie and Lovett were killed outright: Staples was wounded and died next day. From the precise nature of the enemy shelling it was likely that the 'French lieutenant' was a German spy.

238

INSULT TO INJURY

BAILLEUL

During the British retreat of April 1918 under the weight of the great German offensive, some soldiers were standing on the side of the road near Outersteene Farm when three small and youthful Germans appeared as prisoners under escort. Wearing helmets far too big for them and oversize boots, they were on their way for interrogation by the Intelligence staff. As the pathetic group reached the watching British soldiers, one man said, 'Luv us, 'Arry, look what's shovin' our army abaht!'

Bailleul, mentioned in this story, was a major British depot centre and R.F.C. air base. During the German breakthrough of spring 1918 the British fought desperately to hold it. Here men of the Middlesex Regiment man a barricade in the main street. Unlike most towns in French Flanders, Bailleul had not been badly damaged by shellfire.

REFERENCE UNDERSTOOD

BETHUNE

In April 1918, during what was to be the last great German offensive of the war, two soldiers of a field Survey Company of the Royal Engineers were on the top of a colliery chimney. At 130 feet above ground it was an ideal observation post – and a terrifying one. Heavy gunfire was in progress and every time a big shell screamed past the chimney it swayed. A direct hit was possible at any time.

The men's job was to locate enemy batteries and, by giving a map reference, telephone the location to H.Q. One of the pair was trying to give the reference 'Q.20' to a corporal at the other end but the wind, noise and faults on the line frustrated him.

He kept shouting 'Q! Q! Q!' and when that didn't work he tried 'Q words' – but 'Quince and Queen' didn't reach the corporal either. Finally the engineer burst out in exasperation, 'Q! Q! Queue . . . Blimey! You know – the bloody thing wot the poor blighters at home wite abaht for mawgarine in!'

That did the trick.

The story was told by Private B.W. Whayman, the other man on the swaying chimney. The Bethune chimney was one of the few close to the front which survived the most intense fighting. It was knocked down by British guns when it seemed possible that the Germans would use it as an O.P. during their breakthrough.

A SPY IN THE LINE

VILLERS BRETONNEUX

Australian units held the Villers Bretonneux sector in April 1918. Trench sentries of D Company 54th Battalion noticed a dog coming from the direction of the German lines and heading towards Corbie. This excited no real interest the first time or the second. When the dog was sighted a third morning a sniper shot the dog. On its collar was found a note addressed to a Private Wilson, who was a runner with 8th Brigade H.Q. *And the note was written in German.* When Military Police reached the brigade's H.Q. to interview Wilson he had disappeared.

Some time later it was found that Wilson had enlisted under that name in Australia but that his correct name was Wolfram and that he had left Germany and gone to Australia as a migrant just before the war. Obviously he had turned spy and as the dog was well trained he had been operating for some time. 'Private Wilson' was never seen again but it was assumed that when the dog failed to arrive he feared that he had been found out and made his way to the German lines.

A MATTER OF DEFINITION

VILLERS BRETONNEUX

On 11 April 1918, the 14th Australian Infantry Brigade received an order signed by Brigadier R.A. Carruthers, Deputy Quarter-Master General, Australian Corps, It read: 'During the present phase of operations the regular supply of fresh meat presents such difficulties that the men will receive only a small percentage of their rations. There is additional supply of fresh meat available in the form of horses killed by shellfire and the Corps Commander sees no reason why this should not be taken advantage of and used as is freely done in the French Army . . . '

Certainly, a British cavalry regiment had charged up a valley to the east of the town while trying to check the great German advance and many of their horses had been killed, but this had occurred on 5 April, *six* days before the G.H.Q. order.

14th Brigade sent a terse reply to the D.Q.M.G. 'Reference eating of horse flesh: Please define *fresh*'.

LAST WORDS

AUBIGNY AU BAC, SOMME

Corporal E.C. East, M.M., took part in the attack by the 2nd London Regiment on the village of Aubigny au Bac and was hit by shell splinters. While he was looking for somebody to dress his wounds he came across one of his platoon lying by the road with wounds that were obviously mortal.

As he leaned over the soldier to give him a drink the man noticed East's blood-stained face. 'Crikey, Corp,' he said, 'your barber was ruddy clumsy this morning!'

Seconds later he was dead.

PUTTING HIS FOOT IN IT

AVELUY WOOD, NEAR THE ANCRE RIVER

In April 1918 Private A.M. Burrage, after weeks in the front line was suffering from grossly swollen and sore feet and he mentioned his difficulty to his company commander. 'I believe I've got trench feet', he said.

The O.C. looked worried. 'I don't say it's your fault', he said, 'but I suppose you know it's a crime to have trench feet'.

Burrage said reasonably, 'Just look at the conditions, sir'.

'They're terrible, I know', the O.C. said. 'I'll try to keep you out of trouble if I can. Go and see the M.O.'

Burrage hobbled down the communication trench, where it was usually dangerous to move slowly. On the other side of the hill he ran into the C.O. who pointed a finger at him suspiciously and said, 'What's the matter?'

'I think I have trench feet sir'.

The colonel became almost demented 'How dare you have

242

trench feet! What's your name and number? Why haven't you looked after yourself' You know very well it is the duty of every man to take off his boots and socks every day and rub his feet'.

'This is impossible during the day, sir', Burrage said. And it was – unless the men lay on their backs in the water and held their feet in the air.

'Why haven't you done it at night?' the colonel demanded.

'I have been spending my nights organising stretcher parties and trying to get the wounded away', Burrage said.

The C.O. growled some more, said that Burrage would hear more of his dereliction of duty, and passed on.

All too often even the C.O.s of infantry battalions did not know the extent of the suffering of their men in the front trenches. If they were ignorant it was not surprising that brigade commanders, divisional generals and the even more senior commmanders further back had no conception of conditions in the front line.

DISOBEDIENCE OF ORDERS

YPRES

In 1918 a lady working in a Church Army hut at Boulogne asked a group of soldiers what was the finest thing they had seen in the war. The Church Army Commissioner in France, J.C.V. Durrell, heard one of them describe his 'finest thing'.

'Well, ma'am . . . it happened in the early days of the Boche offensive (in April 1918). There was a Casualty Clearing Station in the line of attack and the Boche was only a few miles away. The roads were all choked with our retreating transport. An officer came in and said, "C.O.'s orders – we have to evacuate at once. Nurses must leave first. We can't get the wounded away, which is bad but it can't be helped".

'The nurses refused to go. They said, "We won't leave our wounded. if they have to stay behind, so do we". The colonel came in and cursed and swore and threatened. He even got red in the face. The nurses wouldn't budge. Then one of them said "Why not *try* to evacuate the wounded?"

'And we all set to work. There were no ambulances to hand but we managed to rake up all sorts of old shacks on wheels and we loaded the men – and some we carried. The nurses worked like heroes themselves. And everyone in the C.C.S. got away. Then a big shell came over and laid the place flat. But thanks to those women everyone was safe.'

HE LIKE A SOLDIER FELL

ARRAS

The 1st Battalion Middlesex Regiment was pushed into the line to help steady it after the tremendous German assault of April 1918. There was confusion in parts of the battalion about where exactly they should go to find the front-line. At this point a veteran of 1914 known as Darky, who had been on the Western Front ever since, told the Regimental Sergeant Major that he did not want to rest as instructed; he wanted to get back to the fighting. He was at once detailed to guide some of the lost Middlesex men to the front trench.

When the group reached the support trench line they were told to be careful of snipers. Twenty yards further Darky was shot through the head by a sniper and moments before dying he said to the Middlesex corporal, 'Straight on lad, you can find your own way now'.

This story was told by Corporal A.H. Walker who many years ago lived at Wilberforce Road, Finsbury Park, London N4.

AT HER POST

ROBECQ, LYS

A party of King Edward's Horse gallantly held the Germans in check for several hours in and near a farmhouse at Robecq when the Germans were attacking with artillery and machine-gun fire in the onslaught of spring 1918. The men were exhausted and there were many casualties. All the civilians had fled except one elderly woman. During the action she milked her cows, took milk to the men under fire and made hot coffee for them. She tended the wounded as best she could. Repeatedly urged to leave, she replied every time, 'Why? I am of use here'. She left only when the troops retired.

FEAR BY NIGHT

VILLERS BRETONNEUX

On the night of 24/25 April 1918 Australian units were desperately trying to stem the German offensive against Amiens. Corporal G.M. Sainsbury, a Tasmanian, of 4th Australian Machine-Gun Battalion – equipped with Vickers Medium Machine-Guns – commanded a gun team and took part in an attack on enemy positions near Villers Bretonneux, where the church was burning fiercely. In the dark and under heavy enemy fire all was confusion and Sainsbury had difficulty in keeping his team together with their heavy equipment. At one point the gun's tripod stand was lost.

As a flare burst (Sainsbury wrote) I saw the tripod at the foot of an embankment. As soon as it had died away, I ran to the tripod, got it nicely on my back with a front leg on each shoulder and the rear leg down my back, when up went another flare. To my horror, there, a few yards in front, stood a German soldier with bayonet pointing at me and a steep bank behind me. Just what were the intentions of this man I had little time to think so I acted quickly. Freeing myself of

245

my burden I reached for my revolver in a holster of my equipment. By this time he had discarded his rifle and had fallen to the ground. Shooting any man was never in my line, much less one unarmed, and on his face on the ground. Getting him to his feet, I passed him over to stretcher bearers and that was the last I saw of him, so perhaps his intentions were only to surrender after all.

Corporal Sainsbury was wounded and was later awarded the Military Medal for his work in the vital battle for Villers Bretonneux. He was the only one of his crew of eight to survive the fighting. The German he confronted might well have been suffering from battle paralysis when he fell to the ground. Sainsbury makes the interesting comment that 'shooting any man was never in his line' yet he could command a Vickers gun which could sweep away scores of men in a single attack. Many machine-gunners, British and German, since they were not aiming at an individul enemy, felt that they were not killing any man 'personally'.

'No Bon'

LYS RIVER

During the battle of the Lys – the result of the German offensive of spring 1918 – there was much confusion and civilian refugees as well as troops were retreating. A British officer, dodging his way across country amid enemy shellfire, thought he noticed movement in a shell hole. He found an elderly couple clad in their Sunday best – as the local people often dressed when fleeing from their homes – and crouching at the bottom of the hole. The lady wore a bonnet fringed with beads and cherries which dangled and bobbed as she ducked at each explosion. Recognising her visitor as a British officer and wanting to express herself in a way he could understand, she said feelingly, 'No bon! Ah! No bon!'

The officer had the pair rescued when the situation was a little less dangerous.

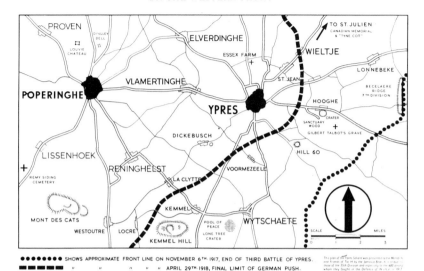

● ● ● ● ● ● ● SHOWS APPROXIMATE FRONT LINE ON NOVEMBER 6ᵀᴴ 1917, END OF THIRD BATTLE OF YPRES.
▬ ▬ ▬ ▬ ▬ ▬ "   "   "   " " APRIL 29ᵀᴴ 1918, FINAL LIMIT OF GERMAN PUSH.

By 29 April 1918 the Germans had nullified all the costly British gains in the Ypres Salient and had advanced to within a mile of Ypres itself. There they could go no further. This map shows the final positions and includes the Toc H 'Pool of Peace', which had been one of the 19 enormous·mine craters blown by the British in June 1917.

A BITE OF THE BATTLE

OVER NIEPPE

Late in June 1918 Captain Elliott White Springs, an American in the R.F.C., flew his fighter in under a German two-seater but his guns would not fire. As he struggled to clear the stoppages the German observer-gunner hit Springs' oil pipe. His motor did not stop at once but brought him back a little way before the bearings melted. He

247

glided back across the British lines and crashed downwind in a machine-gun emplacement.

The butt of his Vickers gun knocked a hole in his chin and he got a crack on the top of his head and a pair of black eyes. One of his longerons tore his flying suit right up his back, just grazed his neck and removed his helmet. Some Tommies fished him from the wreckage.

Running his tongue around his mouth Springs let out a yell because he couldn't find any front teeth. 'What's the matter sir?' a Tommy asked.

'My teeth!' Springs sobbed. 'They're all gone'.

'Oh no they ain't', the obliging Tommy said. 'Here they are, sir'.

And he pulled Springs' lips off his teeth. The teeth were all right; they were just on the outside of his face, through his lips.

The army post where they took him had no anaesthetic but somebody found a bottle of cognac. Everytime he tried to take a swig it would run out of the hole in his chin. He spent the morning with his mouth open while an Irish padre poured the cognac down his throat. He reached a telephone in the Forest of Nieppe that afternoon and called Wing for a tender to collect him. His wounds were stitched at the Duchess of Sutherland's hospital near the airfield and though he was supposed to keep 'absolutely quiet' he was back in the air in a few days.

Of the 210 Americans who landed in England and trained with the Royal Flying Corps, 51 were killed, 30 were wounded, 14 became prisoners of war and 20 broke down mentally under the tremendous stress of aerial combat. Because they served with the R.F.C. they returned home without medals – the British were sparing with decorations and they suffered by comparison with the much decorated pilots of the American front who returned with rank and headlines. Some of the fliers in the U.S. Air Force got a Distinguished Service Cross and a Croix de Guerre for each German plane they shot down. Captain Springs did well. His 12 victories ranked him fifth among American aces; he won the British D.F.C. and the American D.S.C.

SUFFERING ENOUGH

AMIENS–ALBERT ROAD

In the summer of 1918, after the great enemy drive of the spring had been checked, and before the Allied offensive, the main Amiens–Albert road was the British front line. One hot day, when there was little action, Sergeant Paul Maze* crawled along a spur to a forward observation point which had a plunging view of a German trench on the other side, An able artist, he wanted to make a military sketch for Army H.Q.

While he was at work he saw the bald head of a German framed against a shirt laid out to dry on the parapet of his trench. In a loud, tense whisper Maze called to the sentry and pointed towards the enemy soldier.

'I know', the Tommy said casually. 'He's been there all the morning doing nothing but picking fleas off his body. Lousy, that's what he is'.

'He's a good target', Maze said.

'Gawd!' the sentry said. 'The poor bastard's got enough trouble without me shooting him'.

See story entitled 'Firing Squad' (p. 20)

EASY DISPOSAL

BELLEVUE, NORTH OF EPERNAY

During the second battle of the Marne, in the summer of 1918, a French Senegalese was run over by a lorry and killed on the main road near Bellevue. To find out which padre should bury him, a British R.C. chaplain attached to the Royal Army Medical Corps sent a Senegalese N.C.O. to his unit H.Q. to find out his religion.

The N.C.O. came back and reported, 'No religion, Monsieur – heathen'.

The R.C. chaplain asked how the deceased soldier would be buried in his own country. His comrade said,

'Killed in battle – not buried – eaten'. The padre passed on the job to a C. of E. confrère. 'More in your line, I think', he said. 'You people have done more missionary work than we have'.

Lest the story seem apocryphal, and in case it might be regarded as a slur on the Senegalese, it must be said that the story was told by Col. David Robie, who had it from the R.C. padre at the time.

A DISH FOR GOURMETS

LA HOUSSOY, ALBERT–AMIENS ROAD

Mac was the food hound of an Australian company and though a lean man he had a prodigious appetite and was never satisfied. When his platoon was at low strength he would eat the food of the absent men and still be hungry. He often threatened to give himself up if Fritz came over, on the grounds that he would be better fed as a prisoner.

When his unit was in bivouac at La Houssoy in 1918 he spent a lot of time at the company cooker trying to get more than his lawful issue. The cooks were completely fed up with him. About this time the men had to go off to Querrieu for the brigade sports. The cooks promised Mac that during the day they would make for him, and him alone, a dish of Irish quail – if he cared to pay them five francs. He was happy with the deal and spent the day drooling over the meal to come that night.

Reporting to the cooks, he was handed his large parcel of Irish quail and went off alone into the woods to relish it. When he reached what he thought was a large secluded place he opened the parcel and found five large roasted potatoes, each with a feather stuck in it – Irish quail.

Mac was killed at Villers Bretonneux on 8 August, the first day of the final British offensive. A piece of steel went through his chest while he was devouring a huge chunk of bread and cheese. His mates said he would have been happy to go that way.

250

WITHIN RANGE

MERVILLE

All one morning, near Merville in 1918, several German aeroplanes had been annoying the Australian lines despite the efforts of a British anti-aircraft battery nearby. The failure of the battery drew forth many encouraging – and other – remarks from the Australians and the sergeant in charge was getting slightly hot under the collar. As one of the enemy pilots dropped to a couple of hundred feet to enfilade the trenches one of the Diggers yelled out, 'Now's your chance Tommy! Throw the bloody gun at him!'

A STEP TOO FAR

ST QUENTIN

In the middle of 1918 a lightly wounded German soldier was being carried on a stretcher to the dressing station by an Australian and an American. He spoke a little English and was talkative. 'English no good', he said, 'French no good, Americans no good'.

The stretcher-bearers walked on without answering. The German began again. 'The English think they're going to win the war – they're wrong. You Americans think you've come to win the war – you're wrong'.

The American spoke for the first and last time. 'You think you're going to be carried to hospital – you're wrong. Put him down, Digger!'

This story was told by an Australian infantry colonel to a British artillery colonel and was recorded in January 1919 by the writer 'Quex'.

251

CHANGE OF HEART

DARGUIES

A unit was resting in Darguies when 'Snowy', the hard-case of the company yelled out, 'Fall in those I owe money!' A dozen of his mates lined up. Snowy looked hard at them, then shouted, 'Creditors, shun! Dismiss!' And then he beat a hasty retreat to the estaminet.

DOWN IN ONE PIECE

OVER LILLE

74 (Tiger) Squadron Royal Air Force was famous for its dash and the spirit of its individual fliers. On 26 June 1918 the commander, Major K.L. 'Grid' Caldwell, and Captain Cairns collided during a fight. Cairns brought his damaged fighter under control and landed safely but the whole squadron saw Caldwell spin down and disappear. That night the mess had a wake and all the fliers became drunk, but then the wake turned into a celebration. About midnight Caldwell staggered in, covered in blood and with his uniform torn to pieces.

He had survived by astonishing coolness and courage. Having set his tail stabiliser, he got out of his seat and crawled out onto the wing and somehow counter-balanced his plane out of a spin. His aileron control was jammed and part of his wing tip was gone but he 'balanced' the aircraft down. He landed it on the British side of the trenches by reaching in and pulling the stick back before the wheels hit the ground.

The plane turned over and threw Caldwell into a clump of bushes. As he had crashed about 30 miles from his own airfield he had taken

252

until midnight to get back. He resumed command, took charge of his own wake and the drinking and when the squadron went out for dawn patrol he led it. Then he went to hospital.

Caldwell shot down 25 German aeroplanes and twice won the Distinguished Flying Cross as well as the M.C. Apart from 74 Squadron he also served in 8 and 60 Squadrons.

PROFITABLE ENTERPRISE

MOUSSY, NEAR EPERNAY, MARNE

In mid-July 1918 Moussy and other villages became frontline Allied towns as the Germans moved back. Battles were expected and most of the inhabitants had been evacuated by the civil authorities. The town was thronged with English, Scots, French, Senegalese and Italians and the Provost Marshal's men were kept busy maintaining discipline in the fair-like atmosphere.

Two Scots discovered a large and varied wine cellar. Dressing themselves as French peasants, they set up a stall, just outside the house. Regardless of brand or vintage, they sold each bottle for two francs. To give the enterprise the air of legality and to promote confidence among their customers – as well as to keep order – the two Jocks employed a mate to stand sentry with fixed bayonet. Of course, he had the added duty of watching for the arrival of military police.

Men clamoured to buy wine but the entrepreneurs closed down the establishment when other Scots started to object, with threats of violence, to their high prices. According to rumour they cleared a profit of 2,000 francs.

PRIVATE PROPERTY

TANK WOOD, SOMME

Just before the big Allied push of August 1918 the Royal West Kents were resting in Tank Wood, which was dotted with shellholes. One was filled, unusually, with fairly clear water, evidently from a nearby spring. Near the edge of the pool was a board with the stark notice MINE. The West Kents carefully avoided it. All sensible soldiers kept away from places marked as dangerous, whether from unexploded mines, concealed well openings or other hazards.

A little later the R.W.K.s saw a soldier bathing naked in the hole and one of them yelled. 'Hey, stupid, can't you read?' And he pointed at the notice.

'Of course I can', the unworried soldier said. 'I *would* be stupid if I couldn't read my own writing. This 'ole's *mine*'.

SAVING THE TANKS

VILLERS BRETONNEUX

8 August 1918 was the day of the battle described by Ludendorff as 'the blackest day of the German Army'.

On the day before in a small wood near to but not part of the Bois l'Abbé, on the left of Villers Bretonneux, 13 English carrier tanks loaded with ammunition, bombs and petrol were parked in preparation for the next day's advance.

That morning a crowd of gunners from Australian artillery brigades stationed in the area were invited to look over the tanks and received some general information about steering and control from the Tommies in charge. Later in the day the Germans who had been doing some perfunctory shelling dropped a stray shell in the wood. It hit one of the tanks and hurled up a tumult of soil, trees, exploding ammunition, burning petrol and machinery.

An artist's contemporary impression of the episode described in this story. While the Germans had been lucky in destroying many of this group of tanks they did not discover that the British, Australians and Canadians were about to launch a major attack. Within hours of the tank incident 1,000 guns opened up on a 12 mile front and 100,000 infantry went over the top. It was the beginning of the offensive which broke the Germans' Hindenberg Line.

Thinking they had discovered a dump, the Germans concentrated on this area and peppered it with furious bombardment. The tank drivers wisely ran for safety.

The Australian gunners, not under attack, were interested spectators for a time but soon tired of watching. About 20 of them then rushed into the woods to try to save the tanks. Their only knowledge of tank driving had been gathered during their visit of inspection that morning. A wild bombardment of screeching shells was lifting up the earth in weird fountains and trees were being tossed about like twigs.

The gunners disappeared in the smoke and flame and everyone watching thought they had virtually committed suicide. Then one of the tanks came lumbering through to safety, followed in grotesque procession by four more – five magnificent gestures in a place accustomed to brave deeds.

Then the camouflage on one of the tanks caught alight. With complete disregard for his life the driver stopped the tank in the midst of the

German shells, ripped off the camouflage and stepped inside again.

An English officer who saw the episode was so overcome with exul- tation that he threw his arms around the neck of an Australian major. 'Those chaps aren't men', he said. 'They are bloody archangels!'

CONSIDERATE TO THE LAST

ST QUENTIN

A soldier named Tich was the life and soul of a Royal Fusiliers Battalion until he was seriously wounded on the Somme during the British advance in August 1918. As he was carried off on a stretcher he waved his hand feebly to his mates shelter- ing behind a ditch. 'Hey!' he said in a hoarse whisper. 'Don't tell 'Aig! He'd worry somethin' shockin'.'

Stories about soldiers' last words before death or after wounding are legion but this one is particularly poignant – if only because it shows that the soldiers knew that their Commander-in-Chief would not worry in the slightest.

EVERYBODY'S WAR

SOMME

A platoon of the 9th Royal Fusiliers became isolated from the rest of the company during the final British advance on the Somme in August 1918. The men were under shellfire for about three hours and could do nothing but cower under the scanty shelter. When the shelling stopped the platoon stood up but within a minute a German spotter plane came over. Again the Fusiliers scrambled for cover and lay still.

After the aeroplane had circled a few times, a soldier, new to war and unable to resist the temptation to fire at the machine, jumped up and did just that. He fired three quick rounds before a corporal pulled him down. 'You bloody fool, you've given away our position!' he said.

The young soldier gave him an aggrieved look. 'Blimey!' he said. 'Ain't I in this bleedin' war as well as 'im?'

AH, WELL

VILLERS BRETONNEUX – MONT ST QUENTIN

In 1918 the waggon lines of an Australian gun battery had been established between these two places and an incident occurred there concerning a well. The story was told, tongue in cheek, by one of the gunners.

Thirst had driven Bluey to break a serious order and drink at an unauthorised place, a well. Within an hour he was taken with fierce stomach pains and rushed to the M.O. The doctor diagnosed poisoning, sent him to hospital and had the well marked with a grid sign saying POISONED WATER – DO NOT DRINK.

This led to lengthy surreptitious visits to the well by members of the battery.

Just imagine it, so-called soldiers who had sworn to suffer, fight, and kill their fellow men, prepared to risk their health and strength for a few weeks of hospital life in preference to the discomfort of active service and a good chance of death in any case. Anyway, not one of the shirkers derived any benefit from the duty-dodging scheme, for there was not another seizure in the unit.

The well was not poisonous at all, because I drank about 12 pints of the water by way of experiment and it didn't do me any good – I mean harm.

'WE PAID HEAVILY'

MOISLAINS

In September 1918 Colonel Rowland Feilding (already represented on more than one occasion in this book) was Commanding Officer 1st Civil Service Rifles. The village of. Moislains had been reduced to rubble during the fighting of September 2 and with some of his officers, Feilding retraced the last lap of his battalion's attack and identified the trenches through which the Germans had tried to outflank his men.

He found the enemy bombing-posts with the stick-bombs still lying on the firestep, ready to throw. Feilding wrote: 'All had indeed gone well for us but that last exposed slope was a sorry sight. There were our Lewis guns, many of them still mounted and pointed towards the enemy positions – the gunners dead beside them. The dead lay thick,

their packs opened and the contents scattered; their letters and little souvenirs they had carried . . . littered the ground beside them. Beside one boy lay a black earthenware cat, his mascot, which had not saved him. We certainly paid heavily for this little scrap of trench.

'We buried an officer and 24 men of the Civil Service Rifles we found there, and many others of the brigade were left lying. There was no time for anything elaborate, so the poor bodies with their blackened faces were lifted into shell-holes or into the trench, one or two or three or four together, and earth was put over them. Then a rifle, with bayonet fixed, was stuck into the ground, butt uppermost, to mark each grave, with the names on a bit of paper attached to the trigger guard'.

Feilding's description of this field burial helps to explain why so many bodies were permanently lost. The rifles would fall down or sink into the mud and the pieces of paper blew away or were smeared by rain. War Graves Registration teams could never keep up with the slaughter. The still living often rifled the packs of the dead for anything useful such as socks, food or ammunition.

THE BEST AUTHORITY OF ALL

CAMBRAI

When the Germans retreated under the Allied offensive of September–October 1918 they left behind several dumps of coal. Many British units and individual soldiers were soon scrounging it in readiness for another bleak winter. One 2,000-ton dump of coal was disappearing so rapidly that a guard was placed on it. A British infantry colonel and a captain were walking past the dump one day and saw a big Australian busily shovelling coal in the G.S. (General Service) waggon. The dump sentry, with rifle and fixed bayonet, was marching up and down a few paces away.

The colonel stopped and as the sentry saluted him he said, 'What are you supposed to be doing?'

'Guarding the coal dump, sir'.

'Then what about this Australian? Has he any authority to draw coal? Did he show you a chit?'

'No sir', replied the sentry. 'I thought, as he had a government waggon, it would be all right'.

'Upon my Sam!' the colonel said, astonished. Then he tackled the Australian. 'What authority do you have for taking away this coal?'

The Australian rested on his shovel, pushed back his slouch hat and wiped his brow. 'I don't need any authority', he said, 'I bloody well fought for it'. And he continued shovelling.

The colonel began to speak then changed his mind. 'Extraordinary fellows', he said quietly as he walked off.

They really were remarkable men and noted as much for their quick, dry sense of humour as the Cockneys were for their more cheeky, pungent humour. On one occasion a padre was addressing a large group of Diggers, at Amiens, before they left for Blighty on leave.

'My comrades,' he said, 'remember that hell is a frightful place and it's filled with drink and loose women.'

One of the Australians said loudly and piously, 'Oh Death, where is thy sting?'

THE LOST BATTALION

ARGONNE FOREST

On 2 October 1918, the U.S. 77th Division attacked northward in the Argonne Forest. A force of 700 under the command of Major Charles W. Whittlesey, consisting of Headquarters scouts and runners, two companies of the 1st and 2nd Battalions of the 308th Infantry, two platoons of the 306th Machine-Gun Battalion, and a Company of the 307th Infantry, reached its objective east of the Mouloin de Charlevaux.

Neighbouring units and supporting troops had been stopped far short of the line reached by Major Whittlesey. The Germans seized this opportunity to work their way behind the isolated unit and cut its communications with American troops to the rear. It was thus cut off and surrounded, and had only one day's rations.

Enemy artillery and trench mortars constantly shelled the position. The situation was reported by carrier pigeon message and the force disposed for all-round defence. The following message was then sent to all company detachment commanders:

Our mission is to hold this position at all cost. Have this understood by every man in the command.

Fire from enemy machine-guns and trench mortars continued. About 3.00 p.m. the next day the Germans launched a frontal attack supported by fire from the flanks and rear. The attackers got close enough to throw grenades, but the assault failed. At about 5.00 p.m. another attack came from both flanks and this too was repulsed but with heavy American losses.

The Americans had three medical orderlies but no medical officer. All dressings and first-aid bandages were exhausted on the night of the 3rd.

Daylight of 4 October found the men tired and hungry. All, especially the wounded, had suffered bitterly from the cold during the night. More enemy trench mortars opened a steady fire, causing heavy casualties. Scouts reported that the Germans were all round the position in large numbers but no word from the rear had been received. Again the situation was reported by carrier pigeon.

During the afternoon of the 4th an American barrage, starting in the south, swept forward and settled down on Whittlesey's position

260

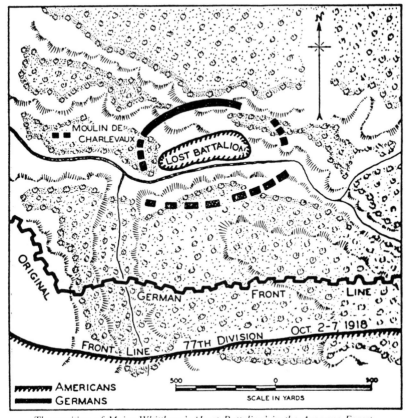

The position of Major Whittlesey's 'Lost Battalion' in the Argonne Forest.

causing more American losses. The last pigeon was released with a message giving the location of the force and stating that American shells were falling on it.

At about 5.00 p.m. a new German attack was repulsed. Water was being obtained from a muddy stream along the ravine below the position; often at a cost of one casualty per canteen, for the enemy had laid guns

to cover the stream. Accordingly, guards were posted to keep men from going to the stream during daylight. A chilly rain on the night of the 4th added to the discomfort. About 9.00 p.m. a German surprise attack failed. The wounded were now in terrible condition and, like the rest of the force, were without food.

Indications of American attacks

from the south had been noted, but no relief came. Actually, several battalions of the 77th Division had been almost wiped out in valiant but vain efforts to reach the surrounded unit.

During the afternoon of 5 October, French artillery located to the southwest opened a heavy fire. The Germans waited until the French fire lifted and then launched another attack which the Americans again stopped.

Shortly after this, American aeroplanes attempted to drop packages on the position but these fell in the German lines. Bandages for the wounded were by now being taken from the dead; even wrap-leggings were used. It became increasingly difficult to get water.

On the morning of 6 October the enemy's rifles and machine-guns started early and his trench mortars again took up their pounding. Another American aeroplane came over and dropped packages, but again they fell in the German lines. Soon afterward there were signs that the Germans were forming for another attack, but this was broken up by American artillery fire.

During the afternoon of 6 October a murderous machine-gun barrage plastered the position and took a heavy toll. This was immediately followed by an attack which, though beaten off, added to the roll of dead and wounded.

By this time ammunition was running low but despite everything, courage and morale remained high. The men were determined to fight to a finish. About noon on the 7th another attack was repulsed. At 4.00 p.m. enemy fire ceased. From the left flank an American soldier appeared limping toward the position, carrying a long stick with a piece of white cloth tied to it. This soldier had been captured while attempting to obtain a package of food dropped by the planes. He brought a letter from the German commander, neatly typewritten in English.

SIR:
The bearer has been taken prisoner by us. He refused to give the German intelligence officer any answer to his questions, and is quite an honourable fellow, doing honour to his Fatherland in the strictest sense of the word.
He has been charged against his will, believing he is doing wrong to his country, to carry forward this present letter to the officer in charge of the battalion of the 77th Division, with the purpose to recommend this commander to surrender with his forces, as it would be quite useless to resist any more, in view of the present conditions. The suffering of your wounded men can be heard over here in the German lines, and we are appealing to your humane sentiments to stop. A white flag shown by one of your men will tell us that you agree with these conditions. Please treat this messenger as an honourable man. He is quite a soldier. We envy you.

Major Whittlesey made no reply, and ordered that two white panels which were being displayed for U.S.

aeroplanes were to be taken in at once. Nothing white was to show on the hillside.

The fiercest attack of the siege followed. Wounded men dragged themselves to the firing line, and those who could not fire loaded rifles for others. The Germans used flame throwers in this attack, and nearly took the position, but finally they were driven off.

At dusk on the 7th it seemed impossible to hold out. Only two machine-guns were left of the original nine and no gunners remained to man them. Ammunition was almost exhausted; the next attack would have to be met with the bayonet. There had been no food since the morning of 3 October. The water obtained was slimy and bad. Still these men were willing to fight on.

That night the enemy withdrew and American troops arrived soon afterward. Out of 700 men who jumped off on the morning of October 2nd, 194 were able to walk out of the position. Many of these were wounded.

Whittlesey's force became known as 'the Lost Battalion' while it was still surrounded and the label has stuck in military history. This Argonne action achieved little but it is a superb example of leadership and courage.

OTHER MEN'S DISCARDS

CORBIE, SOMME

Some Australian soldiers did everything possible to take a rise out of officers even when it went against their own interest. 'Stonker' Evans was one of these men. He reported for sick parade one day and when he confronted the M.O. that officer eyed him suspiciously. 'How long have you been sick?' he asked.

'About six weeks sir', said Stonker hoarsely.

'Six weeks! Why didn't you come to me before?'

'I've been treating myself, sir'.

'Why would you want to do that? That's what I'm here for. Anyway, what did you treat yourself with?'

'Well, sir, I've been waiting around outside and picking up all the pills the other blokes have been throwing away after sick parade'.

CHALLENGE

ETAPLES

A soldier on guard at the big Etaples camp in 1918 saw a figure approaching about two in the morning and made the usual challenge. 'Who goes there?'

'Chaplain', was the answer from a padre.

'Right, Charlie', the sentry said. 'But crikey, mate, I didn't know *you* was over 'ere! Do your act, mate, and give us a laugh'.

TAKE AND HOLD

ST PYTHON, FRANCE

The final Allied advance of the war was in progress and for the first time since 1914 gains were measured in miles rather than in yards. On October 13 the 2nd Battalion Scots Guards were held up by German strongposts in the French village of St Python. Machine-gun fire raked the streets and many men fell. Command of the leading platoon fell to Corporal Harry Wood, M.M., when his sergeant was killed.

The company's task was to clear the western side of the village and secure the crossing of the River Selle. But first the ruined bridge had to be captured and success depended on Wood's leaderhip. Well concealed German snipers were picking off every man who approached, so Wood carried a large stone into the open space, lay down behind it and began a duel with the enemy snipers. At the same time he shouted to this men to work their way to the bridge while he covered them. Wood was an old regular who had been with the battalion since 1914 and he kept up such well-aimed rapid and disciplined fire that his platoon reached the bridge safely. Then they covered him while he sprinted to their position.

The Germans tried several times

264

to storm the post but each time Wood, with a superb display of tactical leadership, held them off. His effort was the key to the day's success and he was awarded the Victoria Cross.

In October 1918 Wood had been one of a small party which had been cut off near Ghent. They evaded capture by dressing as civilians and bluffing their way through the encircling Germans. His bridge at St Python still exists.

SHELL SHOCK

SOISSONS

In October 1918 the Americans made a major attack against the German lines at Soissons. On the first night, a soldier of the Machine-Gun Company, 28th Infantry, succumbed to shell shock and began to lunge violently about him with his fixed bayonet and the rifle butt.

Sergeant Ray Smith shouted a warning to the men of the platoon, who tried to trip or disarm the maniacal soldier. They did not want to hurt him but when he cornered one of his comrades and thrust at him with the bayonet the soldier fired a snap shot from the hip. The bullet landed flat and tore a big hole in the man's right side.

There was no possibility of getting him to the rear; behind the 28th infantry were eight miles of country 'carpeted with our wounded and dying men', Smith said later. The wounded man, now recovered from his madness, lay among his comrades without a moan.

In the morning a messenger was needed to carry a report back to headquarters. Leaning against a tree his face haggard under its sunburn, the wounded man pleaded with the company commander to let him take the report. 'I can't go on with the boys, captain', he said. 'If I take back your despatch it will save you a whole man – and you'll need all your whole men'.

'All right, son', the captain said. 'And good luck'.

With a hole in his side that would take two fists the soldier struggled eight miles to deliver the despatch and then died before the medics could help him.

LONE SURVIVOR

LILLE

On 14 October 1918, during the final British push of the war, the 36th Battalion Northumberland Fusiliers was attacking an enemy-held ridge near Lille and suffering casualties.

At 10 a.m. Lieutenant James Johnson asked Sergeant Eddie Foulkes to try to get the wounded out. 'The Germans may let you pass provided you are not wearing any equipment,' he said. Foulkes agreed to try and took with him 16 wounded men, mostly able to walk, and four stretcher-bearers.

They had covered about 150 yards out of the battle when a machine-gun pinned them down. To encourage his frightened party – wounded men are always worried about being hit again – Foulkes started to sing, 'Jesu, lover of my soul let us to thy bosom fly'. The only one who could join him in the hymn was the wounded boy on the stretcher.

The Germans must have realised that they were firing on wounded men, if only because they were not returning the fire, but they gave the party no respite. Foulkes tried to get the men under cover but one by one they were hit and hit again. In the end Foulkes was the only survivor. He won the D.C.M. for his courage in the action, both in the advance and then for his brave attempt to extricate the wounded.

Lieutenant Johnson won the V.C. for his work that day. Eddie Foulkes finished the war not only with the D.C.M. but the M.M and the Croix de Guerre. He served in World War II and founded the Manchester & District branch of the Dunkirk Veterans Association.

WAR DOGS

YPRES/ARMENTIERES SECTOR

War dogs were used by the British army in most sectors and fairly intensively in the Ypres Salient.

Working over rough ground chewed by shellfire and laced with barbed wire, a dog could carry a message in

While dogs were the most frequently seen animals on the battlefield, either as mascots or duty animals, soldiers would adopt any creature. This group, somewhere on the Somme, has a pet fox. (Author's collection and copyright)

about a quarter of the time a man would need, and in greater safety. And they could get through gas with less danger of being killed or disabled.

Keeper Sergeant Brown had several fine dogs in service in the Salient. One little bitch, Silky, had her leg badly cut but brought in an important message calling for artillery support. Another dog, Vulcan, went out on patrol with an officer and a runner. The officer was killed and the runner wounded but he sent Vulcan back with a message giving

his position so that another officer could be sent out.

Near Kemmel, Vulcan went out with a patrol on a bombing raid, the objective being to find out the identity of the German units on that front. The only survivor of that patrol, Vulcan came back with some papers in his message box and between his teeth a shoulder strap from a German uniform with the regimental number on it.

The first news of the capture of Hill 60, Ypres, was brought in by a dog. In this fight the troops had attacked a German sap and needed more bombs to hold it. A dog brought in the request, as well as a casualty report.

In July 1918, a dog covered the 13½ miles from Vieux Berquin to the western edge of Nieppe Forest, where Corps H.Q., was situated, in 50 minutes, a feat of navigation as well as endurance. A duplicate report was sent off by runner at the same time; a fit and experienced soldier, he reached Brigade H.Q. – which was closer than Corps H.Q. – one hour and 35 minutes *after* the messenger dog arrived at Corps H.Q.

BREAKING POINT

FRANCE

Several soldiers have left accounts of the way the stress of battle breaks some men. One of these writers was a young infantry officer who wrote a series of letters, which were never posted, to an American nurse he had met on leave in Paris. The letters were found after his death in action but his identity was never established.

There comes a point in the career of every fighting man when he can endure no further. He may be perfectly healthy, but he knows that the day is surely coming when he will break. It may not come for a long time; but the certainty that the break is coming fills him with dread. Inadvertently he betrays this dread in little ways. Officers who have trusted him begin to watch him – they begin to doubt his courage.

We had such a man on our B.C. (Battery Communication) party. The B.C. party consists of expert signallers and linesmen, chosen out of the battery for their pluck. As the English say, they have to be 'stout' fellows. Their job is to go forward and sometimes over the top with the observing officer to direct fire. At all costs and at whatever risks, they have to keep up the communications with the battery. If the line goes down, no matter how bad the shelling, your linesmen are expected to go out and mend it. This man of whom I speak was a linesman. He'd been in the war from the first and had made a record for his daring. He had stood the racket for two years, and then his nerve began to go from him. We wouldn't believe it at first; soon it became patent to everybody. His eyes would become vague. You could see him making an effort not to run. He quivered like a highstrung horse under shellfire.

Of course the just thing would have been to send him out; but we had too many casualties and couldn't spare him. In such cases the last thing one dares to do is to show pity. Pity is contagious. The army expects every man to do his duty; it takes no excuses, and only notices him when he fails. So this poor chap, who had been a hero, had to watch himself hourly becoming a coward. Worse still, he was kept wondering just how many of us knew it. He must have been very brave, for he played the game to the end.

We were in a position where the Huns pounded us day and night. The B.C. party's quarters were under a ruined house which might fall at any moment. The enemy had already scored several direct hits on it. Suddenly, in the middle of a strafe, he began to undress. When he was asked what he was doing, he paid no attention. When he'd got rid of every stitch of clothing, he dashed out into the area where the shells were falling. He was stark mad.

For most soldiers who fought on the Western Front the mud was the worst enemy. Many of them lost their lives in it. A soldier wounded and helpless on ground such as this would slowly sink into the mire. It was virtually impossible for stretcher-bearers, often working under enemy fire, to locate their wounded mates in such a morass. Yet, amazingly, Australian soldiers captured the German blockhouse shown here. Tens of thousands of square miles of France and Belgium were a quagmire repeatedly churned up by shellfire.

JOURNEY'S END

Pilgrims to the Western Front should visit Ypres, south-east of Bapaume near Barrastre, and go to the road near the railway station. While standing there read this description, by Private A.M. Burrage, Artists' Rifles, of what he saw at that spot in March 1918. The Germans had broken through and two of their shells had exploded on the road.

Screams and yells were ringing out all around and the inevitable cry for stretcher-bearers. My own company came first so I hurried back to my own platoon, or rather to the spot where I had left it.

I had seen ghastly sights but nothing to equal the one which awaited me. The road was strewn with fragments of men, torn-off limbs, and the trunks of men which seemed only half to fill their tunics. It was the only time I ever saw a gutter literally running with blood. And the scene was lit up by the fitful red flames of the burning (R.E.) dump and station.

Only one man out of the platoon was left alive . . . He was lying on his back, crying, and another fellow was hanging on to a severed artery in his thigh above a gaping wound from which the blood pumped at every heart-beat. I had nothing to make a tourniquet and our clumsy attempts to hold the artery were useless. We could do nothing but watch him bleed to death. He died crying for his mother. 'Mother' was the one and only word he uttered.

When all the stories of humour and irony, pathos and drama have been told, this was the real war, the killing of nearly one million men from Britain and its empire – as well as the millions of combatants from other nations. Their sacrifice is the abiding 'story' of the 'Great War'.

HIS MATE

There's a broken battered village
  Somewhere up behind the line,
There's a dug-out and a bunk there,
  That I used to say were mine.

I remember how I reached them,
  Dripping wet and all forlorn,
In the dim and dreary twilight
  Of a weeping summer dawn.

All that week I'd buried brothers,
  In one bitter battle slain,
In one grave I laid two hundred.
  God! What sorrow and what rain!

And that night I'd been in trenches,
  Seeking out the sodden dead,
And just dropping them in shell
    holes,
  With a service swiftly said.

For the bullets rattled round me,
  But I couldn't leave them there,
Water-soaked in flooded shell holes,
  Reft of common Christian prayer.

So I crawled round on my belly,
  And I listened to the roar
Of the guns that hammered
    Thiepval,
  Like big breakers on the shore.

Then there spoke a dripping
    sergeant,
  When the time was growing late,
'Would you please to bury this one,
  'Cause 'e used to be my mate?'

So we groped our way in darkness
  To a body lying there,
Just a blacker lump of blackness,
  With a red blotch on his hair.

Though we turned him gently over,
  Yet I still can hear the thud,
As the body fell face forward,
  And then settled in the mud.

We went down upon our faces,
  And I said the service through,
From 'I am the Resurrection'
  To the last, the great 'adieu'.

When a sudden light shot soaring
  Silver swift and like a sword,
We stood up to give the Blessing,
  And commend him to the Lord.

At a stroke it slew the darkness,
  Flashed its glory on the mud,
And I saw the sergeant staring
  At a crimson clot of blood.

There are many kinds of sorrow
  In this world of Love and Hate,
But there is no sterner sorrow
  Than a soldier's for his mate.

By Padre G.A. Studdert Kennedy M.C., C.F.
(Woodbine Willie)

GLOSSARY

Abbreviations and some of the terms used in this book

A.I.F.   Australian Imperial Force; that is, Australian soldiers serving overseas.

Anzac   An Australian or New Zealand soldier, from the acronym formed by A.N.Z.A.C. (Australian and New Zealand Army Corps), first used during the Gallipoli campaign of 1915.

B.C.   Battery (artillery) Communication.

Blighty   The soldier's term for England. It is based on the Urdu word vilayati or bilati, meaning 'away' or 'removed at some distance'. A 'blighty one' was a wound which was bad enough to have a soldier sent to England – and therefore a welcome wound. Soldiers also referred to 'Bailleul, Boulogne and Blighty.' Bailleul was the transit camp, Boulogne was a leave port and then came Blighty.

C.C.   Commander-in-Chief.

C.C.S.   Casualty Clearing Station; generally not far behind the front lines.

C.F.   Chaplain to the Forces.

C.O.   Commanding Officer; usually a lieutenant-colonel in command of a battalion.

C.Q.M.S.   Company Quarter Master Sergeant, generally addressed as 'Quarter'.

C.S.M.   Company Sergeant Major; the senior non-commissioned officer of an infantry company.

D.C.M.	Distinguished Conduct Medal; awarded to non-commissioned ranks.
D.F.C.	Distinguished Flying Cross; an officers' award.
Diggers	The most freqently used term for Australian soldiers and the one they themselves approved; they often shortened it to 'Dig'. The term is believed to have come from gum-diggers in colonial Australia. The author's mother, a nursing sister on the Western Front, said that many soldiers told her they were Diggers because they were forever digging trenches.
Don R	Army parlance for Despatch Rider; 'Don' was signalese for D.
D.S.O.	Distinguished Service Order; an officers' award.
Dum-dum	A bullet with its nose cut off or scored across so that it will make a larger wound. Such bullets are banned by the Geneva Convention. A soldier taken prisoner with dum-dum rounds in his possession was generally shot during World War I.
Fighting Order	The Tommy's battle gear generally weighed more than 66lb. Apart from rifle and bayonet, steel helmet, trenching tool and normal clothing, pack and greatcoat, it comprised: ground-sheet, waterbottle, haversack, mess tin, towel, shaving kit, spare socks, message book, two gas masks, teargas goggles, wire-cutters, a field dressing, iodine phial, 220 rounds of .303 ammunition, two empty sandbags and two Mills grenades. The second gas mask was for a comrade who might be wounded and without his own mask.
F.A.N.Y	First Aid Nursing Yeomanry; trained nurses operating first aid posts.
Firestep	The step in a trench on which soldiers stood to fire at the enemy.
Fritz	A soldiers' commonplace term for any German. Frederick the Great had been

274

known as 'Old Fritz' and German soldiers often used the term when speaking of each other.

G.S.   Ground Strafing.

H.L.I.   Highland Light Infantry.

Howitzers   High-trajectory guns which lobbed heavy shells into trenches and over hills.

H.Q.   Head Quarters.

Hun   A derogatory and abusive term for the Germans during World War I.

Jerry   Another name the Tommy gave German soldiers; their helmets suggested a chamber pot.

K.C.B.   Knight Commander of the Bath.

K.C.M.G.   Knight Commander of the Order of St Michael and St George.

K.R.R.C.   King' Royal Rifle Corps.

Lewis Gun   Designed in 1911 by the American, Issac Lewis, this light machine-gun was extensively used by British frontline troops for close support fighting; it was fitted to many British aircraft.

L.P.   Listening Post; a dangerous forward post where two or three men were stationed to listen for enemy activity.

Maxim   The machine-gun invented by Hiram Maxim. The weapon was used by the British in colonial wars and the Germans used it extensively in World War I. In 1917 Maxims were being produced in Germany at the rate of 14,000 a month.

M.C.   Military Cross; an officers' award.

M.M.   Military Medal; an other ranks' award.

Mills bomb.   Officially this is the H.E. (high explosive) 36 grenade. It was the most important British grenade and from the spring of 1915 to November 1918 British and British Empire troops threw 33 million of them.

Minenwerfer	A German shell which the Tommies called a minnie or moaning minnie, from the noise it made in flight.
N.C.O.	Non-commissioned officer.
New Army	In September 1916 Lord Kitchener appealed for 100,000 volunteers to join the small and battle-depleted regular army for three years. This was the beginning of the New Army, often called Kitchener's Army, first used on a large scale in 1916. The New Army grew into a force of millions.
No Man's Land	The area between the front lines of the opposing armies; it varied from time to time as territory was won or lost. A man badly wounded in No Man's Land had little chance of being rescued.
O.C.	Officer commanding; usually a captain commanding a company.
Old Contemptibles	This was the first contingent of British troops to join the Belgian and French forces against the Germans. According to stories of the time – August 1914 – the Kaiser ordered his troops to 'exterminate the treacherous English and walk over this contemptible little army.' The troops turned the epithet into a an accolade and styled themselves the Old Contemptibles.
O.P.	Observation Post; a dangerous position from which artillery spotters and others observed the enemy positions.
pavé	The cobbled roads of France and Belgium; the cobbles were difficult to march on but better than mud.
R.A.M.C.	Royal Army Medical Corps.
R.A.P.	Regimental Aid Post.
R.E.	Royal Engineers.
R.F.C.	Royal Flying Corps; it became the Royal Air Force in 1918.
R.M.O.	Regimental Medical Officer.
R.Q.M.S.	Regimental Quarter Master Sergeant.

R.T.O.	Railway Transport Officer.
R.W.K.	Royal West Kent Regiment.
Shrapnel.	In this book the word shrapnel is used in the correct way – it refers to the hundreds of thousands of lead balls the size of marbles which filled the case of a shrapnel shell. Pieces of exploding shell are not shrapnel and should be referred to as shell shards, shell splinters or shell fragments.
S.R.D.	The label on all army rum jars. The letters stand for Special Ration Distribution but frontline soldiers said cynically that they meant 'Seldom Reaches Destination', because the rum was stolen by base-area troops.
Straffin	(see page 5) Tongue lashed or the parade ground; from strafing or being under artillery attack.
Toc H	Army signalese for Talbot House, a soldiers' rest house in Poperinge, Flanders, and referred to several times in this book. Toc H later became a major international welfare and charitable organisation.
Tommy	The nickname of the British soldier, from Thomas Atkins, the name filled in by the Duke of Wellington on the first sample soldier's paybook.
Uhlans:	German lancers.
V.C.	Victoria Cross: the highest British award for military valour. During World War I roughly half the V.C. awards were posthumous. It is open to all ranks and it precedes all other awards, distinctions and orders.
Whizzbangs	German shells with a flat trajectory which made a *whizzbang* noise.
Y.M.C.A.	Young Men's Christian Association.